# You Are There . . .

. . . on the luxury cruise liner *Morro Castle* as she moves out of Havana harbor on her return trip to New York. You are among the passengers, determined to squeeze the last ounce of pleasure out of the voyage. You are among the crew, simmering with discontent and rebellion. You are among the officers, torn by bitter hatreds, rivalries, and suspicions. And you are face to face with the strange and sinister man who is planning the captain's murder and the ship's destruction as the *Morro Castle* steams toward her fearful and tragic rendezvous with destiny. . . .

"One of the most horrendous crimes in maritime history . . . a monumental job of research!"
—*Seattle Post Intelligencer*

"Minute-by-minute excitement . . . a heady brew!" —*Rocky Mountain News*

"A non-fiction thriller . . . buy it and read it!"
—*Best Sellers*

# SHIPWRECK

## The Strange Fate of the Morro Castle

_Gordon Thomas and Max Morgan Witts_

A DELL BOOK

Published by
**DELL PUBLISHING CO., INC.**
1 Dag Hammarskjold Plaza
New York, New York 10017
Copyright © 1972 by Stein and Day, Incorporated
All rights reserved.
For information contact Stein and Day, Incorporated
New York, New York 10017
Dell ® TM 681510, Dell Publishing Co., Inc.
Reprinted by arrangement with
Stein and Day, Incorporated
Printed in the United States of America
First Dell printing—December 1973

# CONTENTS

PROLOGUE      7

HAVANA: SEPTEMBER 5, 1934      9

1. *A Likely Suspect*      11
2. *Charade*      34
3. *Rumors of Sabotage*      50

AT SEA: SEPTEMBER 5—SEPTEMBER 7, 1934      63

4. *Playing with Fire*      65
5. *Poison*      84
6. *The Storm Rises*      97
7. *A Fatal Evening*      112
8. *Who Killed the Captain?*      126
9. *The Smell of Smoke*      137

FIRE AT SEA: SEPTEMBER 8, 1934      151

10. *Panic*      153
11. *The S.O.S.*      167
12. *Out of Control*      179
13. *Nightmare*      189
14. *The Rescue Armada*      199
15. *Jump!*      209

16.   She's Worth a Fortune to the Town      220
17.   Abandon Ship                           230
18.   Beached                                241


**ON THE BEACH**                             249

19.   Indictments                            251
20.   The Verdict                            266


**APPENDIXES**                               279

Acknowledgments                              281

Special Thanks                               287

Bibliography                                 291

# PROLOGUE

In 1884 an editorial in the *Daily Spray,* a journal circulating in the Asbury Park area of New Jersey, suggested one way for Asbury Park to improve its resort status.

> We want a first-class shipwreck. Why? To make Asbury Park a famous winter resort. There is a very comfortable berth for a big ship between the fishing pier and the Asbury Avenue Pavilion.
>
> She should strike head-on, so that her nose would ram the Baby Parade grandstand, and her tail might hop around even with the end of the pier.
>
> We could accommodate her all winter.
>
> Pontoon or suspension bridges could be built from the pier and the pavilion, so that the ship could be used as a casino.
>
> We need a spectacular ship.

Fifty years later, almost to the day, the newspaper's demands were fulfilled.

This is the story not only of *how* it happened, but of *why*.

# Havana:
# September 5, 1934

# 1.
# A LIKELY SUSPECT

Somebody on board wanted to kill him.

No record exists of the exact moment Robert Wilmott, captain of the *Morro Castle,* a cruise liner shuttling between New York and Havana, Cuba, finally came to this conclusion. But by the time the ship docked in Havana on September 4, 1934, the captain had decided that somebody on board did want to kill him.

Robert Wilmott, ponderously firm and earnest, lacked imagination. To the passengers aboard the *Morro Castle,* however, he was a public-relations press release come true, a dream of what a liner captain should be. He epitomized the advertised enchanted world of a sea cruise, in which there is no death or danger, where the seams between reality and magic are always caulked.

For four years Captain Wilmott's ship, launched during the Depression, had been the flagship of the Eastern Seaboard smart set, a haven for those eager to avoid Prohibition and forget about the Depression. On this, the 174th voyage, her reputation as a floating gin mill remained intact. As usual, nearly every stateroom was filled.

Robert Wilmott was responsible for no small part of the *Morro Castle*'s success. Passengers frequently made sure that he was still in command of the ship before buying a ticket. He was the perfect ship's captain for passengers who had never been on anything bigger than the ferryboat to Staten Island.

In an era when many of them expected a liner captain to be either a Valentino or an old sea dog, he had chosen the latter role. His image of himself had not seemed to hurt him, though: he had something to offer everyone. For the well-off he was worldly-wise; he was the cosmopolitan who could produce an out-of-town twang; he could always act the hick inside the dinner jacket to accommodate any wealthy farmer. He enjoyed his work.

But during the summer of 1934, a series of events had occurred which endangered not only the *Morro Castle,* but also her master. On July 29, a meal had been served that made Wilmott ill enough to suspect poisoning; on August 4 an attempted strike had threatened to wreck the liner's tight schedule; on August 27 a fire had started in a hold containing high explosives.

At first Robert Wilmott tried to isolate each of the incidents, as if this would minimize them. But on the present run from New York to Havana, they gradually became linked together in his mind.

Since the ship's departure from New York on the afternoon of Saturday, September 1, 1934, he had shunned virtually all social obligations on board. He confined himself to his cabin, not eating, drinking only bottled water. Apart from visits from the first officer, who reported at regular intervals, his only caller was the chief radio officer bringing messages from the radio shack. Otherwise Captain Wilmott relied on the telephone switchboard to keep in touch with the bridge, the engine room, and the rest of his ship.

His absence aroused immediate speculation on the first-class decks. By the time the *Morro Castle* berthed at the Ward Line pier in Havana that Tuesday, even the tourist passengers were wondering why their captain had relinquished the helm, temporarily at least. The ship's officers' bland reassurance that there was nothing to worry about succeeded in pacifying only the least skeptical.

Meanwhile, in assessing responsibility for the attempted arson, murder, and strike action, Robert Wilmott had made one grave mistake.

He suspected the wrong person.

By midmorning on Wednesday, September 5, Eban Starr Abbott, chief engineer of the *Morro Castle*, was well into his normal routine in Havana. Satisfied that all was functioning smoothly in the engine room, he bathed and dressed carefully. He selected one uniform from his small wardrobe: an immaculate white affair with gold braid at the cuffs and epaulettes.

For four years, the boxlike cabin between the ship's two smokestacks had been his home at sea. At the end of the last voyage, Eban Abbott had removed an item of property which distinguished his from other officers' cabins: a photograph of his wife Ada. Packing for this voyage—the 113th he was to make on the *Morro Castle*—he had explained to Ada why he was leaving her picture behind. "There were goings-on in the ship that he didn't want me to be any part of," Mrs. Abbott later recalled. "The passengers were a fast crowd, he said—men with other people's wives and that sort of thing."

Her husband's attitude toward the passengers—as far as Mrs. Abbott could tell—was that they were to be avoided at all cost. He cringed, he told her, at their loud bonhomie on the boat deck and the gin-and-sin-

13

ning at the nightly gala balls. Naturally, she took him at his word.

Many of his fellow officers believed he regarded the *Morro Castle* as little more than a showcase for his engines. More than once he had sharply rebuked the helmsman for his steering when the ship's navigational position did not jibe with what he calculated it should be from engine revolutions.

Eban Abbott, the son of a seaman, was raised for the sea. In 1909, the year he got his chief engineer's license, he joined the Ward Line. He was assigned to cargo boats that sweated through the tropics or buffeted across the Bay of Biscay. For twenty years, freighting was Eban Abbott's trade.

Then in 1929, he was given one of the key posts in the American merchant marine. Henry E. Cabaud, the executive vice-president of the Ward Line, told Abbott that he was being promoted to chief engineer of the *Morro Castle,* the fastest turbo-electric vessel afloat.

Eban Abbott followed the *Morro Castle* through every step in her gestation. By her maiden voyage on August 23, 1930, he knew the capacity and caprices of every generator and armature, the position of every switch and circuit breaker. The promises of the drawing board and trial runs were realized: on her first trip to Havana, she clipped twelve hours off the record.

Only one thing marred the situation for Eban Abbott: the first officer of the *Morro Castle* was William Warms.

Abbott and Warms actively disliked each other. In the four years since the maiden voyage, the dislike had deepened to the point where Abbott openly referred to that "worm on the bridge." Warms talked of that "stuffed tailor's dummy in the engine room."

Eban Abbott squared his white cap and hurried ashore. Waiting for him on the pier was the ship's surgeon, Dr. de Witt Van Zile. The two men headed toward the most famous tavern in the Caribbean, Havana's Sloppy Joe's.

Over lunch-time drinks the chief engineer planned to raise once again with the doctor the real reason why he disliked First Officer Warms.

Deep in number five hold, storekeeper William O'Sullivan and seaman John Gross sat on a pile of sacking and watched the Cuban stevedore gang stack a cargo of bananas, eggplants, and peppers. The laborers worked fast, keeping pace with the derricks and winches that lowered the cargo into the hold.

Ever since the discovery of the fire—the one that Captain Wilmott now believed was arson—O'Sullivan and Gross had been detailed to guard the huge steel-lined hold whenever it was open. From where they sat the two men could clearly see the scorch marks on the bulkhead near where the fire had started a bit over a week before.

They, too, had no doubt it had been deliberately started. Both were inclined to believe some sort of device had been planted in the hold just before it had been closed in New York. The *Morro Castle*'s smoke-detecting system had alerted the bridge; the flames were extinguished by an automatic firefighting mechanism which pumped pressurized carbon dioxide gas into the hold. The incident had been over in moments.

The theory of incendiarism was supported by several clues: a small train of charred pieces of cardboard led away from the initial fire point; the heat generated was unusually intense, considering the small size of the blaze, suggesting a chemical agent had been used. The fire had been extinguished only a few feet from crates marked "sporting goods," a regular consignment in the *Morro Castle*'s Havana-bound cargo.

Gross and O'Sullivan agreed the fire had been set deliberately; it was on the question of motive that they disagreed.

Gross maintained that the arsonist must have been a former crew member seeking revenge for being sacked. The Ward Line had a notorious reputation for hiring and firing: in an age of mass unemployment a man on the breadline could, and often did, behave irrationally.

O'Sullivan rejected this idea. He felt that more than one man had been needed to set the fire in that particular hold. Whoever did it would also have to have had special knowledge, for the crates of "sporting goods" contained cargo a good deal more dangerous than their labels would have told an uninformed observer.

O'Sullivan had discovered the trail of cardboard shreds, and the sight made it difficult for him to sleep on the run down to Havana. In his words: "My bunk was only a few feet from those crates and they contained enough guns and ammunition to blow the ship all over the Atlantic!"

The storekeeper understated the situation. For a whole year the *Morro Castle* had been a floating arsenal. Certainly none of her passengers had any inkling of this; neither did the Bureau of Navigation and Steamboat Inspection, nor the American Bureau of Shipping. Built with a low-interest government loan of $3,422,181, the liner had been designed for conversion into a troop carrier in the event of war. But at no time had the Ward Line or its parent company, Atlantic Gulf and West Indies, ever informed the government that a vessel "certificated for ocean passenger service" was also going to be actively involved in gunrunning.

It was not a case of sporadic moonlighting, nor merely an effort to raise the profits of shareholders. The *Morro Castle* was regularly engaged in a traffic in armaments. The shipments were used by the Cuban dictatorship of Gerardo Morales Machado to suppress a growing Communist influence on the island. There are strong indications that the shipments were organized by powerful U.S. business interests concerned about the threat Communist activities would pose to the handsome profits coming from Cuban tobacco and sugar.

Such trading was not without risk. The year before, in July 1933, as the liner slipped into Havana Harbor, it had been caught in the cross fire between a group of Communist guerrillas fleeing in a boat and the pursuing police cutter. Bullets ricocheted off the liner's decks and superstructure; fortunately nobody on board was hit. Ward Line officials calmed the passengers by reporting the incident as just "a little local bother."

The "sporting goods" shipments—kegs of high explosives, drums of gunpowder, cannon powder, smokeless powder, belts of machine-gun ammunition, cartridges, bullets, and shells—continued. In one month, August 1934, the *Morro Castle* transported over one hundred crates of assorted weapons to Havana.

This arsenal was always unloaded at night by soldiers of the Cuban Army; often a convoy of trucks was needed to carry away the crates.

Storekeeper O'Sullivan had literally stumbled on this arms traffic in July 1934. Just before sailing from New

York a hoist of drums had been gently swung aboard. Because the holds were already sealed, Captain Wilmott ordered O'Sullivan to stash the drums in the forepeak storeroom.

In the process, O'Sullivan tripped over a drum and a longshoreman revealed the contents of the cargo. "The way he talked," O'Sullivan told Gross, "led me to believe that this wasn't the first time they had loaded this kind of cargo in this kind of place." Since then O'Sullivan had kept a careful tally of weaponry going to Cuba.

To him the motive for starting a fire near the "sporting goods" was clear. To prevent these explosives from reaching Cuba, somebody was desperate enough to risk sacrificing a whole ship's crew and passengers; to murder, if necessary, up to 750 people.

Exactly who would take such chances, O'Sullivan could not say with certainty. But he hazarded a guess.

"Communists," he told Gross. "They're the ones behind it!"

Gross listened attentively as the storekeeper told him what he knew about the cargo. When O'Sullivan finished, the seaman made an immediate decision: as soon as the *Morro Castle* berthed in New York three days later, he would sign off the ship, even if this meant being unemployed again. Better to starve, as far as he was concerned, than run the risks entailed in serving on the ship.

In the meantime Gross offered O'Sullivan a piece of advice: he should keep his mouth shut. Communism had already gotten a toehold in the fledgling seaman's union. Every day its influence increased; it was better not talked about.

Communism had had a toehold in Cuba, as well, for

some years before the *Morro Castle* was launched. In May 1919, a handful of professional revolutionaries from Haiti slipped ashore at Guantanamo Bay. These *cacos,* who were for the most part peasants, came to Cuba to spread a "workers' revolution," which they had declared months earlier against American domination on Haiti. They preached the doctrine that Cuba, like Haiti, belonged to the people.

Since 1903 American interests had exercised virtually complete control over Cuba's political and economic affairs. For $2000 a year the United States rented military bases at Guantanamo and Bahia Horda.

During this time, Americans did little to improve conditions for the local population. Statistics showed that in 1920, there was only one doctor for every 3000 people; a third of the population had intestinal parasites; the average per capita income was two dollars a month; six out of every ten rural children never went to school; 75 per cent of Cuba's arable land was controlled by American companies; U.S. control in the telephone and electric services exceeded 90 per cent.

Dedicated to the abolition of colonialism, the *cacos* rapidly gained ground in the 1920s through a series of propaganda exercises. By 1930 the slogan *Cuba libre* had become the rallying cry of guerrillas who waged sporadic urban warfare in Havana.

Their immediate goal was to overthrow the corrupt and repressive regime of the president, General Gerardo Machado; their ultimate hope was the removal of American influence from the island.

In the interests of stability, successive American administrations openly supported the dictatorship. In turn, Machado raised no awkward questions of independence. Politically, he concerned himself with the exile or assassination of hostile labor leaders—or anyone suspected of being a Communist; economically, he embarked on a reckless and enormous increase of the public debt.

In the 1930s American policy on Cuba was to "veto revolution, whatever the cause." On the occasion of a threatened rebellion by a Negro political party—the Independent Party of Color—the United States sent troops to Cuba to crush the uprising. U.S. Secretary of State Knox stated, "The United States does not undertake first to consult the Cuban government if a crisis arises requiring a temporary landing somewhere." In 1933 American Ambassador to Cuba Sumner Welles said that the prime qualification for any Cuban president must be "his thorough acquaintance with the desires of the [U.S.] Government [and] his amenability to suggestion or advice which might be made to him by the American legation in Havana."

Cuban Communists, who preached revolution against what they called "American tyranny," were supported covertly by the Communist Party in America through advisors and funds.

Seaman Joseph Spilgins had made a discovery. Politics had nothing to do with his keeping it to himself, though; it was "simply a matter of having a full belly. When you have starved for a few weeks, even a dollar a day and all the stew swill you can swallow is mighty tempting."

The twenty-six-year-old deckhand had sailed on the *Morro Castle* for three day trips. Although he held no able-bodied seaman's certificate, he was carried as one—but paid the salary of an ordinary seaman: thirty dollars a month. Breakfast was coffee warmed up after the officers' mess and soggy stale bread. Lunch and dinner were stew. His bunk was between two steampipes; the blankets were filthy, and he rolled up his trousers for a pillow. Still, Spilgins found it "the most comfortable place I'd had for a long time; I didn't want to do anything to lose it."

On the second run down from New York, he was put in charge of the six starboard lifeboats. Questioned later, he admitted that he had no clear idea what this meant, other than that they should be "always on the shackles, ready to be lowered."

He had, however, carried out an inspection of the lifeboats, something no officer of the ship had done since Spilgins had come aboard. He found that several of the boats had rusted buoyancy tanks. Where the rust had become too severe, red lead had been daubed on and covered with a slick of paint.

Based on what he saw, Spilgins believed that the boats would be useless in an emergency. In his words: "Taking a chance in them would be as bad as jumping into the water. The material put in the tanks by the shipowners in this country is unbelievable."

Spilgins did not voice his fears to any of the ship's officers. He feared that to do so would cost him his berth.

The tall, raw-boned first officer knew that nothing would ever induce him to give up the sea. Though William Warms surrounded himself with mementos from land—photographs of his wife, his small son, Donald, their home, and scenes in New Jersey—he knew he could never completely fulfill himself in any land job.

Warms had gone to sea at the age of twelve; his wages were two meals a day and a dollar a month. He had immersed himself in sea lore to cushion some of the hard knocks that a turn-of-the-century sailor had to take. By the time he was sixteen he had buffeted around all the oceans of the world. He had sailed with captains who carried Bibles under their arms like telescopes and with some who forbade drinking, gambling, or "going with dirty women."

Those wrathful skippers had molded Warms into a God-fearing man who had little enthusiasm for fancy living or manners—which was one reason he disliked Eban Abbott. Warms believed the engineer was not a "proper seaman." As far as Warms could tell, Abbott was a man "who liked the uniform and not the job; he tried to speak Cambridge English as if he was ashamed of coming up the hard way."

William Warms was intensely proud of his own climb up the promotion ladder. In 1918, after nine years of service, the Ward Line rewarded him with a command: they made him captain of a fruit boat. He did well, bringing the ship home on time, satisfying the profit needs of the stockholders. Other commands followed: his enthusiasm for his work overcame the discomforts of shunting around the world picking up anything from copra to lemons.

In 1926, Warms became the master of his first passenger liner, a small ship named *Yumari*. He worked the crew as hard as he drove himself. Yet, unaccountably, he ignored the cardinal rule of sea captaincy: take every precaution to ensure the safety of passengers and crew. He never held any lifeboat or fire drills on the *Yumari*.

Three members of the engine-room staff filed a complaint with the Steamboat Inspection Division of the Department of Commerce in New York, stating that their lives had been endangered by the captain's behavior.

Warms pleaded that "the weather was bad and I had no time to hold the drills."

He lost his license for ten days; the Ward Line took away his command. For the first time since he had gone to sea, Warms was forced "on the beach." His year ashore was agonizing, made worse by the fact that it was the first blemish on his otherwise exemplary record.

Then he was given command of the Ward cruise liner *Agwistar*. In 1928 two fires mysteriously broke out on board. Once more the issue of proper fire precautions came under scrutiny; again Captain Warms lost his command, was demoted to first officer, and was forced ashore. To his dying day he would maintain he had been a scapegoat, a victim of intrigue.

In 1929 he returned to the sea, working on a Ward Line freighter. His dourness had become more marked. He tended to divide people into two categories: "professional seamen," and those "better left on the beach."

Warms was determined that he would never become involved in any situation which would drive him ashore again. For a year he had gone about his business, a mere name on the list of employees to those in the Ward Line's head office. But with seamen, William Warms had quietly established a reputation as probably the best cargo officer in the American merchant marine.

It was this reputation that influenced Captain Wilmott to choose him as his first officer. With the cargoes the *Morro Castle* carried, he needed an officer who knew the fastest way to load a hold—and how to keep his mouth shut.

What Robert Wilmott had not banked on was a deep-rooted personal clash between his first officer and chief engineer—two key men in any emergency.

After four years of increasing tension, Captain Wilmott told Warms he planned to settle it the only way he could: he would recommend that Eban Abbott be transferred as soon as possible to the Ward Line's other turbo-electric liner, the *Oriente*.

William Warms was pleased with the decision. In the privacy of his cabin, he wrote a page in an exercise book which he used from time to time to log important events in his life: "The seafarer in America is a race apart and neither the man nor his calling is thoroughly understood, and the most tragic part of the entire business is that nobody wants to understand."

Having written his soliloquy, Warms became concerned with a new idea: if Captain Wilmott continued his strange behavior, the company was bound to make him take a rest. If this happened, would the Ward Line give First Officer William Warms a third chance?

That Wednesday morning George Ignatius Alagna, the ship's first assistant radio officer, learned that for him any promotion within the Ward Line was out of the question. Indeed, his whole promising career appeared to be in jeopardy. At 11:30 A.M. he received a message from his employers, the Radiomarine Corporation of America, that he was to be relieved of his post when the voyage ended. There was no mention of a new assignment. At the age of twenty-two, the slim, dark, handsome Alagna faced a bitter lesson: his concern for the welfare of others had probably cost him his future.

Alagna had joined the *Morro Castle* in June 1934. Like all radio operators, he was leased to the ship by the Radiomarine Corporation, which had a virtual monopoly on radio men within the American merchant marine. The pay was good—eighty dollars a month— and the working conditions were reasonable. Alagna was one of three operators on the *Morro Castle*.

He soon discovered "there were not-so-hidden snags. The wireless shack was small. The three of us shared a tiny cabin next door to the transmitting room. And the food they served us was revolting."

There were other drawbacks, about which the instructors of the Indiana School of Technology at Fort Wayne had neglected to warn him. On the *Morro Castle,* fifty feet separated the bridge from the radio room, but in terms of personal contact they might as well have been a "billion fathoms apart."

There was also a separation—though not by distance —between Alagna and his radio-room colleagues. The junior member of the communications team was a nineteen-year-old, heavily muscled, blond Finn named Charles Maki. Maki still had problems with the English language which often made it necessary for him to spend an extra hour transcribing messages he received on watch.

Off duty, his favorite pastime was to trade punches with a fellow Finn. Maki and his friend took turns landing sledgehammer blows on each other until one of them collapsed, unconscious. Between these frequent contests of strength, Maki would lie on his bunk contemplating the bulkhead overhead, which he had covered with pictures of muscle men in countless poses clipped from a score of body-building magazines. Maki would lie there and flex his biceps, giving an excellent imitation of his heroes.

Stanley Ferson, chief radio officer when Alagna first joined the *Morro Castle,* was an altogether different personality. A lifetime of crouching over a transmitter and coping with static seemed to have permanently isolated him from ordinary human contact. Alagna exchanged no more than a handful of words with him.

In June 1934, Ferson was taken ill shortly before the *Morro Castle* sailed. She left for Havana with only two operators. Alagna was designated acting chief radio officer.

On the next trip Maki became ill. Ferson returned, taking over again as chief radio officer, and a newcomer was drafted into the radio room. To Alagna's fury, he found himself reduced to the most junior post. Only one thing stopped him from making a heated protest—the attitude of the newcomer. George White Rogers exuded understanding and sympathy for Alagna's situation.

Physically, Rogers was an extraordinary sight. He had a fringe of gray hair around his ears, and blue eyes buried in a mass of fat tissue. His neck was a fold of flesh connecting a massive head to shoulders that sloped sharply. Rogers spread outward to hips that were many inches wider than his chest. Overall, he resembled a pear.

By contrast with his almost repulsive figure, Rogers had a quiet, cooing voice and a smile which seemed to have been permanently set years before.

On his first night aboard Rogers had taken Alagna aside: "He said he was specially assigned by the Radiomarine Corporation to get information allowing them to sack Ferson and myself. I gathered that somebody on board had stuck a knife into us. Before acting, the Radiomarine wanted positive proof that we were no good. That was why Rogers was there." Rogers said, too, that he had already formed a favorable impression of Alagna, but still reserved judgment on Ferson.

It was an extraordinary tale, but to Alagna, new to the sea, inexperienced and not a little gullible, it was believable.

Perhaps it was naïveté which prompted Alagna to speak favorably of Ferson when Rogers expressed reservations about him; perhaps it was a genuine sense of grievance over working conditions aboard. Whatever the reason, George White Rogers had tapped a well of resentment in the young Alagna, who angrily spit forth a catalog of complaints: the food was little better than pig swill; working conditions were appalling; the officers seemed to have stepped out of the nineteenth century.

Rogers suggested a simple solution: "Organize a strike just before the ship sails on the next trip from New York. You will get all the backing you want on the ship and ashore."

Because of his "special position," Rogers said, he would be unable to participate. His involvement might compromise his "undercover work" for the Radiomarine Corporation.

That, too, seemed reasonable to George Alagna.

Exactly a year before, militant action by seamen—like the action Rogers was suggesting—had shattered the complacency of American shipowners. In August 1933, the crew of the *Diamond Cement* had staged the first sit-down strike in America. They demanded higher wages and better working conditions before they would go back to work. Waterfront workers along the entire East Coast backed them. A scab crew was prevented from boarding the ship. The shipping line finally capitulated and granted all the crew's demands. It was one of the great victories for militant American seamen.

The foundations for that strike had been carefully laid; the reinforcements to sustain it had been readily available.

George Alagna had neither of these prerequisites. All he had was his enthusiasm.

On the afternoon of Saturday, August 4, 1934, Alagna approached a number of the crew and junior officers an hour before sailing time. He urged them to walk off. Clutching a copy of the *Marine Workers'*

*Voice,* the official organ of the Marine Workers International Union, the radioman tried to duplicate the success of the *Diamond Cement*'s crew.

But by the time he had walked the length of the ship he had earned the enmity of Captain Wilmott and every senior officer. They looked on him as a saboteur, a dangerous radical willing to risk their livelihoods in an era when ships' officers would sign on as watchmen to make a living.

The deck crew was not much more sympathetic. Alagna's conditions on board were undoubtedly better than theirs; most of them had nothing in common with the well-spoken college graduate and his talk of a confrontation with the men who paid their wages.

The call to strike was a total failure.

Captain Wilmott wanted to fire Alagna at once, but Ferson and Rogers intervened. They argued they could not work a constant radio watch between them. The Radiomarine Corporation said it was impossible to find a replacement at such short notice.

So George Alagna was temporarily reprieved. But he was shunned by virtually all the officers and crew. The only exception was George White Rogers.

The radio shack continued to be a center of ferment. On August 11, 1934, Stanley Ferson walked off the *Morro Castle* when she docked in New York. His sudden departure baffled Alagna and a number of ship's officers; thirty-seven years would pass before the extraordinary circumstances behind Ferson's resignation were revealed.

With his departure, Rogers became chief radio officer, Alagna regained his old position as first assistant radioman, and Maki—absent during the furor—returned to complete the team.

As far as Maki was concerned, "Rogers ran an

easy shop. You did your job, and you relaxed the way you liked." Alagna, on the other hand, found it difficult to relax. He had started to get "the creeps."

He believed somebody was trying to waylay him, possibly even kill him, for the trouble he had caused. "I thought several times that I heard footsteps hurrying along behind me in the shadows of the deck. But each time, when I swung around to investigate, the deck would be vacant. I could neither see nor hear anyone when I was sure someone had been there but a moment before."

It may have been this stress which finally sealed the fate of George Alagna. On this trip, one day out of New York, as the *Morro Castle* steamed through the Florida Strait on her way to Havana, Alagna had been on radio duty. Suddenly he raced to the bridge and accused the watch officer, Second Officer Ivan Freeman, of tinkering with the radio compass on the bridge, jamming the main radio transmitter.

It was a ridiculous allegation; moreover, it offended Freeman's sense of propriety. Junior radiomen did not come to the bridge unless it was with a specific message; they certainly did not assail the officer of the watch. Freeman complained to Chief Officer Warms, who reported the incident to the captain. Captain Wilmott sent a signal to the Radiomarine Corporation demanding the immediate removal of Alagna on their return to New York.

The Radiomarine Corporation's relationship with shipping lines was impersonal: it was essentially a powerful employment agency supplying specialist staff. A ship was forced to accept a radio operator assigned by the corporation. The corporation was responsible for checking a radioman's qualifications, but no check was

29

ever made into a man's background. His health, political beliefs, and previous employment were of little concern.

By 1934 the corporation had become uncomfortably aware of a new militancy among its employees. The year before, radio operators had taken strike action for the first time—against the American Merchant Line, a subsidiary of the International Mercantile Marine, America's largest operator of merchant vessels.

In spite of their lack of experience—in soliciting assistance from the officials of the thriving Marine Workers Industrial Union, the radio operators asked such elementary questions as "How do we walk on a picket line?"—the strike was a success.

That success undoubtedly influenced the corporation when it was asked to withdraw Alagna from the *Morro Castle* after his strike call failed. The corporation knew that if they sided against Alagna, it could be construed by other militant radiomen as an attack on their right to strike.

But Captain Wilmott's charge of personal misbehavior on Alagna's part was a different matter.

On September 5, after the ship docked in Havana, George Alagna received the message that his service on the *Morro Castle* was to be terminated. For a while he sat alone in the silent radio room, contemplating the events that had brought such a sudden shift in fortune. Then he crumpled up the message and walked into the cramped living quarters he shared with the two other men.

Maki had gone ashore with his Finnish shipmate. George White Rogers lay stretched on his bunk, asleep. Though the wall thermometer read 100° F., the radio chief was fully dressed.

Watching him, Alagna was again struck by the fact

that he had never seen George White Rogers undressed. Whenever the chief radio officer changed from one faded white uniform to another, he always retired to the privacy of the officers' toilet. Into that tiny cubicle he invariably took a small bag. It was Maki who had discovered it contained puffs, powders, and lotions.

"You want something, George?"

With a shock Alagna realized that Rogers had been watching him for some moments without giving any signs of doing so.

Captain Robert Wilmott locked his cabin as soon as his visitor left. His worst fears had been confirmed by the Port of Havana chief of police, Captain Oscar Hernandez: Wilmott's life and ship were threatened.

Hernandez had warned the captain to be on the watch for a Communist agent. Evidently he had just received urgent information that the Cuban Communist Party wanted to sabotage the ship because she was aiding the lawful government, and had probably placed an agent on board.

In Captain Wilmott he found a ready listener. When the master of the *Morro Castle* then recounted the details of the mysterious fire, poisoning attempt, and the strike threat, Oscar Hernandez pronounced them all "classic symptoms of the presence of Reds." The captain accepted the police officer's diagnosis as an obvious explanation of the inexplicable.

In all his thirty-one years with the Ward Line, Robert Wilmott had accepted the obvious. He was the archetypal company man, not given to questioning or probing. Big-boned, with a face crimped by the weather, deep-set eyes and a head of graying, close-cropped hair, Wilmott liked his pipe, instant decisions, and good food. He had a fondness for imagery which delighted his women passengers. Few would have guessed that at home he had a passion for classic literature and music.

Since childhood he had had only one ambition: to command a passenger ship. Born in London, he left England in 1902 as a deck boy on a freighter to New York. Ten years later, on a chilly April day, Third Officer Wilmott was on the bridge of a Ward Line cargo boat when the *Carpathia* came up past the Statue of Liberty into New York Harbor, carrying 705 survivors of the *Titanic,* which had struck an iceberg in mid-Atlantic on her maiden voyage. The loss of over 1500 lives shocked the world. To Wilmott, the aspiring captain, the tragedy had a more significant dimension: the master of the *Titanic* had gone down with his ship.

Wilmott showed a similar dedication as he climbed the promotional rungs of the Ward Line. The reward came in August 1930: command of the company's flagship, the *Morro Castle.* At the age of fifty-two, Wilmott realized his life's ambition.

On his first day aboard, he committed to memory the ship's vital statistics: gross tonnage, 11,520; net tonnage, 6449; displacement, 15,870; length overall, 528 feet; length between perpendiculars, 482 feet; beam molded, 70 feet 9 inches; depth molded to shelter deck, 39 feet; total cargo space, 335,000 cubic feet; type of machinery, twin-screw turbine-electric drive; shaft horsepower, 16,000; boilers, 6 watertube.

Though few passengers even remotely understood these specifications, Captain Wilmott recited them regularly in his speech of welcome after dinner on the first night at sea.

Dinner at his table was a treat for first-class passengers, whom he regaled with tales of rounding the Horn and roaring through the China Sea. It was not all myth: in September 1933, he had spent seventy-five continuous hours on the bridge steering the *Morro Castle* through a hurricane.

On the next voyage that September, he had astonished everybody by falling in love with a first-class passenger, the recently widowed Mrs. Mathilda Howell Reed. He was fifty-five years old; she was a few years younger. They spent their honeymoon on a two-week cruise to Mexico and Havana. Since then, they were usually able to get together only a few hours each Saturday, when the *Morro Castle* took on new supplies for the next run to Havana. While he was away, Mrs. Wilmott occupied her days as a store detective; by night she tuned her radio set to receive classical concerts from Europe.

Both on land and at sea, Robert Wilmott had enjoyed a largely trouble-free life. Now that the events of the past few months had at last been isolated and given a label that he could instantly apply, the captain wasted no time. He picked up the telephone and asked the ship's operator to connect him with Chief Officer William Warms.

"Bill," he said, "there's a Red in the radio shack. Get some irons."

# 2.
# CHARADE

To the passengers, the ship's cruise director—on the *Morro Castle*, his name was Robert Smith—was the front-desk manager, the social bell captain, the man in the blue blazer and raffish cap who was always on hand with some new amusement. The Ward Line's brochures were confident that the passengers' expectations would be met: "The Cruise Director is a genial chap with an abundance of new and smart ideas that he will spring on you at unexpected moments, and that will keep you interested all the time."

At this moment, Robert Smith was in the process of staging one of those "new and smart ideas"—what the ship's itinerary called a get-together.

As cruise director of the *Morro Castle,* Smith spent a great deal of time sizing people up, and get-togethers were an ideal opportunity to do so. Almost intuitively he could sift the important passengers from those who went on a cruise to pretend they were important.

Before the *Morro Castle* docked in Havana on Tuesday, September 4, Smith had completed his calculations. There were 318 passengers. Thirty-two of them, mostly Cuban, were using the ship simply as a means of transport to Havana. They traveled tourist, and Smith had decided to leave them to their own devices in the stern of the ship. Another, larger, group on board consisted of the 102 members of the Concordia Singing Society of East New York. Occupying almost the whole of C deck, they established themselves as a self-contained group, dining, playing, and dancing as a bloc.

That left the cruise director with just under two hundred people to amuse for six days—and a series of get-togethers was a safe, guaranteed way of doing so.

On this particular Wednesday noon, he was assembling most of the two hundred "assorted passengers" on the pier at Havana. He would address them for a few minutes on the delights ahead, bundle them into a flotilla of open cars, and wave the drivers away. Then he could go back on to the *Morro Castle* for three hours' sleep before the convoy returned.

Smith watched, with a glad-eye smile for the ladies, as the get-together assembled.

The group standing before him was representative of the lower and middle brackets of the American urban middle class. A few were obviously rich. Most were from the cities of the Eastern Seaboard, many from the New York City area. About a fourth of them were married, and one third were Jewish.

Most passengers were on the cruise just for "a hell of a big time," but many of the unattached women were searching—in earnest—for husbands. Robert Smith calculated that the single women outnumbered the bachelors by about two to one.

The trip itself was not very expensive. Most of the passengers had spent between $80 and $120 for the return passage; a few had splurged $160 for a deluxe cabin. Some traveled at the minimum fare offered, $65, the price of a twin-bed, inside cabin for the seven nights.

Still, many would have to scrimp for months ahead, as they had done for months before. They were people whose short holiday fell in summer and was swiftly gone. Leisure, not being a customary part of their lives, was precious to them. Fortunately, the ship's designers —or her promoters, at any rate—understood this. The *Morro Castle* was fashioned in the image of her clientele: young, pleasant, and somehow, invincibly fun-loving. She was the sea-going version of a second-string summer resort, a low-priced sports car, or the newest and best hotel in a provincial city. The Line's brochures did everything they could to assure passengers their leisure time would be a delightful "life on the ocean wave."

Once the *Morro Castle* docked in Havana, the majority of passengers spent their time ashore on conducted tours. They traveled through the bewildering maze of city streets at high speed, pausing only at brochure-touted places so that they could at least say they had been to Havana. They trooped in and out of the Church of Our Lady of Mercy and a cigar factory that claimed to hand-roll cigars for Buckingham Palace. They viewed the *Maine* Monument, a game of jai alai, and had a drink at Sloppy Joe's, which no self-respecting Cuban ever set foot in. Bowing slightly to avoid cracking their heads on the low-beamed doorway, the tourists entered the Grand Tomb of Bars, ordered rounds of rum, and commented on the beauty of the woodwork and the exquisiteness of the potted palms.

Taking advantage of the night life in one of the raciest cities in the world was encouraged by the Ward Line's brochure: "You may prefer some of those light-hearted, noisy native cabarets where *criollo* airs are played for the voluptuous *son,* the *danzonete,* the *danzon* and the *rumba.*"

36

Cruise director Robert Smith could steer the passengers any way he wanted. Most of them had no idea what they were missing of the real Havana. Like a cheerleader, Smith led them through a litany by now familiar to all of them:

"Are we happy?"

"Yes," came the chorused response.

"Are we going to have a good time now?"

"Sure."

"Good, good, good! Now listen to this!"

Then, with the air of largesse of a man who had paid for it all out of his own pocket, Robert Smith outlined the festivities ahead.

"First, a visit to a typical Cuban farm. An amazing revelation, folks, of tropical luxuriance. Sugar cane, pineapples, coconuts, tobacco, and, for the ladies, a world of flowers. On the way back you will visit the world-famous Tropical Gardens and taste their unique hospitality, drive down the Avenue of Bamboo Trees and the Royal Palm Drive to the Country Club Park, La Playa, the Yacht Club. On to 'Old Havana,' with its winding streets and balconied houses that might have been brought intact from Seville. Then, back on board ready for sailing time—and new games!"

They shouted approval, climbed into the open-top cars, and thundered away from the pier.

Robert Smith watched them go, beaming happily. Not a single passenger reminded him that the delights of the excursion were memorized word for word from Ward Line brochures available to passengers in any New York travel agency. They were still perfect tourists.

To reward them on their return to the ship, Robert Smith had devised a new and exciting game. All he needed was formal approval from Captain Wilmott.

The game was to be called "Lifeboat Rescue."

For Dr. Joseph Bregstein, the 1168-mile run to Havana had been exactly fifty-eight hours and forty minutes of bitter disappointment.

The thirty-four-year-old widowed dentist had paid out over two hundred dollars for a first-class twin-bedded stateroom on a trip he hoped would be an "exciting time," not only for him, but also for his nine-year-old son, Mervyn. A promise from one of his patients, a high official of the Ward Line, to introduce them to the captain and officers of the *Morro Castle,* seemed to assure the success of the father-son adventure.

Apart from being a holiday, the journey was also intended to be one of personal discovery for both of them. Joe Bregstein faced one of the most difficult situations any father faces—introducing a stepmother into a close-knit family unit.

Two years had passed since the tragic death of Joe Bregstein's wife. The scars were still there, but in recent months there had been a visible healing process. Joe had fallen in love again. It had been a gentle courtship; neither Joe nor his fiancée, Muriel Rubine, an attractive Brooklyn woman, wanted to rush things. But when Joe proposed and a formal engagement announcement was pending, both wondered how Mervyn would react. In New York there had been neither a real opportunity nor the time to find out.

As the *Morro Castle* headed toward Havana, it seemed to Bregstein that something must have gone wrong: nobody seemed to remember the promises of special treatment. No one, in fact, seemed the least bit concerned about the Bregsteins' comfort—or lack of it.

Joe Bregstein, never a pushing man, decided to let matters take their course. After briefly exploring the ship, father and son had gone for an early dinner.

Assigned to a corner table looking out over the ocean, they sat virtually alone in the dining room full of white tables, glittering with institutional silverware. The white-coated stewards, Bregstein thought, seemed distantly polite, but by no means obsequious. Like the room stewards and the rank and file of the crew, they were apparently quite unaware of passengers' needs. The dentist wasn't sure whether their attitudes were intentionally annoying or not.

The food, when it came, was hardly first-class fare: standard, sterile, turgid, "the sort of stuff you would get in a summer hotel," Bregstein recalled later. "There was turkey and duck, both with the kind of stuffing which tastes like kitchen soap. The salads were those fancy American ones, but the dressings seemed to have been bottled years before. The whole thing was an attempt to pass off refrigerated mutton as best-quality spring lamb."

Lamb, in fact, eventually caused the mild-mannered dentist to explode. "Mervyn couldn't eat the stuff they offered on the menu. I asked for a couple of lamb chops. The waiter said they weren't on the menu so they couldn't be served. I reminded him this was first class. He shrugged as if he couldn't have cared less. I insisted, so he went away and eventually returned with the chops.

"In one of them was a nail which had obviously been slipped in after the meat was cooked. I called the head waiter, and he apologized as if he had been doing so all his life on the ship. He said there was always trouble with waiters. We both agreed that the waiter who could slip a nail into a guest's food had no place serving meals."

There were other things which disturbed the dentist

and made him wonder whether the ship he was on was really the *Morro Castle* of the glossy advertisements.

There were no life jackets in his cabin; there had been no lifeboat or fire drills. He also noticed that some crew members doubled up on jobs; deckhands would don stewards' jackets to help out during the evening cocktail hour.

Disturbed by all he saw, Joe Bregstein had not yet found an opportunity to bring up with Mervyn the subject of his forthcoming marriage to Muriel.

Nor had the brief and hectic sojourn in Havana offered an appropriate moment. As soon as father and son stepped ashore, they were surrounded by a bevy of guides eager for their business. In the end they took a conducted tour of the city designed to take the tourist for his last cent. At the Cathedral they ran the gauntlet of priests with collection plates. They had to pay at the cigar factory, and at the monument to the *Maine,* the beggars gave them no rest.

On this last day in Havana, the Bregsteins broke through the ring of guides crowding the pier, fended off the street salesmen, shoe-shine boys, hawkers, and pimps, and lost themselves in the Havana the brochures ignored.

Several times Joe Bregstein tried to raise the subject of the future, but each time Mervyn drew his father's attention to some new sight. Bregstein decided to wait with the heart-to-heart talk until they were back on board and on their way to New York.

Joe Bregstein's discoveries were evidence of a crack in the *Morro Castle*'s façade. The carefully nurtured fable that she was manned by "the cream of American seamen" was apparently just a fable.

In fact, crew troubles had plagued the ship since her second voyage. Her schedule allowed only seven hours in New York every Saturday. In that time the crew had to refuel and load supplies, cargo, and a fresh group of passengers. Only Captain Wilmott and the officers were allowed ashore. Deck crew wishing to leave the ship had to sign off, thereby giving up their jobs in an era of unemployment.

This led to acrimony and dissension, which, over the years, degenerated to the point where the *Morro Castle* increasingly drew only seamen of poor quality. To make matters worse, many of the crew—which on the present voyage included 134 aliens and 64 "foreign-born citizens"—could hardly speak English.

At the end of every voyage there were dismissals. Four days previously while the ship was in New York, making preparations for this voyage, forty deck crew and a dozen stewards had been sacked for a variety of offenses including alleged drunkenness, theft, and assault. Already scheduled for dismissal after this trip were six dining-room stewards, a couple of cabin stewards, an electrician, five deckhands, and radioman George Alagna.

Passenger William Price was a thirty-eight-year-old New York police patrolman on vacation with his wife Mary. The morning of September 5, they had spent several exhausting hours ashore, buying cigars, perfumes, and souvenirs. Now they leaned over the ship's rail, watching men and boys diving for coins in the foul water between the pier and the black-hulled ship.

Bored with throwing dimes into the sewage, the Prices were about to go to their stateroom on D deck when a shrill whistle sounded on the port side. There was a pounding of feet, shouts, and somebody shouted,

"Break out da hose, Chrissake, break out da hose!"

Suspecting trouble, and with a warning cry to his wife to stay where she was, Price raced across the promenade deck, unbuttoning his sports jacket as he ran. The shoulder holster and pistol he wore strapped to his body were in clear view. For a moment Price stood there, hand hovering around the gun butt, taking in a most unusual scene: the *Morro Castle* was having its first fire drill in three months.

First Officer William Warms had given the order. It is almost certain there would have been no fire drill if Captain Robert Wilmott had been in full command. Warms's order directly contradicted a policy the master of the *Morro Castle* first instituted on June 16, 1934. On that day—in violation of the seaworthy certificate issued by the government's Bureau of Navigation and Steamboat Inspection, and at the risk of endangering the lives of everybody on board—Captain Wilmott had banned all further fire drills.

His order could lay him open to prosecution, imprisonment, and the certain loss of his master's license. Confronted by the classic dilemma of the company man, Wilmott had acted in what he believed to be the Ward Line's best interests.

The basis for his decision was simple. In May 1934, during a fire drill, a woman passenger had fallen on a deck wet down by a leaking joint connection between a fire hose and its hydrant. She fractured an ankle and hired a good lawyer, and the Ward Line settled out of court for twenty-five thousand dollars.

Captain Wilmott, after a visit to the shipping line office, ordered the *Morro Castle* deck fire hydrants capped and sealed; 2100 feet of fire hose was locked away, along with nozzles, outlets, and wrenches for each length of hose.

Whether the captain received positive instructions from an executive of the Ward Line, or whether he acted independently, is not known, nor is it important. What is known is that as a result of Wilmott's order, the pride of the American merchant marine, one of the fastest and most luxurious liners afloat, became from that moment on, a floating fire hazard in all but its cargo holds. If a fire started in any of the passenger areas, the only pieces of equipment readily available to fight it were seventy-three half-gallon portable fire extinguishers and twenty-one carbon tetrachloride extinguishers.

How this extraordinary situation could possibly have gone undetected can be explained in part by the fact that the required annual inspection of the ship had been carried out by government inspectors on May 16, 1934, a month before Captain Wilmott issued his order. The inspectors concluded that the *Morro Castle* still had the right to "the highest classification" of the American Bureau of Shipping.

But other questions raised after a routine reinspection by another team of government inspectors on August 4, 1934, remain largely unanswered. There is disagreement on how exacting the inspection was. Crew members, like O'Sullivan and Gross, insisted later that the inspection was little more than "a walk around and then a drink with the captain." Officers Warms and Freeman maintained it was a "thorough going-over." If it was, why were the secured fire hydrants not noticed? Why did the ship's officers remain silent? Why didn't the crew make some effective protest?

It will never be possible to answer the first question:

the reports filed on the August reinspection no longer exist. Concerning the silence of officers and crew, remarks made years later by Third Officer Clarence Hackney and seaman John Gross may provide a clue. "When making a living means not being difficult, then you are not difficult."

The fire drill ordered by William Warms was a charade. He refused to allow any water to be used—in case another passenger should slip, be injured, and collect substantial damages from the Ward Line.

Without water, there was no way to test the single 42-foot length of hose he ordered removed from the ship's storeroom for the drill.

Taking their cue from such lax leadership, the handful of men on the hose treated the drill as if it were carnival time. They did not couple it up to a hydrant; instead they ran up and down the deck, lugging the hose along. Ports, deadlights, convention valves, deck baffles, fireproof valves, and watertight doors—none were tested.

Seaman Gross regarded the whole affair as a "damn fool pantomime. There weren't enough men at the hose. We just rolled it out and played it around. Off-duty stewards lay around the deck sunning themselves, reading books, and just sitting around. Not one of them had any idea what to do in a fire."

The whole exercise was over in moments. Sheepishly, the seamen rolled up the hose—through which not a drop of water had flowed—and carried it back to the storeroom.

During all of this, Gross was particularly perplexed by the sight of police patrolman William Price standing nearby, observing, "as if he had stepped out of the pages of *True Detective.*" Gross could not figure out why a passenger needed to carry a gun on vacation.

In Suite 107 on B deck, honeymooners Charles and Selma Widder slept, oblivious to the "fire drill," happily exhausted after four days of almost nonstop revelry.

The voyage had surpassed the Widders' wildest expectations. From the moment they boarded, JUST MARRIED chalked on their luggage by some of the two hundred guests at their fashionable Brooklyn wedding, they had been caught up in a whirlwind of flowers, champagne, candy, and honeymoon euphoria. The rose-wood-paneled stateroom was part of a scene which, for twenty-two-year-old Selma, was nothing short of a "fairy tale."

By day the couple sunbathed and played shuffleboard and deck tennis. In the afternoon they could be seen waltzing at the tea dances, and in the evening, attending the gala balls. Whenever they paused there always seemed to be a waiter on hand with an ice bucket and a bottle of champagne—Charles' generosity with money saw to that. It was "the honeymoon of a lifetime" in all but one respect. Charles Widder still awaited the promised invitation for his bride and himself to dine at the captain's table.

Embarrassment, more than anything else, made Raymond Aloysius Egan, a twenty-seven-year-old bachelor, reluctant to return to the ship before he had to. Going back meant facing another round of well-intentioned prodding for him to pick up one of the single girls on board and have a "good time."

Raymond Egan did not choose to explain—although his reason was simple enough—out of "genuine consideration for the other passengers," and a confused idea about the traditions of the sea. He had read that seamen and vacationers felt ill at ease when a clergyman was aboard.

Raymond Egan was a Roman Catholic priest. The only two symbols of his calling he had brought with him were his clerical collar and a daily office. Both were packed away in his trunk.

Dr. Charles Cochrane left every symbol of his profession behind in New York. This cruise was intended as his first complete vacation in three years. He was accompanied by his sister, Catherine, a woman of delicate health who, he believed, would benefit from the sea breezes.

Few on board knew he was one of New York's most distinguished general physicians. From previous experience Charles Cochrane knew the inevitable problems which would arise if it were generally known he was a doctor. "A doctor is somebody to be consulted at the first rumble of pain," he told one of the passengers. "People do so without a second thought—though they would never dream of consulting a bank manager about financial problems if he was on vacation with them."

Tall, elegant, and naturally reserved, Dr. Cochrane managed to keep a suitable distance between his sister and himself, and the other first-class passengers. He had ensured privacy for the two of them by booking the most expensive pair of cabins on the *Morro Castle,* staterooms one and two on A deck. Each suite cost $160 for the seven days—the price of indulging in the Ward Line's idea of life on a "millionaire's yacht."

Forward of all other passenger accommodations and immediately beneath the navigating bridge, the location of the Cochranes' suites provided a superb panoramic view of the ocean ahead. Somehow, though, the interior decorators had failed to capitalize on the suites' superb location. The palm-tree green walls were covered with murals of New York and Havana. The furniture, resting on coconut-milk-colored carpeting, was heavy and covered with lace doilies and chintz. Replicas of Colonial fireplaces camouflaged the air-conditioning intakes.

Apart from the absence of the captain from their dinner table, the cruise so far had been what Dr. Cochrane expected. Catherine looked better than she had in years, and he himself had finally been able to relax.

The rumors about the captain did, however, concern him. Some of the gossip, he knew, was fantasy: he dismissed as preposterous the idea that the captain of the *Morro Castle* wanted to be relieved of his command, or that the visit aboard of a senior police officer that morning had been linked with some distant incident in Robert Wilmott's past life.

On the other hand, Dr. Cochrane was disturbed by the captain's behavior: his almost complete seclusion in his cabin and his worried and strained appearance during his few public appearances. Such obvious signs of stress in the man charged with the safety of all on board were not reassuring.

More than once Dr. Cochrane had wondered whether there was any connection between the captain's behavior and that of the crew. After nearly four full days aboard the *Morro Castle,* the physician had the impression that many of them were not competent to handle any emergency that might arise.

On September 5, at five o'clock—an hour before

sailing time—Dr. Cochrane and his sister were alone on the sun deck watching the last hold being filled with a cargo of salted hides. The stench was awful.

Catherine Cochrane wondered aloud whether the smell would spread to the rest of the ship. Whether her brother believed what he said or not, he assured her that "the men on the bridge" knew how to control it.

Third Officer Clarence Hackney had just received orders from Captain Wilmott on how to control the odor. In twenty years at sea, three of which he had spent aboard the *Morro Castle,* Hackney had never received such a baffling command.

He had been instructed that once the hold with the cargo of skins was sealed, the ship's smoke-detecting system was to be turned off and was to remain switched off until the last passenger had disembarked in New York.

The system was the most sophisticated early warning of a fire hazard then available. In the *Morro Castle* it was composed of twenty-seven lines of piping leading from the various cargo spaces to a detector cabinet in the wheelhouse. An exhaust fan drew a continuous sample of air through each pipe to the cabinet: the system was so sensitive that, Hackney knew, "anybody having a smoke in the hold would have been spotted at once."

This system, in fact, had indicated the attempted arson in number five hold two weeks previously. With this order from Captain Wilmott, the cruise liner was no longer afforded such protection. At the time, the only explanation Clarence Hackney could give for the change of procedure was that Wilmott was "putting the passengers in front of everything. If there was a fire in the cargo areas, we would have to rely on our noses."

At 5:15 P.M. he shut the valves in the cabinet tubes.

At about that moment Chief Radio Officer George Rogers lumbered ashore. No one would ever know exactly where he went or whom he met, but when he returned he carried two small bottles. One contained sulphuric acid; the other nitric acid.

# 3.
# RUMORS OF SABOTAGE

At 5:30 P.M., thirty minutes before sailing time, Chief Officer William Warms reported to Captain Wilmott what he knew about the activities of another *Morro Castle* radioman. Warms had been logging every move made by George Alagna, and now he was telling Wilmott that the young radioman had gone to the mess for an early dinner.

Had Alagna known what he was suspected of, he would have laughed incredulously.

William Warms and Robert Wilmott believed he was a Communist agitator, ready at any moment to sabotage the *Morro Castle*.

For those on the watch for evidence—real or imagined—of Communist agitation, the *Morro Castle* had been a special focus of attention since its first voyage. Flamboyant Captain Oscar Hernandez—in his white suit and floppy hat, cheroot clamped in his mouth, looking a little like Groucho Marx—was one who expressed particular concern. The more conservative Harold Brust, for eighteen years a detective-inspector with Scotland Yard's Special Branch, was another.

During his time at the Yard Brust's responsibility was political agitators. In 1929, he retired from police work to join the Cuban National Syndicate, which looked after the interests of the island's tourist trade.

By the end of 1930 Brust had notified the syndicate that the *Morro Castle* was "at risk" for transporting arms. The warning was forwarded to the Cuban government, but no action was taken.

A few months later Brust provided the Havana police with information which led to the arrest of six Spaniards who had booked passage on the *Morro Castle*. Their luggage contained caches of gunpowder and time fuses. They admitted to being Communists.

In August 1933, crowds marched on the Cuban presidential palace, and the Army, too, turned against Machado. He was forced to resign and fled the country, to be replaced by an even harsher dictator. Brust was alarmed to see that the quantity of arms cargo transported by the *Morro Castle* to the new junta increased.

In March 1934, he again uncovered evidence of a Communist plot to sabotage the ship. Prompt action produced a spate of arrests.

Early in September of the same year Brust first warned Captain Hernandez of yet another potential threat to the ship by Cuban Communists. Brust was adamant on one point: his information, which he claimed was extremely reliable, indicated that it would be "at least a full month before they will make a move."

In warning the ship's captain, Captain Hernandez omitted this last detail. Captain Wilmott thought his suspicions against Alagna confirmed; as far as he could see it was only a small step from trying to stage a strike on his ship to actually trying to destroy it.

There may well have been a new plot against the ship. Brust's record as an investigator deserved respect: his previous warnings had been timely and correct. And in fact, the Cuban Communists were anxious to make headlines; destroying an American ship that was secretly transporting arms to Cuba would ensure that.

But for maximum effect, they should strike when the ship was headed for Cuba, carrying its lethal cargo, and not on the return trip. There seems to have been one attempt: the fire in number five hold; it is still unclear whether it was part of a Communist plot, or the work of a madman, or both.

If it was true that the best time to attack was when the ship was carrying high explosives, the real period of danger was the next trip out of New York. By then George Ignatius Alagna would no longer be aboard the *Morro Castle*.


But at this moment, thirty minutes before the *Morro Castle* was to leave Havana for New York, Alagna was still a part of the crew. And Captain Wilmott, obsessed with "radicals and Reds," was pressing William Warms for assurances that "everything was under control."

The atmosphere in the captain's cabin must have been a strange one: the special agent plotting with the master spy about ways to trap a "dangerous" Communist—George Alagna.

The most baffling thing about this scene was William Warms' complete willingness to accept the guilt of Alagna; actually, he had more reason to be suspicious of another member of the crew.

The story he had heard in New York about how George White Rogers, the chief radio officer, really came to be aboard the *Morro Castle,* disturbed Warms. He kept it strictly to himself; "there was something about George that didn't make you anxious to tangle with him."

So First Officer Warms joined his captain in railroading the twenty-two-year-old striker. Whether he did it out of a sense of loyalty to his captain or not, and whether he kept silent about Rogers because of the probability of ridicule or because he really feared Rogers, are matters for speculation.

Both Warms and Captain Wilmott were anti-Communists. Both believed—as did many in the Merchant Navy—that Communism presented a real threat to seafaring. Both men also disliked George Alagna. Warms believed he was no more than a "trouble-making whipper-snapper with fancy ideas." Wilmott, on the other hand, regarded him as a committed Communist who would use arson and poison to get his own way, although the captain had no evidence linking him with the attempted arson or the poisoning.

Yet somehow, during their secretive meeting that afternoon, the two men came to the same conclusion: Alagna was a dangerous *agent provocateur,* either a dedicated party member, or a willing tool of the Communists.

They disagreed on only one thing: the best way to cope with the situation. Captain Wilmott wanted George Alagna clapped in irons for the return voyage and handed over to the FBI in New York. Warms argued against this, not on humanitarian grounds but because of the difficulties it posed: the bad publicity for the line; the possibility of the Radiomarine Corporation's demand for an independent inquiry; undue concern among the passengers; the refusal of the other two radiomen to work with a depleted staff; and, most importantly, the ship's lack of adequate irons.

As an alternative, William Warms suggested keeping a "close watch" on Alagna until the ship reached New York, at which point the radioman would "go on the beach" and become somebody else's problem.

Captain Wilmott finally agreed to the "close watch" policy. In doing so, he committed his most unfortunate mistake since banning fire drills.

Dr. Emilio Giro was late boarding the *Morro Castle;* most of the other Cubans embarking at Havana had arrived at the ship during the afternoon. Dr. Giro, who had planned to travel to New York with another shipping line, was unable to get a berth. Quite by chance he had passed the Ward Line offices, entered, and discovered that they had a vacant double stateroom. He would share it with his brother-in-law, Rafael Mestre.

The tall, dark-eyed Mestre was what the Ward Line brochures called "typically Cuban." His infectious laugh and his enthusiasm for life charmed everyone he came in contact with. In addition, he was twenty years old, rich, and single. As he bounded up the gangway, the first thing he checked was the number of pretty, unattached American girls on board. Mestre was in luck: there were plenty to ensure him a good time all the way to New York.

Emilio Giro was thirty-four years old, well off, married, with an infant daughter Sylvia, named after his wife. He was short and slim and soberly dressed—and not one who encouraged casual social contact. Firmly established as Cuba's outstanding specialist in the field of endocrinology, Dr. Giro was going to America for two months to do further research.

A cautious man, he approached the *Morro Castle* as if she were an interesting patient. First he formed an overall impression of her shape, size, and coloring: black-hulled, rising to a towering white structure, the ship was sleek and graceful and quite the largest he had ever traveled on.

Next he inspected the stateroom. It was compact and planned with care. On the back of the door Dr. Giro read a notice, framed in glass, in English and Spanish:

TO ALL PASSENGERS
The necessary number of life preservers for adults and children will be found in each stateroom.
*Directions for Use:*
Slip the arms through the shoulder straps and secure the belt across the body and under the arms.
Your lifeboat is: No. 10.
Your lifeboat station is B deck.

Emilio Giro located a life jacket under each bed. Then he set off to find lifeboat number ten.

According to her shipbuilder, the *Morro Castle* was a "three-deck, complete superstructure type, with combined forecastle head and long bridge, forming a flush deck forward; double-bridged, with an overhanging promenade deck of steel, as are the companion hoods, enclosures, skylights, domes, and the like."

For their part, the interior designers had succeeded in eliminating any hint of the sea in the passenger compartments. False casement windows accented a decor which stylistically mixed something called "Olde English" with the wilder moments of the Italian Renaissance.

Some public rooms almost captured the mood of Elizabethan England: lutes and mandolins hung on the walls of the first-class smoking room. A shattering canvas of what looked like the Mad Hatter's tea party being held in the forecourt of Windsor Castle dominated the dining room. The first-class lounge resembled the drawing room at Versailles during the time of Louis XVI. Overwhelming sweeps of white mahogany were interwoven with wenching.

The *Titanic* had started a trend in nonnaval interior design which the *Morro Castle* carried to the extreme. Redwood, plywood, satinwood, ebony, and rosewood combined to provide false walls, ceilings, and doors.

Traveling first class on the *Morro Castle* was like putting to sea in the Waldorf-Astoria.

Tourist-class accommodations for ninety-five passengers were located well aft on C, D, and E decks. Here, the rich paneling and carpeting gave way to paint and linoleum. Plain-glass wall fittings replaced diffuse lighting. The ventilation system, which pumped carefully measured doses of sea air into the first-class areas, here carried the sniff of engine-room oil and cooking fat from the kitchen.

Dr. Giro located lifeboat number ten on the port side of A deck. The boat was made of steel; he guessed it would hold at least fifty people (its actual capacity was seventy persons). At first he was puzzled that his embarkation station was below on B deck, the promenade deck. Then he realized that for easy access, seamen would lower the boats to the level of the deck below, where the passengers could "just step in."

Satisfied with his inspection, Dr. Giro went below to the promenade deck to watch the final preparations before departure.

He was not in time to see the huge waddling figure of Chief Radio Officer George White Rogers puffing his way to the wireless shack.

Dr. Giro was probably the only man on board qualified to recognize Rogers for what he was—the victim of an unusual medical disease, adiposogenital dystrophy, also known as Fröhlich's syndrome, a pituitary disorder which frequently produces social maladjustment in which intelligence is not impaired, only warped.

Of all the officers and crew in responsible positions, the chief radio officer was probably the least suited for his responsibility.

George White Rogers was born with the pituitary disorder on June 9, 1901, in New York City. His mother, Lulu, suffered from a similar glandular disturbance.

It gave her a rotund figure—poor equipment for husband catching. It appears also to have affected her personality: she had a self-defending reserve. In 1897 she had met George Rogers, Sr. They married in the fall of that year. He was a reticent man, with strong religious convictions. During the week he drove a dray cart; on Sundays he read aloud from the Bible.

Even before their marriage, there was very little communication between the two members of this badly matched couple. The arrival of baby George four years after their marriage did nothing to awaken any true intimacy between them.

In August 1906, George Rogers, Sr., took his family West to San Francisco. He had been attracted by newspaper reports that there was money to be made —big money—by anyone willing to work hard to rebuild the city shattered by earthquake and fire.

The newspaper reports proved to be untrue. There was work, plenty of it, but there was no fortune to be made hauling rubble with a horse and cart. In the space of six months, George Rogers, Sr., tried three separate haulage firms in the hope of increasing his income.

Meanwhile Lulu Rogers became increasingly withdrawn. Their chubby eighteen-month-old baby grew into a puffy-faced four-year-old. His parents dismissed

George's overweight as "puppy fat."

In the spring of 1907 George Rogers, Sr., died of a chest infection; a few weeks later Lulu Rogers joined him in the municipal cemetery of San Francisco. George was taken to live with his maternal grandmother in nearby Oakland.

At the age of seven he contracted pneumonia, from which he recovered only after weeks of nursing. At this point a new and alarming symptom appeared. In a month he gained almost fifty pounds, most of it concentrated in the abdominal region and around the hips and thighs; the upper arms and the back of the neck were also affected. The disproportions were accented by the thinness of his lower arms and legs.

Taunted increasingly by the neighborhood children, George Rogers must have been a pitiful sight—an enormous boy, wearing cut-downs of his grandfather's clothes. By the age of twelve he had assumed truly monstrous proportions. He weighed 170 pounds, was unusually tall, and was already beginning to go bald. His knock knees, flaring pelvis, soft facial features, and short, pudgy hands made him even more susceptible to ridicule.

He had also become painfully aware of the classic symptom of his illness, the one that haunted him from then on: he was sexually underdeveloped. His genitals were minute and hidden in a heavy fold of fat tissue. His pubes, breasts, and hairless skin seemed inordinately feminine, and his voice never deepened into a manly register. The effect of all this on him was devastating: the fat child who had a tendency to laugh for no apparent reason became a secretive and reclusive adolescent.

By the age of eighteen, the psychological harm was deep and permanent. In an attempt to stimulate sexual growth, George Rogers would rub his organs with various quack lotions and ointments, a practice which became a fetish with him. He refused to wear underpants, believing the friction of his trousers against his skin would encourage pubic hair to grow.

He had a disturbing habit of breaking off a conversation abruptly and falling asleep almost instantly. In his mid-twenties, he added five years to his actual age, in the belief, he once confided, that he would be "more respected."

Respect was the one thing George White Rogers wanted more than anything. He equated it with love, happiness, power, and glory. Respect could compensate for the cruel trick nature had played on him.

By the time George White Rogers joined the *Morro Castle* he was literally obsessed with his sexual immaturity. Although he had married, the union had been a disaster. That failure had increased his hatred of his body, which now weighed 250 pounds; his was a girdle-type obesity, with a predilection for the abdomen and hips. He believed, in the intense, frightening way of the true psychotic, that others hated his bulk as well. The memories of cruel teasing by the neighborhood children became a painful carry-over to adulthood.

Over the years he came to believe that his misshapen body kept him from achieving the other prize he sought: recognition.

At numerous stages of his life, the craving went out of control. At the age of thirteen he claimed he was descended from one of the original Pilgrim families; at sixteen he went around San Francisco dressed as a ship's officer. Three years later, when he applied for a job as a shore telegraphist, he stated he had been a wireless operator since 1910, the year of his ninth birthday.

George White Rogers worked his way through that and other jobs. Invariably he was given his walking papers.

Now, after three months on the *Morro Castle,* it happened again: the Radiomarine Corporation told him a few hours before the ship sailed from New York that this was to be his last trip. His dismissal followed a confidential investigation into his background by corporation executives.

Exactly why the investigation was authorized and who authorized it are still the carefully guarded secrets of the Radiomarine Corporation. But one thing is clear: it was a highly unusual move to have such an inquiry made into the background of a radioman. The details of the final report on Rogers are not available for examination. The report was sent and presumably read by J. B. Duffy, the corporation's superintendent, who gave the order that Rogers should be sacked.

Rogers believed—mistakenly—that a number of people on the ship had been questioned during the inquiries. Unfortunately, Rogers' paranoia on this matter was not just absurd: it was dangerous. At some point during the voyage to Havana, nursing his hatred, believing himself once more the victim of unfounded injustice, George White Rogers finally allowed his fantasies a free rein. By the time he slipped ashore forty-five minutes before sailing time to obtain two bottles of acid, these fantasies were real enough for him to act.

At 5:50 P.M., the customs manifest signed, Captain Robert Wilmott appeared on the bridge. Moments later he was joined by the pilot. Both men took up their usual positions, aware that, as always, the passengers would be watching.

The orderly activity on the bridge centered on a hundred or more switches, dials, contacts, and intercoms. This array of electrical gadgetry was designed to do everything from piping music around the sports deck to ordering up a snack for the night watches. Except for the cargo smoke-detector system which Third Officer Clarence Hackney had been ordered to switch off, all the equipment was functioning normally.

A few minutes before six, two tugs were fast aft and forward. A minute later the cables that held the liner to the land were loosed. The ship's whistle blew a long, sharp blast. The bridge telegraphs rang. The tugs nudged bow and stern, and the gap between the *Morro Castle* and the pier steadily widened.

At exactly six o'clock, the liner slipped past the rock fortress whose name she had taken, and dropped the pilot off in a waiting cutter.

Below, Chief Engineer Eban Abbott acknowledged the bridge's order to increase speed, and watched the engine-room dials register the increase in revolutions.

On the promenade deck, Joe Bregstein turned to his son Mervyn. "Here's to home!" he said happily. The boy smiled back.

# At Sea:
## September 5–
## September 7, 1934

# 4.
# PLAYING WITH FIRE

By 6:30 P.M., life on board the *Morro Castle* returned to its normal cruise pattern.

Aft, on B deck, the ship's orchestra of half a dozen musicians was playing a selection of hits from the twenties. Their efforts elicited intermittent applause from honeymooners Charles and Selma Widder. Both were in a particularly happy mood: on their way to the deck ballroom, the ship's headwaiter, Carl Wright, had told them they were to be the captain's guests for dinner the following night.

While the Widders danced to "Tiger Rag" and "Tea for Two," Wright moved graciously through the first-class dining room. A tall, fine-boned man, he had a European-hotel-trained reserve about him. His aloofness, as much as anything else, gave the dining room the class that many of the more snobbish passengers demanded. They relished his conversation, which was always liberally sprinkled with French words. One of the passengers remarked that he even had the ability to make a bottle of soda pop taste like vintage sparkling wine.

Tonight, Wright was hard pressed to maintain the image of polished sophistication. Five of the liner's stewards had returned to the ship drunk that afternoon.

All would be sacked when the *Morro Castle* reached
New York. For the time being, they were confined to
their bunks. This new depletion in the number of his
staff did not augur well.

Wright's foreboding increased when he was informed
that Captain Wilmott intended that night to keep his
first dinner date with his passengers in three days. The
ship's captain had an unnerving habit of sweeping
through the dining room, mentally noting a knife or
fork out of alignment, and making an issue of it afterward.

One guest would be missing from dinner; for reasons
he did not understand, Father Raymond Egan had returned to the ship feeling tired and depressed. He ascribed it to his disappointment that the trip had not
been as relaxing as he had hoped it would be. It was
doubly unfortunate in view of the fact that it would be
the last such vacation in the foreseeable future; the income of a parish priest did not allow for regular cruises.

Patrolman Price—his gun and shoulder holster hidden under his snappy new lightweight jacket—was
enjoying before-dinner drinks with his wife and the
Charles Menkens, their newfound friends, in the first-
class lounge.

Menken, like Price, was a New York policeman,
attached to a Brooklyn precinct a few blocks from the
beat William Price pounded. The two men had never
met before the cruise.

Menken ordered another round of drinks and continued to talk with his fellow cop about what - the - hell
- people - outside - didn't - know - how - big - the -
force - was - but - it - wasn't - big - enough - to - cope -
with - the - crime - wave.

In stateroom number one, one of the few stewards left on duty served cocktails to the four people seated on the overstuffed easy chairs casually grouped around the false Colonial fireplace. Dr. Charles Cochrane and his sister, Catherine, were entertaining Dr. and Mrs. Theodore Vosseler in return for the Vosselers' hospitality of a previous evening.

The two doctors knew each other by reputation. Dr. Cochrane was chief of the Urological Department at Kings County Hospital in Brooklyn. Dr. Vosseler often referred patients from his thriving private practice to the hospital.

While they discussed medicine, Catherine Cochrane told Mrs. Vosseler that her fears about the smell from the cargo of hides had not materialized. This led to a general evaluation of the cruise so far; all agreed it had been quite enjoyable, marred only by the absence of the ship's master.

Dr. Vosseler volunteered that the root of the captain's troubles lay in the inevitable pressures the job entailed. The strain of conducting the complex affairs of a ship as large as the *Morro Castle* could play havoc with a man's health.

"In that case," Dr. Cochrane suggested, "he should take a cruise."

Early in the evening, cruise director Robert Smith outlined for Captain Wilmott's benefit the new game he had invented for the passengers—Lifeboat Rescue.

The rules were simple: teams of passengers would muster at their boats wearing preservers. At a given signal—perhaps a blast from the ship's whistle—the boats would be lowered to the water level, then winched aboard again. The winning team would be the first one to line up beside their boat. Prizes would be presented at the captain's farewell dinner and gala ball on Friday evening.

As Smith saw it, the game would get passengers involved in "thinking safety." Captain Wilmott rejected the idea as the most foolhardy he had ever heard.

Crestfallen, the cruise director returned to his quarters, midships on E deck, convinced that nobody really appreciated the difficulties of his job.

Chief Engineer Eban Abbott dressed carefully. The ship's publicity blurbs gave passengers the option as to whether they dressed formally for dinner, but for Eban Abbott there was only one yardstick: sartorial perfection.

As he dressed, he thought again about Captain Wilmott's suggestion earlier that evening that the chief engineer transfer to the Ward Line's *Oriente*. The suggestion had been polite but unmistakable.

Eban felt strongly that Wilmott didn't want him to go, but for reasons he couldn't understand, the captain had to please Warms.

At about the same time, Chief Officer Warms decided to stroll past the radio shack to make another check. As he passed by the door to the shack, he saw that George Alagna was on duty.

Suddenly, the bulk of George White Rogers filled the doorway to the shack. Warms saw that Rogers was "smiling, and not smiling, if you know what I mean."

Rogers called out softly, "Mr. Warms?"

The first officer turned. Rogers walked down the deck toward him.

"Mr. Warms. I'd like to see the captain."

"Why?"

"I have some information for him."

"About what?"

"Best I tell the captain first."

During the entire conversation a bland, fixed smile remained on the chief radio officer's lips. It was that, more than anything Rogers said, that Warms found disturbing.

The chief officer promised to arrange an interview after dinner. Only much later did Warms grasp the significant fact about the conversation: as a ship's officer, George White Rogers did not need prior permission to call on the captain.

For some time, William Warms had felt uneasy in the presence of the chief radio officer, and their brief encounter near the radio shack only exacerbated those feelings. Warms could not stop thinking about the story he had heard in New York—that Rogers had played a part in the sudden departure of the previous chief radio officer.

As a matter of fact, George White Rogers played more than a part in that episode: he starred brilliantly in a drama he himself wrote, directed, and staged.

Rogers was a recidivist of long standing. Crime gave some meaning to his life: through it he could gain freedom from the physical restraints that bound him. Crime helped him forget the emptiness and devastating guilt he felt about his sexual underdevelopment; crime boosted his ego and provided a substitute for personal involvement with other people. Outside the bounds of ordinary social mores, he found satisfaction in repeated assaults on society.

That is probably the only satisfactory explanation for the criminal record of George White Rogers, of which the officers on the *Morro Castle* were totally unaware.

The explanation is borne out by the expert testimony of psychiatrists who later examined Rogers, and whose assessment had until now remained unavailable for serious study.

The principal of the Oakland, California, public school George attended did not have the benefit of any medical assessment when he discovered George's first known crime: stealing skates from other schoolchildren.

It was a pointless piece of thievery: fourteen-year-old George, weighing nearly two hundred pounds, was far too clumsy to balance on any rollers. He had stolen to get even with those who tormented him about his size. The date was February 10, 1914. George was let off with a warning.

Nine days later he committed his first serious offense. He broke into a house and stole a radio set. He confessed at once, believing he would again escape with a warning. This time, however, he was not so fortunate: he was committed to a reform school, the Good Templar's House in Vallejo, for correctional training.

Adolescence is an unusually vulnerable time for a developing psychotic personality. It is then that the patterns of moroseness, silence, and purging of normal emotional responses are established.

During this period in George White Rogers' life, the psychotic tendencies he had already shown became more deeply rooted. He began a series of petty thefts from other inmates in the home. Between his unusually long silences, his language became vulgar and salacious. He began to show symptoms of hypomania, a condition in which everything is done at a feverish pace.

A confidential document from the school details the deterioration in young Rogers' personality. According to the report of the superintendent, "he was untruthful; his influence on the other children of the home was bad; he would not work." And, finally, "he was a 'moral pervert.' "

By this time, George White Rogers had already developed a number of regressive symptoms: pulling at his genitals in the hope they might grow; soiling himself; and, in moments of deep frustration, breaking anything within reach—acts which reflected his psychotic nature.

In March 1915, the Templar home asked that Rogers be moved elsewhere. He was committed to the Boys and Girls Aid Society in San Francisco, a place with a policy of firm discipline, where most of his habits were punishable by a beating.

But punishment did not arrest the development of the boy's disturbed personality. Extended silences alternated with a manner often domineering and always intolerant. The conflict between his own inner world and the world around him grew more intense.

The society's reports show that he continued to be "thoroughly unreliable; that he had been involved in several acts of petty stealing, and had also committed sodomy on a younger boy in the home."

Not once was he seen by a doctor. Even a cursory medical examination would have indicated physical abnormality, and a psychiatrist would have recognized the classic characteristics of the psychotic. According to one psychiatrist who later examined Rogers' record, "there was clearly a basic disturbance of the *feelings;* this disturbance was *periodic;* in between there were periods of *normality.*" This assessment was made too late, but it suggests how Rogers might have been impelled to continue his criminal career.

The act of sodomy was the last straw for the San

Francisco Society. Possibly fearing it was contagious, the society quickly dumped Rogers. Almost overnight, the society was able to find him a job—as assistant wireless operator on a schooner sailing out of San Francisco.

By chance it was a job Rogers actually wanted. He was paroled, and on May 12, 1917, he went to sea.

In 1912, five years before, shuddering under the impact of the *Titanic* disaster, Congress had passed the first United States radio legislation: maritime radio came of age.

George White Rogers later said it was the glamour of the job that attracted him. It is doubtful whether he found much glamour on the schooner: he got ten dollars a month and his food. Even so, he acquired sound training in wireless telegraphy.

For the next three years there is a blank in the official records on George White Rogers. Where he went, what he did, nobody knows. Later in life, Rogers delighted in teasing questioners about this period. He hinted at all sorts of wild and romantic voyages— among them, that he had been shanghaied, married a girl in China, and fought in a South American revolution.

When he did reappear, definite changes in him were apparent. He now weighed more than 250 pounds and had started smearing his groin with potions. He had also found religion. In September 1919, when he joined the U.S. Navy, he stated he was a Jehovah's Witness.

Rogers had one of the shortest naval careers on record: eighteen weeks. Poor eyesight was given as the official reason for his dismissal.

His discharge added to his emotional problems. He became increasingly incapable of experiencing appropriate emotions in any situation. All that survived was an ugly eroticism in a man some called "a walking zombie."

From 1920 to 1923, Rogers again disappeared from official view, this time into the strange world of New Jersey's Hoboken. He felt at home among the tacky shops, the foreign sounds, the unkempt streets. Somewhere along the line he met and married Edith Dobson.

It was then that his quest for that mystical respect really began. In March 1923, Rogers sought it in show business. He got a job as a technician with a New York radio station.

Here, in the easy-come-easy-go world of broadcasting, he mistook badinage for personal insult. Once more he felt singled out as a figure of ridicule. Again, he retaliated with a senseless act of theft. In November of that year he stole two fifty-watt radio transmitters valued at three hundred dollars. He made no attempt to sell them. When challenged, he handed them back and was promptly fired.

For six years he drifted through the zany era of ragtime, Dixieland, and the Charleston. He once said that if there had to be a song for him, he would probably have chosen the 1920s hit "Me and My Shadow."

During those years he held one job after another in quick succession. President Hoover's promise of a chicken in every pot and a car in every garage was lost on Rogers. He found it difficult to earn enough to get even the chicken. For him it was a period of drifting into near-poverty and social isolation, a slow and insidious process.

If Edith was ever aware of what was happening to her husband, she said nothing. She had openly questioned her husband's authority only once, shortly after they moved to Bayonne, New Jersey. Edith Rogers wanted to go to a relative's funeral. Her husband forbade her, threatening to kill her dog, to which she was inordinately devoted.

She went. He poisoned the dog.

By 1929 he became especially fascinated with the possibility of murder in which the evidence is totally destroyed. Arson seemed to fall into that category quite nicely. Rogers maintained that his interest was no more than an intellectual exercise.

But there is evidence that he went beyond that. He started a collection of scientific books and magazines on the subject of arson and experimented with delayed-action timing fuses and reactions between various acids and compounds. His experiments reached a climax when he believed he had reproduced the time bomb which caused the famous "Black Tom Explosion" in World War I.

That explosion had occurred at a New Jersey factory producing materiel for the war effort. At the time, it was widely held that the fire was started by a saboteur. Rogers believed the fire could "only have been caused by an incendiary fountain pen clipped to a workman's pocket when his working coat was hung up for the night in a closet."

He advanced a plausible explanation of how it could have been done. "An incendiary fountain pen was filled with acid which ate down into a combustible powder through a thin membrane of copper. The thickness of the copper was the timer; its thickness controlled the time it took for the copper to melt."

The device was designed to produce a chemical reaction that generated intense heat, and simultaneously released oxygen to feed the fire.

Rogers manufactured a number of these devices, each one more exact in its control of the time between setting and explosion.

In March 1929, while he was employed by the Wireless Egert Company in New York, a mysterious fire broke out at the plant. Police files noted: "It was Rogers' custom to arrive for work at 8:30 A.M. The morning of the fire he was on the scene at 7:30 A.M. He unlocked the door and let the firemen in."

By then the blaze was burning fiercely. Salvage experts concluded it had been started by a chemical timing device. Rogers was questioned for days. The set smile never left his lips. In the end he was released. The police file stated that Rogers was "suspected of the arson."

The police could have found the evidence they needed for a conviction in Rogers' home in Bayonne; a back room contained timing devices powerful enough to destroy a dozen factories.

Although he had got off scot-free, Rogers' first real encounter with the police frightened him. The threats, the bullying, the crude jokes about his misshapen body, and the final admonition that next time "they'd throw the book" at him, were traumatic. After destroying his bombs, chemicals, and electronic equipment, he took to his bed and remained there for weeks.

When he reemerged, he returned to his old method of getting even: stealing. Each time he committed a theft, he was caught. He promptly returned the goods, and persuaded the owner not to press charges.

The astonishing thing about every episode is that the owners went along with him. George White Rogers had found that if he presented the "problem" of his body in the right way, it elicited pity. He tried it after his first theft; it worked. After a cautionary lecture, the store-keeper told Rogers he would persuade the police not to prosecute.

The police role was itself a curious one: on at least two separate occasions he confessed and was never brought to court.

But somewhere down the line, George White Rogers may have sensed that his luck could not hold. In March 1934, he decided to return to sea.

In twenty years of intermittent crime, Rogers netted less than three thousand dollars. Financial gain could not have been the motive.

The officials at the Radiomarine Corporation had no inkling that Rogers had a long, undistinguished record of crime and mental disturbance when they renewed his license. Nor could they reasonably be expected to. The same defense can be advanced for Ward Line officials. Under any circumstances, a psychotic is difficult to spot because so often his defenses are superbly constructed.

Rogers, with his set smile or long silences, might have appeared to be an oddball, but there was no way a lay person could know he was genuinely disturbed.

When Rogers joined the *Morro Castle* as first assistant radio officer in June 1934, and related his wild story about being an undercover agent for the Radiomarine Corporation to George Alagna, Alagna—young and impressionable—believed him.

Rogers liked the *Morro Castle*. It took him away from America, away from the police, away from their questions.

There was only one drawback: he was not in complete command. He was answerable to the chief radio officer, Stanley Ferson.

By the end of June, Rogers devised a plan to remove Ferson from the ship. The plot was simple. It consisted of a series of letters written by Rogers, and retyped by an unwitting accomplice, Preston Dillenbeck, in Bayonne.

The two men shared an interest in radio transmitting. Rogers promised Dillenbeck a job at sea, once Dillenbeck had the necessary license. Dillenbeck believed Rogers was already the chief radio officer on the *Morro Castle,* and had the power to appoint his own staff.

On July 24, 1934, Rogers wrote to Dillenbeck from Havana:

> Was in New York last Saturday, but didn't get a chance to see you. Well OM how goes everything in Bayonne? This is my second trip and everything going very nicely. How is the code practice going along? Suppose that service work is keeping you very busy these days. Well, don't forget the fact you need that second class license. One of our juniors is in a jam with the Federal Radio Commission, and I hate to see the fellow get into a lot of trouble. It has to do with the sending of CQ message for the Radio Telegraphers' Union without any authority, and this, of course, comes under the heading of false and fraudulent signals. There is a way that I can help him and at the same time pave the way for you so I want you to do the following. I am enclosing a letter that I have written, and I want you to rewrite this letter on your typewriter and address it, in a plain envelope to the address that I will give you. Then take the letter to New York and mail it from there. This is very im-

portant. Rewrite the letter on your typewriter, address it in a plain envelope, and mail it in New York.

This will tip him off as to what to expect, and at the same time, having been mailed in New York when I am in Cuba, it will not involve me. When I get to New York I will get another junior who will be assigned to the ship temporarily, so that when you get your ticket there will be no trouble getting you assigned here with me. This must be done as soon as you receive this letter, so that he will get the letter in New York when we arrive there. Don't fail me please. Will try to see you this trip.

Enclosed was the letter Rogers requested Dillenbeck to retype and redirect to the "junior in a jam." In fact, it was for the chief radio officer, Stanley Ferson. It read as follows:

Mr. Stanley Ferson,
Radio Operator,
Morro Castle,
c/o Ward Line S.S. Company,
Foot of Wall St.,
New York, N.Y.

Dear Sir:
During the past several weeks the writer of this letter has handled communications from various parties that lead him, in the spirit of fairness, to advise you of the following:

As you probably know, there is an action being taken against you by the Ward Line with the Federal Radio Commission. This action is, primarily, to discipline you for your action in the recent Morro Castle disturbance. Reports are received from the Morro Castle every voyage regarding your attitude in the company and these reports are being compiled in the final summation of your case.

The writer has known you for the complete time you have been on the Morro Castle and, in order to avoid the approaching unpleasantness, I would advise you do the following:

Send in your resignation as operator on the Morro Castle and apply to the R.C.A. for an indefinite leave of absence. This will remove you from the jurisdiction of the Ward Line, who then, from what I have learned, will, necessarily, drop their action against you.

As long as you stay clear of the Ward Line Vessels you will be all right.

Personally, I have watched your struggle with the causes of your disagreement with the Line and I think that they have been complaints that have been just.

For obvious reasons the writer must remain unknown to you although you know him very well.

I don't like to see anyone framed, as they are evidently doing to you.

I am sure that the above course of action is the best for you, and will, undoubtedly, result in all action against you being dropped.

Trusting that the above will be received in the same spirit that it is written. The writer remains:

A Friend

On July 27, 1934, Dillenbeck typed and mailed the letter. The following day Stanley Ferson found it waiting for him in New York. He showed it to Rogers and Alagna saying: "Someone's trying to get me."

He sounded, Alagna thought, very frightened. Rogers commented: "If I knew the bastard who was trying to fix you, I'd have him off the ship in no time!"

Reassured by this show of support, Ferson decided to sail on. Alagna later asked Rogers privately whether, in his capacity as a "special agent" for the Radiomarine Corporation, he could not carry out an investigation as to who sent the letter. Rogers declined; it was, he said, outside the bounds of his responsibility.

On July 31, 1934, Rogers again wrote to Dillenbeck. After complaining about the weather on the voyage he went on:

> Our letter of last week started the ball rolling fine. The fellow is all ready to go home to Mississippi. Here is another to mail him so he won't change his mind. Use a plain envelope and mail it in New York.
>
> Don't get any Bayonne postmarks on it whatever you do. Make it snappy with that license 'cause will need a junior pretty soon.

Enclosed was the following letter:

> Dear Mr. Ferson:
> You, undoubtedly, received my letter when you were in New York last Saturday. I trust you found the contents interesting. The writer knows the origin of the letter the Ward Line received regarding the conditions on the Morro Castle. The

Ward Line firmly believes that you wrote this letter.

The conditions are such that, though the writer of this would like to come out in the open and assist you, he must, through necessity, remain behind the scene and trust that the advice he gives will not be misconstrued.

It has been mentioned in circles already connected with you that the best course of action would be your resignation from the Morro Castle with a request for a leave of absence. This advice was given through accurate knowledge of the facts of the case, and for your own personal benefit should be followed. The suppression of the whole matter could then be accomplished with no difficulty.

This enforced absence would not have to exceed, possibly two months. It would, in no way, affect your status with your own company. The writer has reliable information of the above.

The request for leave and resignation should be given in a natural manner such as need of rest etc., so that the records will show no indication to leave on account of this trouble.

The writer will be one of the main factors in getting this whole thing cleared up. I know all the facts in the case and am not only in close contact from my end of affairs but from your end as well.

There is a certain personal interest taken in your case which cannot be explained at the present time. The Federal Radio Commission has no interest in this matter other than the charges presented by the Ward Line. Should the Ward Line drop their charges, the whole matter will die a natural death.

With you out of the picture, temporarily, this can be accomplished from this end. After all there are plenty of ships in your company's service where the complaints you have made are unknown. Being definitely through with the Ward Line should cause you little concern.

There are jobs much bigger and better than the Morro Castle that you can get.

Believe this letter in the friendly spirit it is written and use your own good judgment. The matter rests entirely with you.

A Friend

Stanley Ferson received that letter on August 4, 1934. It increased his fears. His discreet inquiries revealed that the Ward Line had received no letter, signed either in his name or anonymously, complaining about conditions on board.

Ferson began to have that same "spooky" feeling Alagna had become aware of. On August 11, 1934, the chief radio officer walked off the *Morro Castle,* and did not return. George White Rogers was appointed to his job, with a salary increase to $120 a month.

But this was not enough for George White Rogers. He started to pocket charges to passengers for radiograms. But—and this was characteristic of his entire career as a petty criminal—he failed to make proper plans to escape detection. It is a curious paradox that a man with a mind capable of evolving the fairly complicated ploy to remove Stanley Ferson from his job overlooked the well-known fact that at the end of each voyage, inspectors from the Radiomarine Corporation checked the books against the money a chief operator handed in. Rogers failed to doctor the books and was found out in a bit of thieving worth only a few dollars.

In less than three days' time his career at sea would be terminated, unless something dramatic changed the course of events.

Rogers already had a plan to ensure that there would be. He placed the bottles of sulphuric and nitric acid on the shelf above George Alagna's bunk.

During the evening he casually strolled over to the shelf, removed the bottles, and turned to Alagna.

"What are you going to do with these, George?" asked a surprised Rogers.

# 5.
# POISON

At precisely 7:30 P.M., William Warms and Eban Abbott, immaculately dressed, arrived in Captain Wilmott's cabin. If either was surprised to see the captain also dressed for dinner, he did not show it.

The predinner meeting in the captain's cabin was a nightly ritual at sea, a chance for the ship's three senior officers to discuss informally the day's run and the behavior of the ship, passengers, and crew.

The captain's cabin was designed as a place of special entertainment for carefully selected passengers. Furnished with three sofas upholstered in blue, several easy chairs with matching tables, a couple of stand lamps, a grandfather clock, and blue drapes on the scuttles, it looked like the lobby of a midtown Manhattan hotel. Along one bulkhead stood a long cabinet which converted into a bar. A connecting door led to the captain's night cabin. It held a double bed, bath, and toilet. A speaking tube above the bed was connected to the bridge. A telephone, an extension of the instrument in the day cabin, stood on a side table.

The chief engineer's report was short: the engine room and his men were working normally.

The chief officer announced that five stewards had been logged for drunkenness. There had been a fight in

84

the forecastle between two deckhands. All would be sacked in New York.

Warms made no reference to the "fire drill" he had authorized earlier. And Captain Wilmott did not mention his order to seal off the cargo smoke-detector system.

Nor was there any mention by Warms or Wilmott of the watch being kept on George Alagna. Only several hours later did Eban Abbott learn of their suspicions concerning the radio operator.

At 7:45 P.M. the three men began their evening rounds: a brisk tour of the bridge, the promenade deck, and the first-class dining room. The ritual was an excuse to show both passengers and crew that the ship was under benevolent, yet effective, command.

Their inspection of the bridge area required only a few moments. The complex of equipment—master gyrocompass, course recorder, bearing repeater, steering repeater, and radio-direction-finder repeater— seemed to be in order. The various compasses in the wheelhouse showed a true reading. The azimuth, electric sounding machine, Bassett depth recorder, aneroid barometers and multiple chronometers, and the fathometer all indicated that the Morro Castle was on course and on time.

The three men proceeded quickly to the promenade deck, which was enclosed at the forward end with storm windows. The glass sheeting swept back to midships, where it gave way to 125 feet of open rail, lined with deck chairs, empty at this hour. Beyond lay the deck's ballroom, where the orchestra was playing Gershwin and Berlin tunes.

After a brief look into the verandah cafe—a jungle of potted plants, palm trees, and shrubs—the captain's party strode down to the shelter on D deck.

Captain Wilmott wanted to check the galley area. During the time they had spent on the ship, neither of his fellow officers could recall such a digression from the normal evening rounds. Eban Abbott thought it further proof that Captain Wilmott was still preoccupied by the attempt to poison him.

On July 29, 1934, Captain Wilmott had ordered an afternoon snack of one of his favorite dishes, finnan haddie, brought to his cabin. He had only eaten a mouthful when he became aware of a peculiar taste. He inspected the haddock. It appeared fresh.

Afterward he developed severe stomach cramps, diarrhea, and a temporary disturbance of vision. By the time the ship's surgeon, Dr. de Witt Van Zile, diagnosed it as food poisoning and treated the captain accordingly, the suspect haddock had been dumped overboard with other kitchen garbage.

After recovering, Wilmott conducted his own investigation. It produced more questions than answers.

Finnan haddie had been on the first-class dinner menu the same day; yet none of the passengers who ate it complained of any side effects. That the captain's haddock was deliberately tampered with was a reasonable deduction. But who was responsible?

The portion of fish for Robert Wilmott's snack had been selected from the cold store by a kitchen boy. It was then washed and prepared by another kitchen hand. An assistant chef poached it and placed it on a tray. A steward carried the tray to the captain's cabin. Another steward later removed the uneaten portion. Finally, another kitchen boy dumped the fish.

Four people in all handled the haddock before Wilmott touched it. Apart from the stewards, none of them had come in contact with the captain.

Had one of them doctored it? If so, why?

The captain was a remote figure to the galley staff; he had little direct effect on their lives. Had one of the kitchen hands been acting on behalf of another crew member? There were a number of seamen who hated the captain as the nearest available symbol of the Ward Line. The majority of deckhands looked upon him as, at best, an affliction to be lived with.

Assuming that the attempted poisoning was an act of revenge, another question arose. Had the poisoner carried the drug around with him, waiting for an opportunity?

The tampering probably took place after cooking. Prior to that the fish had been washed and poached, diluting any poison. Furthermore, the usual signs of food poisoning appear several hours after the contaminated food is eaten. Robert Wilmott complained of stomach cramps within an hour of tasting a single mouthful of haddock.

Could it have been a simple case of accidental food poisoning? Was it staphylococcal poisoning, or the more severe salmonella poisoning? It was barely possible. Both staphylococcal and salmonella poisoning undoubtedly would have affected others.

Captain Wilmott, his suspicions already aroused after the strike call by George Alagna, told the ship's surgeon that he believed he had been deliberately poisoned.

Dr. Van Zile took no steps to confirm, or even to report, this extraordinary tale. It was a peculiar state of affairs: the captain had flatly stated that somebody had tried to kill him, and the one man who could have been expected to pursue the matter further—the ship's doctor, with his knowledge of poisons—did nothing.

Dr. Van Zile was, by all accounts, quite fond of drink

and the social side of his work—and not a man of great initiative. Even so, a statement as unusual as Captain Wilmott's would not ordinarily be ignored. Dr. Van Zile had a duty to report the matter to the Ward Line.

He did not. Instead, he told the whole story to his close friend, Chief Engineer Eban Abbott, who made a "mental note of it." Later Abbott discussed the matter with his wife, Ada. She advised him that if somebody was trying to get the captain, Abbott had best stay out of it.

That is precisely what Eban Abbott did.

There is one final question. Why didn't Robert Wilmott report the matter himself? Why didn't he tell the chief officer himself?

There is no ready answer to these questions. But the evidence suggests that even the master and officers of the *Morro Castle* were genuinely afraid that reporting anything untoward to the Ward Line might lead to their dismissal. Among the passengers, Joseph Bregstein was not the only one to notice the apparent lack of concern for passengers' comfort on the part of crew and officers alike. Another passenger remarked, "They acted like it was best to turn a blind eye to most things." Apparently the "blind eye" was turned to more than just passengers' well-being.

Eban Abbott's total silence about the episode is perhaps more understandable, considering the nature of his suspicions. He believed, he told his wife, not only that it had been a deliberate attempt at murder, but that the man responsible was Geroge White Rogers.

There was "something about the man," he told her, "something *peculiar,* that made me feel that Rogers was no ordinary person."

It is perhaps a little easier to speculate on why Rogers would want to poison the captain: a psychotic needs very little provocation to push him into erratic action. It is possible that something Robert Wilmott had said or done was misconstrued by the chief radio officer as a personal slight.

In any case, Chief Engineer Eban Abbott was firmly convinced that another attempt would be made on Captain Wilmott's life, and he told the captain as much.

It was probably Abbott's warning that caused Captain Wilmott to break the routine of his evening rounds to inspect the ship's kitchens.

The main galley, pantry, and mess spaces, entirely enclosed in steel, were located just aft of the first-class dining room. Leading directly off the main galley were the dish scullery, and the glass and silver scullery. Beyond the sculleries was the complex of the vegetable store, cooking-kettle room, galley scullery, coffee and cold pantry, and beverage room.

Captain Wilmott, followed by Warms and Abbott, walked quickly past the bank of eight ovens, broiler, and roasting spit, past the line of baking ovens—each capable of holding forty one-pound loaves—to the zinc-covered dressers, covered with servings of the chef's specialty, a crabmeat cocktail.

Headwaiter Carl Wright, who had come into the kitchen the moment he was alerted of the captain's presence there, hovered in the background, waiting for the inspection party to finish their rounds. Now he moved forward.

"Captain, sir, is everything in order?"

The master of the *Morro Castle* turned, nodded at the headwaiter, and turned back to the rows of crab hors d'oeuvre. He picked a dish at random.

"Serve me this one at dinner," he ordered Wright, and

proceeded into the first-class dining room.

The dining room extended through two decks with a mezzanine supported by tall pillars at the well opening. Above the well opening in the ceiling of the mezzanine was an oval mural depicting Perseus rescuing Andromeda. Captain Wilmott's table was immediately beneath the painting; the tables of Warms, Abbott, and Dr. Van Zile fanned out on either side.

They were the only representatives of the ship's officers on display at dinner; the junior officers, strictly forbidden to go on the passenger decks except in an emergency, dined separately in a bleak mess room far below.

Seventy feet forward of the first-class dining room, with its silver-and-gilt baskets of fruit, the deck crew used the stale bread to sop up the last of the greasy stew.

The air in the crew's mess reeked with a permanent stench that no first-class passenger suspected existed. The accumulated smell of sweat, cigarette smoke, dirty clothes, and liquor pervaded this jungle of bare rivets and steampipes. It was a world with its own laws and its own rules; few of the ship's officers ventured into it. Thieving from the line was permissible; so were drug-running and bootlegging. Fights—some with fists, some with knives and wrenches—were commonplace. During the *Morro Castle*'s four-year history, a number of men had been taken off the ship suffering from severe wounds.

Often drawn together by a common resentment toward authority or toward each other, at sea the crew formed small groups and aired their complaints over their tin plates at mealtime.

One group, composed of storekeeper William O'Sullivan, seaman John Gross, and Joe Spilgins, discussed a recurring theme: the lack of proper safety drills and precautions on the *Morro Castle*. When others joined the discussion, they discovered that things were even worse than they had believed.

Ship's watchman Arthur Pender described the situation as "catastrophic." Pender, a licensed first mate for oceangoing liners, had been to sea for sixteen years. The Depression forced him on the employment market. Four months prior to this voyage he had been hired by the Ward Line, which paid him fifty dollars a month to be partly responsible for the ship from midnight to 6:00 A.M. Since joining the crew of the *Morro Castle,* he had carefully checked out every alleged breach of the rules of safety.

In his years at sea Pender had developed an overwhelming concern about safety regulations. It had made him unpopular with more than one master—and might even have hurt his chances of promotion. On the *Morro Castle,* as he had done on other ships, he compiled a "potential disaster dossier." His concern was that of "a professional seaman who has learned how vital these safety things are."

He had discovered that the fire doors were not equipped with sirens or bells, standard in all first-class passenger vessels. In port the men on gangway watch had never been instructed where the nearest fire alarm was located ashore. He noted that during a fire drill— when there was one—the crew never handled more than two hoses, one forward and one aft.

Most of the crew had no actual training with fire hoses. The fire-screen doors were never closed during fire drill. There was no emergency squad equipped with an iron bar, a portable fire extinguisher, an ax, a blanket, a gas mask, and a bucket of sand. The air ducts in many cases did not function; they were painted over.

Four of the ship's lifeboats were virtually useless because of their position alone. They were the first two forward on either side. In an emergency lowering, they would come down outside the enclosed promenade deck. It might well be impossible, during an emergency, to open the heavy glass windows in order to get into the boats.

The condition of the lifeboats had preoccupied Pender for weeks. He had inspected every one on the ship and come to the conclusion that almost every marine law had been broken. The plugs in the lifeboats were not chained or fastened in some manner to the lifeboat itself. In the port lifeboats, all the Jacob's ladders were thrown into the boats and heavily coated with aluminum paint; the shackles were useless.

Pender also discovered something that dismayed him even more. Third Officer Clarence Hackney had ordered two seamen to move the ship's Lyle gun—a line-throwing apparatus—to a new place.

The gun and the drum of powder used to fire it were originally stored on the bridge. Captain Wilmott ordered it moved elsewhere, as "it might get some Cuban excited into thinking we were an armed ship."

It was then placed in the ship's peak storeroom. When that was taken over for an even more lethal cargo—the arms shipments—the Lyle gun and powder were stored in the cabin of First Officer Warms. After only a short time, Warms had the gun returned to the bridge.

Third Officer Clarence Hackney had some difficulty

finding a new place for it. Then he discovered a dark, empty space between the ceiling of the first-class writing room and the deck above. He ordered the seamen quietly to roll the Lyle gun and the drum of powder into the space. Hackney believed it was a sensible place to keep the equipment. The overriding consideration, as far as he was concerned, was that the space was easily accessible from the bridge in an emergency.

He overlooked the fact that all that was between twenty-five pounds of dangerous explosive and the writing room below were thin sheets of board covered with plaster.

The seamen who dumped gun and powder barrel into the hiding place Hackney had found carried the apparatus past the wireless room. When Chief Radio Officer George Rogers stopped them to ask what they were doing, they told him the purpose of their mission. He expressed interest, saying he never knew the space existed.

Discussion in the crew's mess reached a new intensity after storekeeper William O'Sullivan described the fiasco of the "fire drill" held earlier that day.

"It's playing with fire, that's what it is, playing with fire," insisted seaman John Gross. "I just hope I get off this ship before anything happens."

"Well, if you're going, make sure you don't take a lifeboat," said Spilgins.

In the first-class dining room, dinner was in full swing. Headwaiter Carl Wright had solved the problem of the shortage of stewards by drafting waiters from the tourist-class restaurant, among them Sydney Ryan.

Ryan, who had never worked in first class before, was astonished at the variety and apparent quality of the food offered: the crabmeat hors d'oeuvres were followed by a choice of roast goose, baked ham, or steak; trays of vegetables accompanied each entree.

Ryan's job was to assist with the bar service by replenishing wine and liquor glasses during dinner. By the time the ice cream and fresh fruit compote were served, it was clear to Ryan that many of the passengers were quite drunk.

In a corner, members of the Concordia Singing Society had linked arms and were singing the classic German drinking song, "Ein Prosit, ein Prosit, der Gemütlichkeit."

Above the noise, loud conversation, and laughter came the refrain:

> Trink, trink, Brüderlein, trink,
> Lass' doch die Sorgen zu Haus!
> Trink, trink, Brüderlein, trink,
> Leere dein Glas mit mir aus!

Ryan marveled at their boisterous freedom, at the casual way they ordered up rounds of drinks, or pushed aside plates still half covered with the remains of dinner.

He calculated each singer had consumed in one meal's food and drink the equivalent of his week's salary.

All evening, attention centered on Captain Wilmott's table. For three days his empty chair had aroused intense speculation. His presence now caused an understandable stir, not least of all among the physicians present.

Dr. Emilio Giro, seated two tables away from where the captain sat, observed that Wilmott ate very little and sipped only ice water.

The two doctors at the captain's table, Charles Cochrane and Theodore Vosseler, were both aware of what seemed an unusual nervousness in his conversation. He seemed preoccupied, his mind elsewhere. Captain Wilmott told his table guests that the "pressure of work" was responsible for his absence during the outward-bound voyage.

Others were equally interested in the master's behavior. When the Right Reverend Hiram Richard Hulse, missionary bishop of Cuba, seated at the table of Chief Officer Warms, mentioned to Warms that the captain looked excessively tired, Warms directed the conversation to other topics.

During dinner Dr. Joe Bregstein had come to the conclusion that the adjectives that peppered the ship's brochure—"delightful," "splendid," "delicious"—were altogether relative.

The food continued to appall him. His steak was tough and the baked potato barely warm. His son's meal was not much better. And the headwaiter's solution to the steward problem, while it meant more waiters, had no visible effect on the quality of the service, which remained abysmal.

The dentist, who had quickly become one of the most popular people on board, made a perceptive discovery about many of his fellow passengers: they did not act as they were supposed to according to the brochures.

People didn't become well acquainted, he noticed. Many of them seemed to be too shy or afraid of getting stuck with someone boring. And some of them didn't seem to have a good time simply because they did not know how to.

He noticed, too, that in spite of the efforts of cruise director Robert Smith, the passengers were left to their own resources a great deal of the time. Often those resources revealed a colossal lack of imagination, energy, or taste. On the outward-bound trip, a game of musical chairs caused the greatest excitement. The largest gatherings were for bingo.

Even the ship's orchestra was grinding out the sort of schmaltz one could hear in any second-rate summer hotel. After dinner Joe Bregstein went into the first-class lounge, sat down at the piano, and hammered out honky-tonk renditions of "They Called Her Frivolous Sal" and "Let Me Call You Sweetheart." His performance was greeted with appreciative applause.

In the deck ballroom, couples danced tangos and foxtrots. In the verandah cafe, converted for the evening into a movie theater, a good-sized audience watched Joan Lowell treasure-hunting in *Adventure Girl*.

In the ship's public rooms, other passengers gathered to do some serious drinking.

More important things occupied Captain Wilmott's mind. As soon as dinner was over, he excused himself and hurried to his cabin. He was anxious to keep his appointment with Chief Radio Officer Rogers, to find out "what other tricks that radical's up to."

# 6.
# THE STORM RISES

At exactly 8:45 P.M., George Alagna tuned the receiver in the radio shack to the six-hundred-meter frequency, the distress wave band for ships at sea.

The mandatory three-minute period of silent "listening out" is an international watch kept by all ships at sea. For three minutes at precisely fifteen minutes past and fifteen minutes before each hour, every marine radio operator on duty stops transmitting and tunes to the emergency channel, listening for even the weakest distress signal.

Junior Operator Charles Maki watched carefully as Alagna fine-tuned the instruments. Maki himself sometimes found it difficult to locate the frequency; on several occasions Chief Radio Officer Rogers had noticed Maki's hesitation, and he used each occasion to give Maki a tongue-lashing.

Ever since Rogers had assumed command of the wireless room, his hostility toward Maki had increased. The chief radio officer made special note of each of Maki's faults: he was slow on direction finding, decoding meteorological bulletins, and switching smoothly across the transmitting and receiving wave bands.

Maki knew his career as a radioman would be terminated abruptly if Rogers made a report to the Radiomarine Corporation. Rogers chose not to file any official complaint; instead, he kept Maki on as a personal whipping boy, somebody he could verbally castigate whenever he wanted to.

Maki took it all quietly. If anybody had suggested that the perfectly proportioned body and the he-man pictures over his bunk were a constant reminder to Rogers of his own physical failings, Maki would undoubtedly have shaken his head in bewilderment.

At 8:48 P.M., Alagna again adjusted the apparatus to maximum sensitiveness—standard procedure before transmitting—and turned it over to Maki to send a handful of passengers' messages. For a moment Alagna watched Maki working. Satisfied that the Finn was on the proper frequency, Alagna left the radio room to go into the small adjoining room.

Through the open door he caught a glimpse of Rogers strolling down the deck outside.

Two things had bothered Alagna all evening. How had the bottles of acid gotten onto the shelf over his bunk? He was positive they had not been there until Rogers had returned from his quick trip ashore. And how had Rogers been able to tell they contained acid? There were no labels on the bottles. Alagna had unstoppered the bottles earlier; the contents were odorless. He had pondered about that, too; he understood that acids gave off a distinctive smell.

He had gone from the radio shack to the room next door where the three operators slept, determined to resolve the mystery.

His bunk was below a porthole. Just above his pillow was the small shelf holding his toiletry; Rogers claimed to have discovered the two bottles there.

Alone in the room, Alagna was struck by something else. The porthole had been closed all day; for any stranger to reach the room he would have had to come through the radio shack. There had been no callers that day. There seemed to be only one answer: either Maki or Rogers had placed the bottles there.

He searched the shelf over his bunk. The two bottles were gone. And when he slipped out on deck again, so was George White Rogers.

After dinner William Warms set out to do what he made a point of doing every night: "walk the ship." He set out from the bridge alone, pacing along the decks and companionways.

Warms, like Alagna, had a sense of foreboding. Everything on board appeared normal enough. Subdued chatter and bursts of laughter emanated from the public rooms, alternating with the rattle of the stewards' trays and the sound of the orchestra. Yet the vague feeling of uneasiness remained.

The intrigues, fears, and machinations on board the *Morro Castle*—some Warms was aware of and others he only suspected—had reached a dangerous level. What the chief officer did not know was that while he strolled, a meeting was taking place that threatened to bring it all to a very unpleasant head.

George White Rogers' interview with Captain Wilmott exceeded Rogers' wildest hopes.

He had planned it with care in order to achieve just the right balance of distaste and distress in relating the story. It was a simple one: for weeks, he told Wilmott, he had suspected that George Alagna was quite capable of stirring up trouble. But he would never have suspected the trouble would reach the proportions it had. Now he even had proof: the discovery of the two bottles of dangerous acids.

Captain Wilmott was so shaken by the revelation that he accepted without question the chief radio officer's statement that he had thrown the bottles over the side immediately on discovering them.

The story of the bottles reinforced Robert Wilmott's fears tenfold.

"I think the man is crazy!" he ranted to Rogers. "We have always had trouble with that man! In New York he went down the gangway and started a riot when the passengers were getting off because he wanted to get off the ship without having his crew pass stamped by the immigration authorities . . ."

The weeks of strain showed clearly on Captain Wilmott's face. The more he talked about Alagna, the more irrational he became. The most trivial rumors and details were magnified, until Alagna suddenly became the epitome of every Communist agitator the captain had ever heard or read about.

Rogers listened gravely. He had no need to do anything else; the captain's fears were now firmly established, and nothing would shake them.

The captain finished his tirade, "Mr. Rogers, he is nothing but an agitator in any organization where he is serving. I want you to take the key to the emergency room and I want you to put it in your pocket. I do not want that key to the emergency room anywhere that man can get it, because I do not trust him."

What precise damage George Alagna could do to the radio compass, which was the only item of importance kept in the emergency room, Captain Wilmott did not explain, nor did George White Rogers press for an explanation.

The captain already had Alagna under surveillance by Warms. Now the chief radio officer had effectively established his own role in a worsening situation. He would be the captain's contact within the radio shack, reporting regularly on the operator's activities.

As Rogers left the cabin, Captain Wilmott thanked him again for disposing so promptly of the two bottles of acid.

He had no reason to suspect that the chief radio officer had retained them for his own use.

Around 11:00 P.M., the orchestra slowed down the tempo on the deck ballroom. A medley of soft, romantic numbers announced the end of the evening's official musical entertainment.

Charles and Selma Widder planned to retire to their stateroom, which was equipped with a loudspeaker offering a selection from the ship's library of records. A sticker on the speaker announced that the *Morro Castle* was the first passenger ship in the world to be so equipped.

As they left the ballroom, Charles Widder asked a steward to send down a bottle of French champagne; at $1.50 a bottle, the honeymooners rated it the best value on board.

Steward Sydney Ryan never sipped champagne. He could not afford it on his salary of $40 a month. Even at this rate of pay, Ryan was comparatively well off. In a good month he could double his income in tips.

The Ward Line paid the lowest possible wages and drove the crew as hard as it could. Ordinary seamen earned $35 a month; firemen, $52; quartermasters, $55; engine-room oilers, $60.

The ship's officers were in a substantially higher bracket. First Officer Warms earned $180 a month; Captain Wilmott, the princely sum of $300 a month. Chief Engineer Eban Abbott's paycheck was $220 a month.

For that salary Abbott was expected to keep the engines running smoothly, and play his part in entertaining the passengers, particularly the women on board.

He was good at both. In the engine room he was served by a competent crew; on deck he relied on his own considerable charm and wit.

Joe Bregstein remembered him as a very passable sleight-of-hand artist with a handkerchief or coins. "Quite a number of people became fond of him," the dentist recalled. "Abbott would buy them a drink, and they would set him up a drink."

As the orchestra played the last dance, the chief engineer whirled one of the beautiful young female passengers around the dance floor. Of all his social assets, Abbott was proudest of his dancing. Even the Cubans admired his ability in executing a 3/2 rumba.

Like many ship's officers who came into contact with women passengers, Eban Abbott had long understood the fine difference between easy familiarity and inappropriate intimacy. His job was basically to cheer up women whose expectations had not been fulfilled. Harmless flirtations relieved Abbott's boredom, too. Problems arose only when some of the women passengers demanded more than he was ready or able to give.

On this particular evening, however, the chief engineer's problems were of an entirely different sort.

The Prices and the Menkens spent the evening playing pinochle and discussing life insurance. William Price revealed that if he were to die that night he would leave his wife Mary fourteen hundred dollars plus what she would get as a policeman's widow. Mr. Menken wondered aloud how an insurance company calculated something as involved as the coverage of a ship.

In all, seventy-one insurance companies throughout the world had insured the *Morro Castle* for $4,200,000. One third of the total was underwritten by British companies, principally by Lloyd's of London. But under the complicated limited-liability law of 1851, the Ward Line had little responsibility for insuring the passengers.

In the event of disaster, the law stated that "only by proving the owners to have possessed knowledge of the unseaworthiness of the vessel or the inadequacy of the crew before the fatal sailing," could passengers collect any insurance. In practical terms this was almost impossible.

The real owners of the *Morro Castle* had virtually no knowledge of the ship—a state of affairs which, given the terms of the law, was very much in their best interests. The Ward Line was just one subsidiary in the powerful shipping complex of Atlantic Gulf and West Indies—AGWI. The involvement of Franklin D. Mooney, president of AGWI, with the *Morro Castle,* gives some indication of just how little the owners knew —or cared to know—about this particular piece of property.

Since sailing on the *Morro Castle*'s maiden voyage, Mooney had only once had anything to do with the ship. In 1932, he was accused of violating the White Act, which prohibited any officer of a company with a mail subsidy (which the *Morro Castle* received for ferrying mail to and from Cuba) from receiving more than $17,500 a year in salary. Mooney was drawing $128,000. During the government investigation, Mooney said he believed the average seaman on the *Morro Castle* received $32.50 a month, but he couldn't be sure, because it really was not his province.

Mooney had muscle where it mattered in Washington. His lawyers knew how to argue a persuasive case: if there had been a violation, it was not intentional; their client was willing to make a substantial gesture by reducing his salary to $85,000 a year. More important, he would raise the crew's wages to "around $50 a month for a seaman." The investigators were satisfied. Nobody ever pointed out that a salary of $85,000 a year was still many times more than the White Act allows—nor was Mr. Mooney ever again asked to account for his income.

Under the terms of employment, the crew stopped drawing their pay the minute they stepped off the ship. There was no provision for compensation for any injuries sustained while on duty.

Passengers were in a similar situation. If they wanted insurance protection, they had to take it out on their own. Not one passenger had done so on this present voyage. Most of them probably assumed they were covered.

They were not.

As midnight approached, Joe Bregstein played one last tune on the piano, acknowledged the applause, and left the first-class lounge for a brisk stroll around the deck before turning in. In spite of his complaints about the food, the dentist felt he had adapted well to life at sea. He hadn't once felt sick on the cruise, not even when the ship cut through the Florida Strait.

He leaned over the port rail, peering into the night.

Far in the distance a light broke the darkness. Breg-stin wondered what it was.

Farther down the deck, Father Raymond Egan was also watching the light. The priest had slept fitfully, awakened often by the sounds of music and laughter coming from the public rooms. He hoped a stroll around the deck would relax him. But he still felt list-less and tired—and regretted now that he had missed dinner.

"Miami."

Father Egan turned around, startled. Standing be-hind him was George White Rogers. The chief radio of-ficer explained that the light came from the city of Miami, ten miles away on the Florida coast. The next landfall to watch for was Port Everglades, he told the priest.

Nodding good night, Rogers proceeded down the deck. Father Egan marveled that such a big man could move so quietly.

At midnight the ship's bell on the bridge announced a change of watch. A new squad of oilers and firemen scuttled down to the engine room. On the bridge, Fourth Officer Howard Hansen assumed command, checking the deck log, course recorder, and fathometer.

Moments later he was joined by student engineer William Wesley Tripp from Dorchester, Massachusetts. This was Tripp's twelfth trip on the *Morro Castle;* the previous eleven had been spent entirely in the engine room, where he made copious notes for his work-study project on operating procedures. Tripp was now taking notes on the bridge.

Tripp, an engineering student at the Massachusetts Institute of Technology, had persuaded the Ward Line to sign him on because he wanted to know "how ships run."

What he had learned fascinated him. He told Hansen it was enough to convince any man never to set foot on land again.

At the moment Hansen had more immediate things on his mind. The barometer was dropping; the wind was shifting and stiffening.

Bad weather was on the way.

From where he stood far in the stern, night watchman Arthur Pender noticed the change in the *Morro Castle*'s course. For a few minutes the ship yawed as she fought the Atlantic swell. Then the motion eased as the ship increased speed.

Pender approved of the navigational tactics: apparently a decision had been taken to push the *Morro Castle* hard through the night. If the weather was still bad when the daybreak came, speed would be reduced to keep the passengers happy.

Pender walked through the tourist class, pausing at regular intervals to punch a time clock connected to the bridge. Except for the muted throb of engines or the hum of a ventilator, everything seemed quiet. Occasionally, a murmur came from behind a cabin door, but otherwise the tourist passengers appeared to be asleep.

At around 1 A.M., the night watchman came to the first-class area. The public rooms were still filled with drinking parties, although most of the first-class passengers had retired to their staterooms. Stewards moved in and out of the public rooms, carrying drinks to the cabins.

Pender was shocked to see that the two other night watchmen, who should have been on deck, had been drafted to help with cabin service.

The *Morro Castle* was now protected by only four men: Fourth Officer Howard Hansen, the officer of the watch; a helmsman; the bow lookout; and night watchman Pender.

Pender regarded this as the most flagrant breach yet of the rules governing safety at sea.

Another violation of those rules kept First Officer William Warms awake in the early hours of Thursday morning. His previous uneasiness had crystallized around one thing: the lack of boat drills on the *Morro Castle*.

Like the fire drills, lifeboat drills had been suspended by Captain Wilmott because the captain insisted they "upset passengers." As a reminder of the potential cruelty of the sea, they were not in keeping with the balmy world of the pleasure cruise.

Warms had been concerned about this decision for months. The memory of his own suspension in 1928 for failing to carry out similar drills on another ship haunted him. He had developed a premonition that the situation could repeat itself, and that along with Captain Wilmott, he could again face censure.

As he lay there in his bunk, Warms decided that rather than risk another such censure, he would take almost as big a gamble. When the ship docked in New York he planned to confront Captain Wilmott with the dangerous situation the captain had allowed to develop. If that failed to set things aboard ship right, he proposed laying all the facts before the Ward Line itself.

And while he was in New York, the first officer planned to make full inquiries into just how George

White Rogers came to be on board the *Morro Castle*.

Having resolved to do something about these problems, Warms found it a bit easier to fall asleep. As he drifted off, he was aware that it was beginning to rain.

Within moments, wind, rain, and waves were crashing against the *Morro Castle*'s starboard freeboard with thunderous violence.

Chief Engineer Eban Abbott awoke with a start as a burst of spray flew through the open cabin porthole. He listened for a moment to the sounds outside and then reached for the emergency speaker tube linking him with the engine room.

From below a voice told him what he wanted to know: orders had come from the bridge to reduce speed.

Eban Abbott closed the porthole and went back to sleep.

On the bridge Fourth Officer Hansen plotted the new course Captain Wilmott had just ordered. Hansen had awakened the captain shortly after 3 A.M. with news of the tropical storm. The course he ordered brought the ship head on toward the wind and seaway, then reversed the process a few moments later, completing a zigzag to port.

With satisfaction Hansen noted that the maneuver reduced the roll considerably, while at the same time it kept the ship on a mean, or true, course.

By 4 A.M. the storm had blown over.

Without awakening the captain, Fourth Officer Hansen gave his first solo order of command that night; speed was to be increased and the ship brought back on its original course.

Student engineer William Tripp wrote it all down in his private log.

As he finished writing, the first streak of dawn separated sky and sea.

Dr. Emilio Giro awakened early out of habit. He looked out of the stateroom porthole; the ship's progress along the Atlantic swell was almost imperceptible.

He dressed quietly, anxious not to disturb his brother-in-law, Rafael Mestre, who was sound asleep after a long night of dancing and drinking.

At 7 A.M., Dr. Giro stepped out on deck. The sun was coming up behind a bank of clouds. In spite of its warmth, Dr. Giro shuddered involuntarily, remembering his fear during the storm. Lying in his bed, he had suddenly realized he couldn't swim. He wondered what would happen if the ship sank.

Now he found himself walking down A deck, toward lifeboat number ten. The boat was still there, still intact.

Feeling relieved and just slightly foolish, Dr. Giro began a leisurely stroll around the decks.

By 7:30 A.M., cruise director Robert Smith was putting on a brave show of losing a game of shuffleboard to Mrs. Thelma Hulse, wife of the missionary bishop of Cuba. Smith was probably one of the best players on the Eastern Seaboard—but he also knew when it paid to lose.

Farther down the sports deck, Mr. and Mrs. Charles Menken played a furious set of deck tennis before a growing crowd of onlookers. The Menkens played a fast and skillful game, earning generous applause.

Drawn by the noise, Father Raymond Egan stopped to watch for a moment and then went on to the first-class dining room.

At exactly 8 A.M., he strode into the room and told a bleary-eyed Sydney Ryan that he felt like eating his way through the whole menu.

The dining room filled rapidly. Breakfast was a time for appraising clothes, class, and temperament, and for starting—or ending—a brief fling. This morning headwaiter Carl Wright noticed a number of new couples. The thought crossed his mind that the storm last night might have had something to do with the inordinate amount of chatter going on this morning.

At nine o'clock, cruise director Smith's voice came over the loudspeaker in the dining room:

"Good morning, everybody. This is your cruise director speaking. Are we happy? Everybody? Good, good, good! . . ."

First he gave them the weather forecast: it looked like a wet day. Never mind, he told the passengers, there was plenty to do: miniature horse racing, bingo, indoor quoits. For the ladies, the beauty parlor was open all day. And "don't forget, folks, tonight there's the grand elimination dance with lots and lots of prizes!"

Immediately after breakfast, Selma Widder booked an appointment with the ship's beautician. She wanted to look her best that evening for dinner at the captain's table.

That morning Captain Wilmott locked himself in his cabin. He opened it only to Chief Officer Warms, to whom he announced: "Acid—that's what they'll use. Acid to destroy me with!"

Baffled, Warms beat a hasty retreat, convinced the captain was having some kind of breakdown. If he continued to behave like this, the Ward Line was bound to retire Wilmott. For William Warms that could mean only one thing: a real chance of sewing an extra stripe of gold braid around his cuff.

The thought was a heady one. He was as excited as he had been that day, long ago, when he had first gone to sea.

On the sports deck, the first officer took cruise director Robert Smith aside and told him, "You might well have those lifeboat drills after all."

# 7.

# A FATAL EVENING

By lunchtime on Thursday, many sensed there was trouble on board.

Dentist Joe Bregstein believed he also knew the cause of the passengers' restlessness: the appalling lack of service everywhere.

The voyage was becoming unbearable to him; his feelings about the food had long since been overridden by his worries about safety on board. That morning a number of the more seasoned passengers had remarked on the absence of boat drills. It only heightened his apprehensions.

Joe Bregstein's concern would undoubtedly have increased still further had he noticed a seaman sorting through a locker outside the first-class lounge.

Night watchman Arthur Pender was collecting another piece of evidence for the list he was compiling. The locker held extra life preservers. They were all useless, he discovered, because the canvas flaps used to keep the life preservers from falling off were knotted.

Nevertheless, Joe Bregstein felt worried enough by lunchtime to question the first ship's officer he came across, Chief Engineer Eban Abbott.

When the dentist asked Abbott about boat drills, and told him what some of the other passengers had said, the chief engineer just smiled reassuringly. Like a bank manager when you have money in your account, Bregstein thought—polite and helpful. He asked Bregstein if this was his first trip, and when Bregstein told him it was, he nodded and said the dentist's fears were very natural among first trippers. There was absolutely no need for any worry, Abbott told him: "The *Morro Castle* is the *safest* ship afloat."

As a measure of good faith, he offered to give Bregstein a guided tour of the ship.

The gesture was typical of the chief engineer. On most days he singled out a passenger or two—often a pretty girl among them—for a conducted jaunt around the ship. Like the harmless flirting at the ship's dances, it was a way of breaking up the prolonged periods of boredom during the voyage.

Before going to lunch, Joe Bregstein arranged to meet the chief engineer the following morning. The excursion would be a last-minute surprise for his son Mervyn.


At many of the tables, the lunchtime gossip focused on Captain Wilmott's absence from the meal. Two theories were advanced more often than others: either the captain was not well or he was on the bridge, plotting the fastest possible course to New York to avoid the worst of the bad weather.

Both had some truth in them. By no means could the captain be said to be his usual balanced self. He had also told the bridge to plot alternative courses that could take them around the worst of the weather front—plans which were abandoned early Thursday afternoon when the radio room received a meteorological report warning of a gale, force seven, bearing down toward the ship in a wide sweep from Newfoundland.

News of the storm's approach was conveyed to passengers by cruise director Robert Smith. "But," he assured them, "that won't spoil the fun. A tea dance, extra sessions of bingo, and the fun of indoor horse racing in the verandah cafe are still scheduled."

A group of Concordia Society singers applauded, but elsewhere discussion still centered on the missing captain.

Headwaiter Carl Wright placated guests at the captain's table: "The master is on the bridge making sure everything is shipshape if the storm becomes really bad." Wright had no way of knowing if this was true; he was just repeating what Chief Officer Warms told him to say.

Warms issued similar instructions to the ship's officers. The captain's absence was to be played down. He told Clarence Hackney that Wilmott had expressed a desire for "peace and quiet" until the ship reached New York. The third officer passed this on to Fourth Officer Hansen, adding that the "routine handling of things will be in the chief's hands."

Hansen found it a gloomy prospect. Over a prelunch drink in the mess room, the ship's surgeon had indicated that the tension between Warms and Eban Abbott went back to the time Warms lost his license for neglecting the safety of passengers and crew. That only confirmed Hansen's lack of confidence in Warms.

Nevertheless, the fourth officer saw no real reason for concern. Every officer on the bridge held a master's license: every officer there was—in theory, at least—capable of bringing the ship home safely.

Some of the other crew members had a different view of Warms' capabilities. His dining room steward, James Pond, regarded the chief officer as "a real sailor, a man who made it the hard way. He may have been a bit rough on the edges," Pond recalled, "but he was the seadog type who could get away with it."

At lunch that day, there was nothing rough-edged about William Warms. He seemed to be in a very cheerful mood.

Others at lunch were more or less concerned about the approaching storm. Chief Engineer Abbott played down the expected bad weather. In any event, he insisted to his table guests, the Menkens and the Prices, *his* engines could withstand any amount of pounding.

At the table hosted by Dr. Van Zile, the ship's surgeon, news of approaching bad weather, the captain's absence, and extra bingo sessions made no impact, favorable or otherwise. By the end of lunch, his guests had worked their way through several pitchers of planter's punch and interminable toasts to a "wonderful time."

In the forecastle a number of crew members were, of course, already aware that everything was not wonderful. Willing to accept that the *real* troublemaker was radioman George Alagna, they were nonetheless intrigued by the possibility of exploiting the situation to create additional trouble.

Storekeeper William O'Sullivan and seamen John Gross and Joe Spilgins, among others, listened as several disgruntled members of the crew discussed means of "getting even" with the Ward Line. Someone suggested planting a "stench bomb" in each of the public rooms as soon as the ship berthed in New York. If the "bombs" were powerful enough, a large area of the *Morro Castle* would be inaccessible to new passengers for up to a day. Sailing time would have to be delayed, and as a result, the Ward Line would lose thousands of dollars of revenue and suffer severe damage to its reputation.

It did not matter that there would be no direct benefit to the seamen for this childish piece of sabotage. It was enough for them to cause disruption.

In the end the idea of the stench bombs foundered on a technicality. None of the men knew how to make them.


"I did the best thing possible by dumping them overboard, George, the best thing all around. You've got to believe that."

Alone, sitting on his bunk, George Alagna recalled the words of the chief radio officer.

They did not make sense.

Alagna had not brought the bottles aboard, nor had he known of their contents. There was only one way to interpret the way Rogers phrased things: in dumping the mysterious bottles, the chief radio officer had apparently helped Alagna—and at the same time implicitly accused him of intending to commit a crime.

"I did the best thing possible . . . ," Rogers had said. The longer Alagna thought about it, the more upset he became.


At 4:15 P.M., George Rogers tuned into the six-hundred-meter distress wave band, ordered Charles Maki to "listen out," and left the radio shack.

He walked the few feet to the chart room, unlocked the door, entered, and locked the door behind him.

Precisely what he did in the chart room is not known. There could be a perfectly innocent explanation: he could have been checking out the radio compass. He might even have been using it, as he had done previously, to pick up a shore music channel, possibly a radio station in Jacksonville or Charleston, both some little distance off on the port side.

Or George White Rogers might have escaped to the chart room to brood—and plan. For he had just realized his role as the captain's informer was over.

Earlier he had gone to Captain Wilmott's cabin to make his first report of the day on Alagna's activities. He knocked and found the door locked. When he knocked again and identified himself, Captain Wilmott ordered him to go away and stay away. Whatever his reason, Captain Wilmott had literally locked out the chief radio officer from further consultation.

Rogers found himself in an all too familiar situation. When he reached New York he would be out of a job, would again face harassment by the police, would have to endure the neighborhood jests, imagined or real. All the scheming, planning, and sheer duplicity which gained him the chief radio officer's job had come to nothing.

For a reasonably well balanced man, facing unemployment in a jobless world would be a difficult test. For George White Rogers, physically and mentally disoriented, the prospect could well have been too much.

If anything could turn his mind once more to thoughts of revenge, the moment when Captain Wilmott ordered him away was tailor-made.

In the locked privacy of the chart room, Rogers' mind could well have turned to the most practical way to execute that revenge.

In the verandah cafe Selma Widder was having a phenomenal run of success. Coiffed and expertly made up by the ship's beautician, she spent the afternoon horse racing. At the racetrack, a large table with toy horses which were cranked around the course, the excitement was in the betting. By the end of the afternoon Selma Widder collected twenty-five dollars—exactly the weekly salary of cruise director Robert Smith, who paid over the winnings.

When the races broke up, passengers drifted to the bars and other public rooms. Dr. Emilio Giro noticed that, after just twenty-four hours at sea out of Havana, boredom was setting in again.

Outside, the rain was also returning, falling steadily from a leaden sky.


On the bridge the watch changed. Third Officer Clarence Hackney made up the log and handed it over to Second Officer Ivan Freeman.

On the complex of electronic equipment that made up the bridge control board, the rpm indicator showed 145, giving a speed of nearly twenty knots. With the weather closing in, it was too fast for passenger comfort. Freeman ordered a reduction to seventeen knots.


The reduction in speed came too late for Catherine Cochrane. The plunging and pitching had finally made her sick. Her brother, Dr. Charles Cochrane, prescribed sips of ice water, salted, and rest in bed.

Other passengers relied on different remedies to combat the seasickness brought on by the gale. William and Mary Price chose a large brandy apiece; Mr. and Mrs. Charles Menken settled on whipped egg with a dash of rum. Selma and Charles Widder lay in their bunks concentrating hard on the ceiling, willing the sickness to go away. Both knew it scotched their plans for dinner at the captain's table.

The gale was a relief to headwaiter Carl Wright. It considerably reduced the number he could expect for dinner, and provided a cast-iron story, should the captain continue to be absent from meals.

The gale, in fact, brought Captain Wilmott out of his cabin.

When he joined Warms on the bridge, the first officer gave him the latest weather report: east nor'east gusting to force eight, blowing through the night. Captain Wilmott authorized a further reduction in speed. For a while he stood silently staring ahead into the storm.

Then he turned to Warms and said: "I don't feel good. I will take an enema and lie down."

Without waiting for a reply he walked back to his cabin and locked the door after him.

At midnight the watch changed. Student engineer William Tripp noted that for the last 73.5 miles the run north had averaged a speed of 16.2 knots.

Watch Officer Howard Hansen ordered an increase to 18 knots: most of the passengers were probably in bed, anyway.

Night watchman Arthur Pender welcomed the rain because it excused him from a regular chore: from 3 A.M. until 6 A.M. he usually had to help wash down the decks between fire-watch patrols.

Tonight he passed the hours between rounds in the comfort of the ship's pantry, sipping hot coffee and wishing life could always be so peaceful.

On the bridge, Fourth Officer Howard Hansen ordered regular course corrections which took the ship first past Frying Pan Shoals, and then Diamond Shoal at 5 A.M.

Ahead lay the most difficult part—navigating past Cape Hatteras, the most treacherous stretch of coastline. The Cape Hatteras lighthouse had still not been sighted. Hansen handed over the watch to Third Officer Clarence Hackney and went below for an early breakfast and a morning's sleep.

After breakfast alone in his cabin, the chief officer called on Captain Wilmott. The captain now complained of a number of new symptoms: a vague ache in the back and a general feeling of tiredness. He had already seen the ship's surgeon that morning. Dr. Van Zile prescribed "some medicine."

A more astute clinician might have wondered about the symptoms, might have linked them with the captain's obvious anxiety. But the questions were not asked.

Warms reported that surveillance of the radio room continued, and that Alagna had done nothing untoward.

Warms now suggested—in a curious reversal—that the radioman should be locked up. The captain—in an equally curious reversal—resisted the idea, telling Warms, "No, we will get rid of him in New York. I don't want any trouble with him. He held the ship up once"—a reference to Alagna's attempted strike call.

Given the increasingly volatile situation aboard, perhaps Warms should have pressed the captain for an explanation for his change of attitude. He did not.

Nor did the first officer discuss any further his suspicion about how George White Rogers became chief radio officer. It was no more than a hunch based on a few chance remarks, but if he had mentioned them to Captain Wilmott, they might have provided the trigger for him to reveal his own doubts about the chief radio officer.

By noon, the *Morro Castle* had less than fifteen hours of normal living left.

"In the event of collision, five electrically operated watertight bulkheads seal off the ship. They just press a button on the bridge!"

For an hour Joe Bregstein and his son listened as Chief Engineer Eban Abbott recounted an endless stream of "safety facts."

He told them the decks were covered with about sixty-seven thousand square feet of selbalith, a fire-proof lightweight sheathing laid on the plates. An electric fire-detecting system was installed in all passenger staterooms and in the quarters of officers and crew; thermostats provided early warning of any temperature increase. There was also the smoke-detecting system and a network of pipes leading from cargo spaces to the wheelhouse. Seventy-four steel cylinders of carbon dioxide gas, located at strategic points around the ship, fed a complementary smothering system through which the gas could be pumped under pressure.

Abbott did not tell the Bregsteins, of course, that the system had been rendered virtually useless from the moment Captain Wilmott ordered the smoke-detector system turned off. Nor did he say that the protection offered by the fire-detecting system did not extend to the public rooms.

All the same, the list of life-saving gear Eban Abbott itemized was impressive: in addition to the life-boats, there were a dozen box floats, each capable of carrying seventeen people; eighteen ring lifebuoys, each capable of supporting two people; and 851 life preservers, of which 78 were designed for children. In all, there was enough equipment to save 1907 lives—nearly three times the ship's complement.

Like any good performer, the chief engineer reserved until last the tour's climax—the engine room.

There was something boyish and infectious in the way Eban Abbott described *his* engines. It is debatable whether a nine-year-old boy would fully grasp the chief engineer's talk about "continuous-rating shaft horsepower," "solid nickel-steel flanges," a "three-phase torque margin," and "momentary excitation when phasing in the propeller motors at 240 volts," but quite obviously the chief engineer never tired of explaining it.

He led them across catwalks and down clanking steel ladders, pausing briefly for a lecture on the generators that supplied electricity, air conditioning, and refrigeration.

To Joe Bregstein it seemed a different world from the one he saw topside. It was a hot and noisy place and, he thought, "the men had that honest look about them which comes from a hard day's toil."

He would probably have retained that image of the engine-room crew, but for one incident: he noticed a Cuban, with an open paint pot next to him on the floor, painting a pipe adjacent to an open furnace door. It was an obvious fire risk, he pointed out to Abbott. The officer looked unhappy and said he couldn't really say anything. "I just don't start up anything with these people," he told the dentist.

Joe Bregstein wondered how the chief engineer would face a real crisis, if he found it so difficult to exert his authority in such a simple situation.

By Friday afternoon the continuous rain, the cold gray sea, and the whistling wind had all combined to produce an almost universal gloom among the passengers. Many of them had missed lunch, their appetites gone because of the weather and the pitching and tossing of the ship.

The tea dance had been a gelid affair; the sessions of bingo and horse racing were poorly patronized. For cruise director Robert Smith it was the worst day he had had for a long time. Nothing he suggested lifted the depression. He tried musical chairs, spot prize dances, mixed piggy-back races, *anything* that encouraged physical contact between sexes. All failed.

By five o'clock he was reduced to making regular announcements:

"Remember, folks, this is Friday—the *last* day!" The reminder was relayed to every corner of the ship. "It's certain that you still have a lot to do—like taking names and addresses of those you have met on the cruise. But remember, there is still one last grand fling left—the captain's farewell dinner and gala ball. Come one, come all to the crowning event of your week—the end of an epoch in your life."

At exactly 5:15 P.M. Captain Wilmott understood the one social obligation he could not avoid—the traditional farewell cocktail party for a favored few of the first-class passengers.

On this trip there were only four: Dr. Charles Cochrane, his sister Catherine, and Dr. and Mrs. Theodore Vosseler.

It was a brief and restrained affair. Catherine Cochrane was still recovering from seasickness. None of them had come to know the captain as well as was normal on such cruises. Furthermore, none of the guests were great social drinkers.

Captain Wilmott apologized for his continued absence from the ship's social life, but pleaded that weather conditions made it imperative for him to remain on the bridge. He repeatedly assured his guests that any storm could not be as bad as the hurricane he faced a year before, when the waves had been up to sixty-five feet high.

The party broke up around 6 P.M. If any of the guests suspected that Captain Wilmott's excuse was less than the whole truth, they were too polite to comment.

Chief Engineer Eban Abbott was about to dress for dinner when the engine room called. Assistant Engineer Antonio Bujia reported that one of the battery of fire boilers had a fuel blockage.

"Can you clean it?"

"Not without shutting down."

Eban Abbott climbed into a boiler suit, and stepped out of his cabin and into the express elevator specially installed to take him down to the engine room in an emergency. When he stepped out of the elevator, he noticed that the buffeting from the sea sounded like not so distant artillery and the motion was wilder than on deck.

The blockage was in the forward fire room boiler. The chief engineer checked the mechanically atomizing burners and the regulator controlling the flow of fuel. After thirty minutes' inspection, Eban Abbott knew the only way to clear the blockage was to strip down the feeder system, something which could be done only in port.

He ordered the faulty boiler closed down. It would have an effect on the ship's speed. The *Morro Castle* would not be able to reach 20 knots for the rest of the voyage. Nor would the engine room now be able to meet any sudden call for maximum water pressure. The boiler was part of the system which fed the fire hydrants.

He walked over to the operating platform, with its telegraphs, speaking tubes, gauge counters, and clocks. Some of the instruments were already recording a reduction of pressure. He picked up a telephone and dialed the captain's cabin.

There was no reply.

He called the bridge. Second Officer Ivan Freeman told him Captain Wilmott was not there. Again, Eban Abbott dialed the captain's cabin. He could hear the number ringing. After a few minutes he called the bridge and reported the loss of boiler pressure. He also said he had been unable to get a response from the captain's cabin.

In the engine-room log he noted the closing down of number three boiler. Eban Abbott took the elevator back to his cabin, washed, and dressed. Only after completing his toilet did he set out to discover why Captain Wilmott had not replied.

It was exactly 7:45 P.M. when he stepped out of his cabin.

Moments later First Officer William Warms stood in the captain's night cabin, shocked and horrified.

Slumped over the side of the bath, half dressed, lay the body of Robert Wilmott, his eyes open, but obviously dead.

# 8.
# WHO KILLED THE CAPTAIN?

William Warms closed the captain's eyes and hoisted up Wilmott's trousers. He wanted the body "to look decent," he explained later.

He retreated to the door of the night cabin, uneasy. "Peculiar," he muttered to himself. "I just saw him alive, and now he is dead."

Warms looked at his watch, noting the time: 7:48 P.M. About three minutes had passed since he knocked on the cabin door. Receiving no reply he had pushed it open, walked across the day cabin, and found the body.

On that basis Warms put the time of death at 7:45 P.M. His estimate was based on the fact that eighteen minutes earlier—at precisely 7:30 P.M.—he had seen Captain Wilmott alive.

Warms had gone to the captain's cabin with the latest weather report. He found Wilmott seated on the toilet in the night cabin, apparently in good shape. Nearby was a tray of food that Wilmott had picked over: a slice of melon, scrambled egg, toast, coffee, and a pitcher of ice water.

Warms delivered his weather report: "Captain, it is a little thick, but I am here, everything is all right." When he asked the captain how he felt, Wilmott assured him that he felt "all right."

Warms had then left the captain to go back to the bridge, where he discovered the weather had worsened. In addition to the heavy rain, now there was fog. Second Officer Freeman suggested reducing speed. Warms agreed, and ordered Freeman to blow the fog horn as well. When Warms returned to the captain's cabin to report further on the ship's progress, he had found Captain Wilmott dead.

Standing at the door of the night cabin now, the first officer made another observation that he thought was also strange.

It occurred to him that it would have been virtually impossible for Captain Wilmott to have toppled naturally off the lavatory seat and into the bath. Clearly something had forced the captain to move, trousers around his knees, toward the bath.

Had he felt an urgent need for a drink, and tried to reach the bath's cold-water tap? It was possible—yet only a few feet away, on the tray of food, stood the pitcher of ice water.

Had a sudden feeling of nausea driven the captain toward the bath? Persons near death often feel sick. Or perhaps he had eaten something which made him feel ill?

"Peculiar" though it all undoubtedly was, William Warms did not pause to ponder further. He unstoppered the speaking tube linking the captain's cabin with the bridge. The tube was an additional safeguard in case the telephone system failed. Warms used it now because he did not want to run the risk of the ship's telephone operator listening in.

The speaking tube was answered by Fourth Officer Howard Hansen, who was on the bridge to check the weather prospects for his forthcoming watch. Hansen was puzzled by Warms's order to locate Robert Tolman, the ship's purser, and for both men to come to the captain's cabin immediately.

Tolman was the *Morro Castle*'s hotel manager. A dignified man with impeccable manners, he was principally concerned with passenger welfare. He was also responsible for balancing the ship's accounts. Tolman was good at his job; he knew how to soothe a complaining passenger, or curb any fiddling by the bar staff. His contact with the other deck officers was limited.

While Hansen sought the purser, William Warms was forced to use the telephone to locate the ship's surgeon. He ordered him to the cabin, adding: "Bring your bag."

At that moment Chief Engineer Eban Abbott walked into the day cabin.

Eban Abbott came to the captain's quarters via the first-class dining room. The engineer had followed the usual route of his evening rounds. In the dining room, headwaiter Carl Wright reported no sign of the captain.

Mystified, Eban Abbott was surprised to find Warms in the day cabin, looking anxious and a little fearful.

The chief engineer began to explain: "One of the boilers has gone. I'm looking for the old man—"

"He's dead. In there." The chief officer motioned toward the night cabin.

Eban Abbott walked across the day cabin. He stopped short when he saw Wilmott's body.

"Maybe he's just fallen—"

"He's dead! I'm taking over command. Everybody, including *you*, will take orders from me."

In the circumstances Warms, as senior deck officer, was expected to assume command automatically, even though Eban Abbott outranked him. But Eban Abbott regarded the chief officer's words as unnecessarily offensive. It seemed to Abbott that Warms was making a special point of emphasizing his new authority over him.

Perhaps the chief officer had been a little insensitive. In any case, Eban Abbott, who didn't have much use for Warms anyway, believed that he seized on the captain's death as his big chance to have another shot at being captain.

Abbott's feeling was reinforced by the arrival of purser Robert Tolman, followed by Fourth Officer Howard Hansen and Dr. Van Zile.

"The only reason Warms has the purser here," the chief engineer thought, "is to swear him in."

In a group they moved into the night cabin.

Dr. Van Zile knelt beside the body and felt for a pulse.

An examination of a body can be swift and superficial, reflecting preconceived ideas about what is important. Or it can be a very thorough investigation in which every aspect of the body's condition is minutely studied, with no preconceptions allowed to restrict its scope.

The examination conducted by Dr. Van Zile can scarcely be described as falling within either category. The ship's surgeon ordered Captain Wilmott to be lifted on to the bed. At this stage the purser remarked on the change of color in the visible parts of the body. "It's quite blue."

Dr. Van Zile ignored this—as he did Fourth Officer Hansen's attempt to resuscitate Captain Wilmott. When Hansen opened the captain's shirt to do so, he saw that the skin beneath was also blue-tinged.

This time Howard Hansen drew the doctor's attention to it. Again Dr. Van Zile ignored the remarks as he prepared a hypodermic injection. The others watched in silence as Van Zile injected a colorless liquid into a vein in Robert Wilmott's arm.

What the injection was has never been ascertained; it may have been adrenalin. The ship's surgeon probably assumed there was still life in the body, and was attempting to revive the captain.

Tolman noticed that the exposed arm which received the injection was also turning blue. It puzzled him, as it did Howard Hansen, who had ceased any further attempt at resuscitation. The fourth officer also noted that there were no marks of violence.

Finally, Dr. Van Zile announced: "The captain is dead."

It was 8:15 P.M.

Like a court chamberlain invoking a time-honored litany, purser Tolman broke the silence. He turned to William Warms: "I will prepare the necessary papers placing you as master."

Warms nodded, murmuring, "Very good." He stepped to the bedside and glanced briefly at the body. "God bless his soul."

Turning to Howard Hansen, he said, "Lay him out and dress him up."

Then he ordered Eban Abbott to stay and seal up the room. "Leave everything as it is. Turn out all the lights and turn the key over to me."

Without waiting for any reply, the new captain turned and walked from the cabin followed by Dr. Van Zile and the purser. In the corridor William Warms turned to the ship's surgeon and asked: "What was the cause of death?"

"He died of indigestion and heart failure," Dr. Van Zile replied.

Without an autopsy, it would have been difficult for Van Zile to have been more explicit, but his reply was misleadingly simple. The doctor had not been able to diagnose the cause of death. His reply was only a statement of symptoms, not a real answer to the acting captain's question.

Most people die of heart failure. It can happen quickly, as when coronary thrombosis affects a large artery supplying blood to the heart, or it can be the result of chronic heart disease causing a deterioration over years.

Indigestion is a term so imprecise and open to interpretation as to be almost valueless. Robert Wilmott had suffered from a "nervous stomach" and high blood pressure, and was certainly high-strung. But there was no history of chronic heart disease.

William Warms, troubled by Dr. Van Zile's verdict, said to him: "I believe there are other doctors on board. Why not get them to confirm your findings?"

Followed by the purser, Warms walked to the bridge, where Second Officer Ivan Freeman was standing watch. "Wilmott is dead," he said to Freeman. "I have assumed command. You are promoted to first, Clarence becomes second, and Howard, third. Go below and tell every member of the crew you see that I am now the master and to obey my orders."

Next Warms ordered the purser to notify the line.

The purser walked into the chart room and wrote out two identical radiograms: one to Thomas Torresson, the Ward Line's marine superintendent, the other to

Victor M. Seckendorf, the company's passenger traffic manager. The message read:

WILMOTT DECEASED 7:45 P.M. ACKNOWLEDGE.
WARMS.

Warms initialed them and told the purser to take the radiograms to the radio room for instant transmission.

Turning to the business of sailing the ship through appalling weather conditions, Warms told the men on the bridge, "I'm not leaving here, come what may."

In the night cabin Eban Abbott and Howard Hansen completed the task of laying out Robert Wilmott's body. Resplendent in his uniform, his arms folded across his chest, he lay in the center of the bed.

A steward removed the captain's dinner tray, saying news of the captain's death had stunned the kitchen staff.

Why Abbott allowed the steward to remove the tray—particularly in view of the previous attempt on Wilmott's life—is not clear. Undoubtedly the chief engineer, like his colleagues, was under a great deal of emotional stress.

Howard Hansen wondered, as he noticed the captain's face turning black, whether the surgeon's diagnosis of the cause of death was satisfactory.

Hansen was shaking his head as he left the captain's cabin and closed the door behind him.

George Alagna awoke with a start.

Chief Radio Officer George White Rogers was bending over him, shaking him.

"George, George," he said to Alagna. His voice

was hushed and nervous. "George, the old man's dead."

It took a few seconds for the words to penetrate. When they did, Alagna noticed the excitement in Rogers' voice. He also began to think that the captain might have been the victim of a murderer. He didn't know why he thought so, but he did.

Was Robert Wilmott murdered?

Since that Friday evening this question has dominated all serious investigations into events aboard the *Morro Castle.*

In the months following his death, suspicion fell upon the Cuban Communists, who murdered Captain Wilmott, it was said, as a gesture against the Ward Line for shipping arms to the island's dictatorial regime.

Even today, especially among the colony of Cuban exiles in Miami, the view is widely held that Robert Wilmott was the victim of "Red plotters." There are men and women living in Florida now who produce faded clippings from Havana newspapers containing interviews with various Cuban officials who speculated that Communists were responsible for Wilmott's death. Since these officials were a thousand miles from the scene of the crime, however, it would have been difficult for them to be sure.

Captain Wilmott was probably not murdered for political purposes. It would have been pointless: the Ward Line would simply have replaced him with another captain and the arms traffic would have continued.

The cause of death has also been a matter of conjecture. Numerous investigations seem to lead to one significant probable cause: poisoning.

As with the earlier alleged attempt to poison Wilmott, there is no indication what kind of poison was used or who the poisoner was. And, it must be added, the question of whether Captain Wilmott was in fact poisoned is impossible to prove. A more careful investigation by Dr. Van Zile on the scene might have provided some more concrete basis for this hypothesis, but such an examination never took place.

Medical authorities today emphasize the virtual impossibility of determining the cause of sudden death like Captain Wilmott's without an autopsy.

Later speculation on who might have murdered Captain Wilmott centers around the figure of George White Rogers.

Mrs. Ada Abbott, widow of the ship's chief engineer, based her feeling about Rogers' responsibility on discussions she had with her husband. She presented to us a picture of Rogers remarkably like the expert medical testimony already discussed—evidence that Mrs. Abbott was unaware of.

The three volumes on the case compiled by Police Captain Vincent Doyle and exhaustive investigations by Captain Wilmott's lifelong friend Captain George Seeth provide further evidence.

As far as is known, Doyle and Seeth never met. Neither was even aware of the other's existence. Yet, somewhat astonishingly, both came to the conclusion that Rogers poisoned Captain Wilmott as a deliberate act of retaliation.

The evidence presented by Doyle and Seeth differs in certain details. In Doyle's version, the radio officer sought revenge because he believed Captain Wilmott had—and would give to the Radiomarine Corporation —the information which would eventually result in

Rogers' dismissal for dishonesty. Seeth believes Rogers murdered him because Captain Wilmott had discovered Rogers' involvement "as a key member of a smuggling ring among the members of the crew on board," and, according to Seeth, "Rogers murdered him to avoid discovery."

The smuggling ring had operated from the first voyage, smuggling drugs and liquor out of Havana into New York. From time to time New York Customs officers arrested crew members caught red-handed moving contraband off the ship. But the authorities never managed to track down and arrest the smugglers on board. On at least two occasions, suspected informers in the crew had met with "accidents." One had disappeared overboard at sea; the other had been crushed under a load of cargo in No. 2 hold.

Seeth believes that Rogers was responsible for transmitting and receiving details of contraband to an accomplice ashore.

According to Doyle, Rogers obtained the poison used against Wilmott during the ship's stopover in Cuba; he does not indicate what type it was. Seeth believes the poison was an irritant which in ordinary circumstances would not have been fatal; but Rogers knew it was powerful enough to kill the captain, who had a weak stomach. Seeth's hypothesis seems questionable, since such a poison would have worked too slowly.

The Doyle documentation on the *Morro Castle* case is fragmentary. But Vincent Doyle's belief that George White Rogers murdered Captain Wilmott emerges quite clearly. Unfortunately, the police officer is no longer alive to support his contentions or to suggest how the crime was committed.

On the basis of his own investigations, Captain Seeth

believes the essential *modus operandi* of the criminal was simple: Rogers got to the captain's food tray during one of his visits to the galley for coffee, and simply slipped the poison into the master's coffee or scrambled egg.

It is possible: the kitchen crews were in the middle of final preparations for dinner. The sight of the chief radio officer pouring himself another coffee would cause no comment.

Whatever his speculation on these aspects of the case, Captain Seeth was emphatic on one point: "I definitely believe Captain Wilmott was poisoned. I believe he was murdered."

His words sounded very much like Alagna's reaction to the captain's death.

George Alagna was now fully awake. Suddenly desperately afraid, he looked up at the chief radio officer and noticed that Rogers seemed to be smiling.

"Go back to sleep," he said soothingly. "You can't do anything. We'll be in port tomorrow by this time, thank God."

He showed Alagna the cryptic message purser Robert Tolman had brought to the radio shack. Rogers seemed almost in a cheerful mood when he left Alagna.

"Looks like a busy night for me," he called over his shoulder.

# 9.

# THE SMELL OF SMOKE

Father Raymond Egan sensed a growing tension among the diners around him. At first he put it down to the ship's motion: wind and sea combined to send the *Morro Castle* reeling into the darkness. The priest himself was unaffected by the swell, but stewards performed ballets of equilibrium as they carried away trays of uneaten food.

Some of the guests wore costumes—a few sheiks, harem girls, and cork-faced imitators of Al Jolson— but the majority of first-class passengers were in evening dress, a tradition for the captain's farewell dinner.

Father Egan, one of the few men aboard who did not possess a tuxedo, wore clerical collar and vestments. He had carefully weighed the matter before deciding.

There was the question of embarrassment to other passengers, for he still believed they would be uneasy in the presence of a cleric on a "fun cruise." On the other hand, he wanted to do what was "fitting" for such a special occasion. Moreover, his clerical garb would silence repeated suggestions from male voyagers that he "grab a girl and have a ball."

Predictably, his appearance in the dining room had caused a momentary flutter, which was quickly superseded by something more significant.

For some moments all had been aware of the fact

137

that neither the captain nor any of his officers had yet appeared for dinner. Attempts to question the waiters about it proved fruitless: they expressed baffled surprise. The passengers were becoming outspoken and disgruntled. It was, after all, the captain's farewell dinner.

Coffee was being served when headwaiter Carl Wright appeared from the kitchen, white-faced and visibly trembling. News of Captain Wilmott's death had reached the cooks.

Shortly afterward Dr. Van Zile appeared in the dining room, looking like a man about to impart news of a grave calamity to a privileged few. The surgeon whispered something to Dr. Charles Cochrane and Dr. Theodore Vosseler, both seated at the captain's table. The two doctors rose with apologetic smiles and followed the ship's doctor out of the room.

It was a little after 8:30 P.M.

On the bridge William Warms glanced through the papers purser Tolman had prepared for the purpose of formalizing his position as captain of the *Morro Castle*.

Warms paced the bridge steadily, issuing orders in a calm, quiet voice. Tolman was reassured by the new captain's bearing. It seemed that the crisis and the assumption of command had brought a new knowledge and authority to him.

Warms handed back the papers. Needles of flying water hit the bridge windows. Far below the sea was a bubbling mass of white flecks over which the ship rose and fell.

"The passengers, sir . . ." Tolman paused.

Warms turned and looked at him.

"What about them?"

"Shouldn't they be told about Captain Wilmott?"

138

"Not yet." Warms was silent, thinking about something. "Let them have dinner first."

The purser nodded.

"Will you go down and tell them, sir?"

"Mr. Tolman, I'm not leaving this bridge until we get to New York. I'm going to conn her all the way home. I'll get Mr. Freeman to come down and make the announcement later."

Outside the wind whistled through the rigging.

"Can I get you something to eat, sir?" Tolman asked.

"Later," Warms replied.

With a final nod Tolman beat a dignified retreat. Then something struck him: had he imagined it, or had the new captain seemed momentarily surprised that there were actually passengers on board?

By nine o'clock Eban Abbott was accustomed to the ritual: there would be a swift knock on Captain Wilmott's cabin door, it would be pushed open, and Dr. Van Zile would lead yet another distinguished-looking passenger into the night cabin where the body lay.

Abbott, seated in the corner of the day cabin, had been unable to understand the whispers emerging from the next room. The chief engineer had not stirred from the cabin since he and Hansen had laid out the body. He had made no attempt to contact the engine room or the bridge. The death of Robert Wilmott seemed to have induced a severe and deep-rooted trauma in Eban Abbott.

The tragedy for him and everybody on board was that it remained undetected or was misinterpreted.

During the time he sat in the cabin, half a dozen doctors had come and gone. Each had spent a few minutes with the body, and then departed with the solemn air doctors often affect in the presence of death. Later, those who attached any significance to the discoloration of the body ascribed it to a condition sometimes found after a severe heart attack. Although it was an acceptable medical deduction, it was not necessarily the right one: poisoning could also produce discoloration.

If the doctors noticed the silent chief engineer, sunk in his chair in the corner, they made no comment as they left.

News of the death was brought to the engine room by an oiler carrying a case of Cokes down from the kitchens. It was discussed in snatches, often drowned out by the thunder of machinery moving at top speed.

The boiler-room crew was concerned with a more immediate problem: maintaining speed with one boiler out of commission. Very few of the men believed it would make any difference to their work, whoever commanded the ship. Bearings, dials, gauges, reduction-gear housings, condensers, compressors, and pumps were far more dependent on the engine-room crew than on any captain on the bridge.

Acting Captain Warms peered through the bridge windows into the night. There was nothing to be seen all around the ship except black sea streaked with white. But the ship was no longer pitching and tossing so violently through the water. The *Morro Castle* had returned to a rhythmic rolling to starboard and back again.

Warms turned to his new senior officer, Ivan Freeman.

"All hatches battened down and ventilators and everything secured about the deck?"

"Yes, sir."

"Is she washing salt water on deck?"

"No, sir."

"All watches at regular strength?"

"Yes, sir, plus a lookout forward."

Satisfied, Warms nodded.


Night watchman Arthur Pender saw that the change in command, and its reason, had a profound effect on the seamen in the forecastle.

Among the older hands the death was regarded as a bad omen. More than one man told him it would lead to trouble. Several said they would sign off and try to get a berth on another ship for a trip or two until the danger had passed. Others agreed with storekeeper William O'Sullivan that it might mean an extra day's stop-over in New York while "things are tidied up."

Inevitably, the conversation veered to the kind of captain Warms would be. There was a division of opinion as to the first officer's fitness for command, although no one doubted he would be confirmed as captain.

Some, like O'Sullivan, wondered whether he had that "magic thing with the passengers." Others, including seaman John Gross, believed Warms would be a hard taskmaster, cracking down at the first sign of careless seamanship. "He's bound to make for a better ship," was Gross's verdict.

Seaman Joe Spilgins, who was responsible for the starboard lifeboats, hoped the new captain would reintroduce proper safety rules: "Half the guys on the ship never even raised or lowered a lifeboat. Most of them hadn't been showed and wouldn't know how."

Spilgins drew a chorus of approval when he said if it was a choice between a captain with personality and one who observed a stricter adherence to safety standards, he'd take the latter every time.

"Hell," he grinned, "if they want a personality as a captain they should stick Smithy on the bridge!"

While the discussion between the seamen grew more intense, "Smithy"—cruise director Robert Smith—took it upon himself to stop all further speculation in the first-class dining room.

On hearing the news of Robert Wilmott's death, he marched briskly to the captain's table. The room was suddenly very still. Even so, the cruise director clinked a spoon against a glass. When he spoke his voice was flat, almost emotionless.

"Ladies and gentlemen. A great tragedy has befallen us. The captain is dead . . ."

He paused.

"Captain Wilmott passed away earlier this evening. First Officer Warms has assumed command."

Again he paused.

"There is no cause for alarm—only sorrow. I request, out of respect for Captain Wilmott, that all the usual activities of tonight be canceled."

Heads nodded in stunned agreement.

Before any questions could be asked, the cruise director walked rapidly out of the room to repeat the news to the tourist class.

Refused further first-hand information, the first-class passengers quizzed the doctors who had inspected the body. They were no more informative, avoiding all questions on the ground that it would be improper to disclose anything.

Their silence gave rise to rumors of all kinds.

At 10:28 P.M. the tension in the radio room was

broken by an incoming radiogram, addressed to Robert Tolman, the ship's purser. It read:

PLEASE CONFIRM QUICKLY MESSAGE SENT BY WARMS TO SECKENDORF REGARDING WILMOTT GIVING DETAILS. WARDLINE.

George White Rogers looked at the message intently, then shook his head.

"They don't trust him," he said.

George Alagna and Charles Maki looked at each other. Rogers handed the radiogram to Maki.

"Take it to him."

"Warms?"

"It's addressed to the purser. Take it to whom it's addressed. Surely you know that?"

Maki turned and walked out of the room.

"It's bad, George, bad for Warms," Rogers said to Alagna. "It's bad when they cable the purser for more news. It's going over the head of the man in command."

At 10:40 P.M. a priority radiogram was sent to the Ward Line:

CONFIRMING MESSAGE FROM WARMS STOP WILMOTT DECEASED ACUTE INDIGESTION AND HEART ATTACK SEVEN FORTY FIVE THIS EVENING STOP ALL PAPERS FOR ENTRY IN ORDER.

TOLMAN PURSER

At 10:45 P.M. the radio room was again silent as Rogers tuned in to the six-hundred-meter wave band for ships in distress at sea.

Joe Bregstein had left the dining room before the

cruise director made his announcement. He made his way to the ship's lounge and began to entertain a small group of passengers with his piano playing.

The session was brought to a sudden halt by cruise director Smith, who appeared to be hunting down any sign or sound of frivolity in the public rooms.

In the verandah cafe, Rafael Mestre was keeping time to a rumba record with a set of maracas, watched by an admiring group of girls from the Concordia Singing Society. Mestre smiled, shrugged, and walked away with the girls when the cruise director confiscated records, player, and maracas.

On the promenade deck, other members of the Singing Society had formed a circle, linked arms, and were slopping beer as they sang "In München steht ein Hofbräuhaus" at the tops of their voices. The cruise director cut them short in mid-chorus.

By around eleven o'clock most people understood that wild parties were not thought appropriate.

All the same, a number of passengers led by the irpressible Rafael Mestre made an attempt to sustain a festive atmosphere. This was, after all, the last night of the voyage, and some passengers were determined to make the most of it, no matter what had happened. Inhibitions began to dissolve as the drinking and singing continued.

Stewards Sydney Ryan and Daniel Campbell served setups. A few of the passengers broke their glasses as they got progressively drunker. Some of them had their own liquor—rum they had picked up in Havana at four dollars a gallon.

Both stewards wanted the party to break up early. They would have a great deal of work afterward. The public rooms had to be gone over with the electric buffing machine for the new passengers who would board the *Morro Castle* the next day.

But the party showed no signs of abating.

Chief Engineer Eban Abbott had finally left Captain Wilmott's cabin and gone to his own. There he carefully laid out the mess kit uniform he had worn all evening. Then he removed his false teeth and placed them in a glass on his night table.

Next he telephoned the engine room. Without his teeth, Eban Abbott was hard to understand. The voice from the engine room made conversation unnecessary: "All 'kay down here."

Abbott retired, still confused by Wilmott's death, and feeling slighted. He fell asleep wondering why Warms had made no attempt to contact him.

Stewardess Lena Schwarz awoke from a troubled sleep, convinced she smelled smoke.

She lay in the darkness trying to locate its source. It was unbearably hot in the tiny cabin. She moved to adjust the air vent. The merest whiff of smoke was being blown in through the duct. For several minutes she stood by the vent, waiting for another scent. It never came. Puzzled, she climbed back into bed and soon fell asleep again.

Nearly one hundred feet forward of her cabin, Father Raymond Egan also smelled smoke. He too sensed that it came through the vent. He wondered sleepily if it might be coming from either the engine room or the kitchens.

Neither the stewardess nor the priest was aware that around midnight George White Rogers had handed over the watch to his junior operator. He told Maki that, "as the weather was lifting, he would take a breath of air."

Twenty minutes later Rogers returned.

There is strong circumstantial evidence that during the twenty minutes he was taking "a breath of air," George White Rogers prepared an incendiary device —or several such devices—designed to set the *Morro Castle* on fire and threaten the lives of all its crew and passengers.

Rogers had considerable experience in the effects of explosive devices; he knew that to manufacture one and leave it lying around for any length of time was risking not only discovery but also a premature explosion.

Moreover, he would have had no trouble hiding all the raw materials he needed in the chart room beforehand, in the knowledge they were unlikely to cause suspicion. The bottles of sulphuric and nitric acid were unlabeled. The other parts would look equally innocent: a fountain pen, a strip of copper wire.

With his knowledge Rogers would have needed little time to fashion a bomb; the twenty minutes he was absent from the radio room was ample time to make several incendiary devices. A "fountain pen bomb"— of the type he had made in the past—would have the advantage of being totally self-destructive, leaving no clues.

Once having made the devices, Rogers would need not only these plants to feed and accelerate the initial flame, but also trailers to spread the fires.

A locker in the first-class writing room containing, among other things, spare jackets for the stewards and waiters, was a perfect site for an incendiary bomb. The locker was immediately below the false ceiling to which the line-throwing Lyle gun and twenty-five pounds of dangerous explosives had been moved. Rogers himself had watched the seamen dump gun and powder barrel into the space between the false ceiling and the deck. The gunpowder would make a perfect trailer.

Another trailer was even closer at hand. Near the radio room were two gasoline tanks, used to run the transmitting equipment. It would be a simple matter to uncouple the feed line, allowing the gas to trickle down the deck.

Night watchman Arthur Pender, who passed only a few feet from the tanks, smelled a strong odor of gasoline, which he did not report to the bridge, thinking the smell must be the result of late cleaning on the eve of the ship's arrival in port.

If Pender had reported it, even a cursory investigation might have revealed the preparations for sabotage. But he did not.

In his investigations Captain George Seeth—who knew well both the *Morro Castle* and Rogers—suggested how Rogers probably placed his bomb:

"Nobody would be surprised to see a radio officer in the writing room. Rogers or one of his staff frequently took messages to passengers, and walking through the writing room was a short cut from their shack.

"Again, nobody would have been surprised if Rogers had gone to the locker itself. He would have had a ready excuse to say he was looking for a piece of paper to scribble down a message a passenger had just given him for transmission.

"But Rogers would know that the chance of being seen in the writing room around midnight was remote. It was rarely used after early evening; the only person likely to pass through it was the night watchman. It would be a simple matter for Rogers to calculate his movements to avoid detection there.

"Planting the bomb was equally simple. All he had to

do was place his fountain pen device in one of those spare steward coats and walk out again. The whole operation would take less than a minute from radio room to writing room."

Corroborative evidence compiled later into a damning dossier by Bayonne, New Jersey, Police Captain Vincent Doyle supports Captain Seeth's theory:

"George Rogers knows that I know he set fire to the *Morro Castle*. He bragged to me one day exactly how it was done. He told me how to construct an incendiary fountain pen.

"Such a device, he told me, had been placed in the inside breast pocket of a waiter's jacket which was hung in the locker there in the writing room where the fire started. When I asked him why he did it, all he would say to me was: 'The Ward Line stinks and the skipper was lousy.' "

Doyle's research reveals that in 1938 Rogers admitted to Bayonne's chief of detectives, Tom Masterton, while being questioned on a different but almost equally serious offense, that the bomb on the *Morro Castle* had been a "simple" matter to arrange.

The local district attorney's office decided that though the circumstantial evidence on the *Morro Castle* case was strong, it might not be enough to obtain a conviction, and might tend to confuse the charge for which Rogers was then being tried. And, in 1938, the public prosecutor was not concerned with Rogers' previous medical and criminal history.

Captain Doyle died, still convinced he could successfully have prosecuted Rogers for arson. There were others who felt there could be no reasonable doubt of the outcome of such a case. One was Bayonne's deputy chief of police, Edward Adamski. There was little doubt in his mind that Rogers was responsible for the *Morro*

*Castle* disaster. "He struck me as a man who would, who could, be vicious," he said. "He did have a certain amount of charm, yet you could see a certain coldness and cunning about the man."

Adamski revealed another strange facet of the setting of a bomb on the *Morro Castle*—the secret involvement of the Federal Bureau of Investigation in the case.

To this day the FBI denies they ever made any inquiries about Rogers, his background, or his statements later to Bayonne police officers. Yet Deputy Chief Adamski testified that federal agents *did* grill Rogers, hoping to establish why he may have set the bomb.

It is difficult to understand why, unless it is taken in context.

Rogers looked on the *Morro Castle* as a haven from persecution ashore. Yet while on this "haven," petty crime had cost him his job: the Radiomarine Corporation had dismissed him for stealing.

The need for revenge haunted him. The dismissal notice came at a time when Rogers was disturbed to such an extent that he was capable of anything.

Coupled with thoughts of vengeance was the need to preserve his job. At some stage Rogers' mind probably fused both needs into one: when the bomb exploded he would be the key man in the ensuing emergency.

He often contended that "heroes are never sacked."

# Fire at Sea:
# September 8, 1934

The *Morro Castle* (THE MARINERS MUSEUM)

Captain Robert Wilmott, master of the *Morro Castle* (UPI)

Boatload of survivors leaving the burning ship (UPI)

Four of the ship's officers at the inquiry that followed the *Morro Castle* disaster: Ivan Freeman, George White Rogers, William Warms, and Clarence Hackney (WIDE WORLD PHOTOS)

*Morro Castle* lifeboat landing at Spring Lake, N.J.
(THE MARINERS MUSEUM)

Smoldering *Morro Castle* at Asbury Park, N.J. Aground near
the boardwalk (WIDE WORLD PHOTOS)

# 10.
# PANIC

At midnight a new watch came on duty.

Clarence Hackney, newly promoted to second officer, was surprised to find Warms still peering into the night totally absorbed. From time to time Warms walked to the wing, sniffed the wind, and stared out over the sea. Repeatedly he checked the heading.

Hackney could see no immediate cause for concern. The weather had abated. The threatened gale had either bypassed the ship or blown itself out. A "nor'easter" was blowing, skimming squalls of rain over the ship.

Hackney saw that Warms looked tired.

"Have a break, sir."

"Later, Clarence, later. Plenty of time to sleep when we dock."

Warms kept up his vigil, his eyes moving back and forth from the mass of instruments to the darkness outside.

Hackney thought the captain "anxious. He appeared to be on the watch for everything, as if nothing was going to escape him while he had command."

In spite of all his watchfulness, Warms failed to notice that the ship's smoke-detecting system was still switched off so that the smell of raw hides would not

153

disturb the sensitive nostrils of passengers.

Stewards Daniel Campbell and Sydney Ryan were not the only crew members aware that a goodly number of passengers were getting drunker by the minute. Night watchman Arthur Pender encountered a number of drunks during his rounds. From behind the doors of several staterooms came the sounds of boisterous merrymaking.

Later, pausing for coffee in the galley pantry, he was disturbed to hear cabin stewards discussing "wastebasket fires"; they had seen passengers starting them in some of the public rooms.

The fires, caused by half-smoked cigarettes tossed into wastebaskets, were a dangerous hazard. Pender spent between midnight and one o'clock probing and poking all the wastebaskets he came across.

He found no trace of fire.

He checked with the other night watchman, Harold Foersch. Foersch had seen nothing untoward.

At 1 A.M. both men reported to the bridge that all was quiet.

At 2 A.M. Clarence Hackney reported to Captain Warms that the *Morro Castle* was only thirty miles south of Scotland Light. Soon the ship would make its last major change of course, turning into the relative shelter of Ambrose Channel and then up into New York Harbor.

Again Hackney urged Warms to take a rest. "You have been up for over thirty hours."

Warms nodded. He went to his room, sat down for a minute, then got up and walked around again. Shortly after 2 A.M. he carried out his own swift inspection of the ship. He checked the promenade deck, the verandah cafe, and the ballroom. All were deserted.

At 2:30 A.M. he returned to the bridge and told Hackney that all was in order below.

By 2:45 A.M. the party around the bar had dwindled to four—two women in long, trailing evening gowns and their escorts in tuxedos and starched shirts.

Stewards Campbell and Ryan were collecting empty glasses. Campbell looked sourly at the quartet drinking highballs.

"If you're planning to get some sleep before we dock," he said, "you'd better get to bed."

One of the women giggled. "Who wants to go to bed? I'm not going to bother."

Her companions agreed.

At exactly 2:50 A.M. Sydney Ryan paused in his glass collecting and turned to Campbell.

"Dan. You smell it?"

Campbell wrinkled his nose.

"Come on," he said.

Both smelled smoke—coming from a long way forward.

At 2:51 A.M. student engineer Tripp wrote in his log: "Night watchman Foersch reported to captain that he had just seen and smelled smoke coming out of one of the small ventilators on the port after side of the fiddley."

The fiddley was a galvanized-iron duct supplying fresh air to the first-class writing room on B deck, among other rooms.

While Tripp was making his notes, Warms acted. He rushed to the fiddley, near number one stack. A trickle of smoke emerged from the opening. Turning, he ran to rouse his senior officer.

"Ivan! Get up! Fire!"

Warms was calm and collected in responding to the emergency.

Back on the bridge, the acting captain gave his first order to fight the fire. He told Hackney: "Go down below and find the source of the fire and let me know the situation *fast*."

As he ran from the bridge Hackney grabbed a fire extinguisher.

At that moment Campbell and Ryan reached the door of the writing room, puffing slightly from their run. An antique wall clock registered the time. The men paused and surveyed the room. Smoke, like a layer of low-lying smog, carpeted the room.

"It's in that locker!" Campbell shouted.

Opening the locker, he saw a mass of flames inside. Quickly, he slammed shut the door, blistering his hands in the process.

Both men turned and ran from the room to raise the alarm. As they ran, they passed a fire extinguisher placed on the wall near the writing-room door.

It was the first mistake by members of a crew poorly trained in fire drills, rescue operations, or virtually any crisis. If Campbell and Ryan had turned that extinguisher on the fire *at once* it might have made a critical difference.

Three vital minutes passed before Clarence Hackney arrived with his fire extinguisher.

He yanked open the locker door and a wall of flame rushed out. Hackney backed off and emptied his extinguisher into it, but it was a waste of time—a dozen extinguishers could not have contained the inferno now raging around the locker.

Stunned, Hackney watched the flames lick across the false ceiling. It was he who had given the order for the Lyle gun and its deadly keg of powder to be placed immediately above.

Choking from the smoke, he turned and ran from the writing room.

He had made the second fatal mistake.

Solid-steel fire doors had been built into entrances to the public rooms to deal with just such an emergency. It would have taken Hackney only a few moments to isolate the writing room from the rest of B deck by lowering its fire door.

Clarence Hackney did not take that preventive measure. Smoke billowed after him as he ran for the telephone near the door connecting the first-class lounge to the smoking room. He dialed the bridge.

"It's pretty bad," he told Warms. "We better get water on it."

"Break out the hose and I'll get you the men," Warms ordered. "Get all the fire hydrants uncapped—fast!"

The acting captain had reacted swiftly—and he continued to do so. He called down to the engine room: "I want all water pressure possible."

"We've got a boiler still out," a voice replied. "What do you want the pressure for?"

"Fire," retorted Warms. "Get all the pressure you can to the hydrants!"

The bridge itself was an oasis of calm. The sounds of a new storm breaking against the ship drowned out all conversation.

Warms ordered a textbook change of course, turning the ship head on into the wind and sea to reduce the effect of the squall. As the ship lurched and yawed around to its new heading, Warms ordered the bridge lookout to rouse the seamen in the forecastle.

It was 2:55 A.M.

At that moment Ivan Freeman arrived on the bridge, out of breath. He had gone straight from his cabin below to B deck—to be met by a wall of smoke billowing across the lounge. Behind it he could see flames.

He immediately telephoned the engine room and told the duty crew to get up all possible pressure on the fire lines.

Then he ran for the bridge. When he reached it he told Warms: "It's bad. We should run for the beach in case we have to get the passengers off."

For a moment Acting Captain Warms said nothing. Then he walked over to the Derby automatic fire-detecting system. Each light represented a thermostat in a stateroom or the quarters of the officers and crew. The system did not cover the public rooms. Not a single light flashed red on the board. And the smoke-detecting system was still switched off.

Apparently reassured, Warms told Freeman: "We are not going yet. We can hold her. Get down and take charge."

He then spoke to the engine room by telephone. The duty engineer reported a little smoke coming in through the cooling vents.

"Get steam on the main fire pump," Warms ordered. "And have Abbott call me the moment he gets to you."

Warms turned to the helmsman and checked the course: the *Morro Castle* was cutting through the Atlantic at the fullest speed possible with one boiler closed down, on a heading of 2°, almost due north, into a storm which struck the ship head on.

At that moment Clarence Hackney rushed onto the bridge.

"It's getting worse! We'll need every man on the hose!"

This time Warms did not hesitate. He set off the general fire alarm.

"Get all the passengers out," he told Hackney. "Use tin pans! Anything you can get hold of to wake them!"

It was 3 A.M.

The quartet of drinkers from the bar moved toward the lounge doorway, sipping their highballs. They watched, fascinated, as the smoke rolled toward them. Suddenly stewards Campbell and Ryan and night watchman Arthur Pender rushed past them. Each man clutched a fire extinguisher, which he turned on the smoke.

But it was futile. Half a dozen hoses under full pressure would have been required to make an impact on the blaze enveloping the writing room. Even if fire crews had brought hoses to bear on the flames, it would have made little difference: the engine room was unable to provide sustained pressure because of the closed boiler.

The smog in the lounge itself had become so dense that it effectively masked the fire beyond.

"Can't you stop all that smoke?" shouted one of the girl passengers petulantly. "It's going to ruin my dress."

The three crewmen turned and ran back toward the onlookers.

"You best all get on deck," Campbell told them. "Report to your life stations."

"Why? It's raining outside. Anyway, I want another drink . . ."

The man's drunken demand faded as a fork of flame darted out from the smoke.

"Run for it!" he shouted. "The ship's going to go down!"

Seamen and passengers fled.

Panic had arrived on the *Morro Castle*.

Father Raymond Egan sensed the panic the moment he stepped out of his stateroom. The corridor was filling with passengers awakened by stewards hammering on their cabin doors.

They stood, dazed or drunk, in various stages of undress.

Father Egan had managed to put on his clerical garb, believing that in a crisis it would be useful for people to know his office.

He was right. The moment he appeared, people turned to him as a person to lead them out of trouble. But before the priest could act, the corridor lights flickered once and then went out, leaving them in total darkness.

"She's sinking!" a voice screamed.

"She's not!" Father Egan roared. "They're just switching the power supplies."

The conviction in his voice stilled the panic immediately around him.

From farther down the corridor came a chorus of shouts, curses, bellows, moans, and grunts, as passengers became bottlenecked at the foot of the staircase.

Father Egan forced his way down the corridor, deflecting groping hands and stumbling over feet.

"Stay still! All of you! Wait until the lights come on!" He gave the commands firmly.

The bedlam at the staircase slowly died away.

At that moment the lights returned. Father Egan found himself standing above a group of men and women sprawled up the staircase.

The scene was quite terrifying. Ordinary, sensible, thoughtful people had been turned into a pathetic rabble by fear. At the first hammering on their doors by stewards they had given way to panic. Some of them were half dressed.

The priest took charge quickly. He told the passengers they were to return to their cabins, dress in outdoor clothes, put on their life jackets, and go to their boat stations immediately.

"And don't panic," he admonished.

Eban Abbott, awakened by the alarm ringing above his head, walked naked from his cabin to the one next door, occupied by his first assistant, Antonio Bujia.

Bujia was struggling into a boiler suit. He paused, startled by his chief's appearance. Abbott muttered dazedly: "When the bell rings there is a fire—?"

Bujia finished dressing and left without saying a word.

Abbott returned to his cabin. There he carefully dressed in the formal mess kit he had worn the night before. Then he picked up the telephone linking him with the engine room.

Bujia answered. He had already accomplished a great deal: three pumps were working to supply water for the firefighting crews. By then the smoke was drifting down into the engine room, and "every minute seemed like an hour."

"How are things down there?" Abbott asked him.

"Everything is running good."

"Do the best you can and see that everyone is down there and keep things going."

"All right."

Eban Abbott put on his cap with its gold braid and straightened his jacket. Sartorially satisfied, he stepped out of his cabin. He had forgotten to put in his false teeth.

Walking past the express elevator that would have taken him directly down to the engine room, he made his way to the promenade deck. There he watched a fire crew, supervised by storekeeper William O'Sullivan, struggling to couple up a hose to one of the hydrants. The hose had had to be taken from its locker and brought down from the top deck; then the hydrant for it had to be uncapped. Inside, the superstructure glowed a dull red.

"Open the valve! Open the valve!"

Without his teeth, Abbott could not make his words understood. The chief engineer pointed at the valve and motioned to O'Sullivan to open it.

"The valve *is* open!" shouted O'Sullivan.

But the water pressure was low.

"Permission to throw deck chairs overboard?" asked seaman John Gross. "Something to cling to if we have to jump."

The chief engineer nodded and walked past the men. The firefighters abandoned their hoses and started to hurl the chairs over the side. Caught by the wind, the canvas furniture flapped clear of the boat, dropping into the sea well astern.

Abbott continued on his way, still shocked, unable to comprehend the mounting crisis. He walked down a companionway to C deck where he was surrounded by a group of girls from the Concordia Singing Society. They asked what they should do. Abbott pointed to a doorway and told them to go up to the boat deck and wait there.

Moving down to D deck, he continued his unhurried journey, keeping to the crew stairways, where he was unlikely to meet any more passengers.

Coming up the stairway was Antonio Bujia. Eban Abbott peered at him.

"What are you doing? Where are you going?"

"To the bridge. I called you through the telephone

and speaking tube and got no answer. Everything is running good. But we cannot stay down there much longer."

The two men looked at each other. Wisps of smoke were drifting around the staircase.

"Go back and stand by. I'll go to the bridge," said Abbott.

With those few words he changed his whole future; he would regret them all his life.

Shocked and disoriented though Abbott still was by Captain Wilmott's death, he had been moving, albeit slowly and in a roundabout way, down toward the engine room. If he had been challenged about his movements, he could defend himself by pointing out that, as chief engineer, it was also his job to ascertain the extent of the fire so that he could organize the water supplies accordingly.

But Bujia had brought Abbott head on with the reality of the situation: the engine room, in his assistant's estimation, had shortly to be abandoned. There was only one course of action open to Eban Abbott. It was to go down to check out the situation himself.

Abbott was charged with the responsibility to ensure that the men in the engine room performed their duties fully in operating the fire pumps, lights, and power to steer the ship through the growing crisis. He abandoned this responsibility when he ordered Bujia back down below and rapidly climbed to the safety of the open deck.

Dr. Emilio Giro was also making his way up to the boat deck. The first sharp whiff of smoke had been enough; he knew there was trouble.

He turned to his brother-in-law, Rafael Mestre, and smiled encouragement. Mestre grinned back, but Dr.

Giro could see the fear in his face. As they climbed, they noticed a phenomenon others would also notice: the smoke was being driven down on them.

Near the first-class lounge, two Cubans watched fascinated as the fire moved through the room. It ran along the paint, wood, and chintz—and there was no one there to stop it.

"Remember, if we get separated, we are in lifeboat number ten," Dr. Giro repeated. His brother-in-law nodded and crossed himself as they continued upward.

On C deck, cruise director Robert Smith found near-panic among members of the Concordia Singing Society as smoke suddenly swirled overhead and down the corridor.

He moved quickly among them.

"Down! All of you. On your knees! Hold on to the ankles of the person in front of you. And keep your heads down!"

He took position at the head of the crocodile, leading it in a painful crawl along the corridor under the smoke and up a stairway to the ballroom on B deck.

"Get to your lifeboat positions. They'll swing the boats down to you," he said.

Then the cruise director turned and ran back to help the other passengers up from below.

Ever since seaman John Gross had seen the deck chairs disappear off the stern of the ship, he, like many other members of the crew, had been gripped by terror.

He went up the port side and across the promenade deck. Black smoke enveloped everything. Pungent and acrid, the smoke crept down passageways, up stairs, across the wet decks. He could hear a man shouting from behind a wall of smoke—then there was silence.

Out on the open deck the rain was pelting down. For a moment the seaman could smell the land. Then a curtain of black smoke swept across the deck.

He turned and ran.

Beyond the curtain of smoke that sent Gross running, storekeeper William O'Sullivan hefted a fireman's ax, swung it in a wild arc, and smashed the glass corridor window of stateroom number two on A deck. Behind him stood Dr. Charles Cochrane and Dr. and Mrs. Theodore Vosseler. All three were nude under topcoats.

Smoke poured out of the shattered window. At that moment First Officer Ivan Freeman appeared.

"Up top. All of you!" he ordered.

"My sister is in there," said Dr. Cochrane.

"We can't get to her from this side, sir," O'Sullivan told Freeman. "I'll try from the other side!"

"Very well! But the rest of you up top!" repeated Freeman.

Dr. Cochrane started to protest. Freeman cut him short: "We'll get her, sir."

Without waiting for further discussion Freeman followed O'Sullivan around to the port side of the luxury-stateroom complex. Dense smoke billowed everywhere.

The two men felt their way down the deck, barely able to breathe. Finally they reached the cabin Catherine Cochrane was believed to be trapped in. Freeman lifted O'Sullivan through the window.

Inside, the seaman's flashlight was useless. He called out, but there was no answer. When O'Sullivan found the bed it was empty, but it seemed to have been slept in. He searched the floor of the stateroom and, finding no one, assumed Dr. Cochrane's sister must have escaped.

O'Sullivan was almost unconscious by the time he got back to the window, where Freeman waited to drag him out.

The brave rescue attempt had failed—because of the smoke. Unable to see, O'Sullivan had entered the wrong cabin. Catherine Cochrane had been overcome by smoke as she slept two staterooms away.

Soon others would die, with terrible speed and finality as the fire roared down passageways and sealed them off.

On the bridge, Warms looked on the smoke as a good sign, an indication that the fire was being doused. "Subduing it is bound to produce a temporary increase in the amount of smoke," he thought.

As he turned to check the ship's course, a light on the Derby fire-detecting system flashed red: a temperature of 160° F. was being reported from stateroom number five.

Suddenly the whole system flashed on.

"My God! They're all going," Warms cried.

166

# 11.
# THE S.O.S.

Acting Captain Warms' first terrible miscalculation came when he executed the textbook turn into the wind to meet the storm squall. Warms had either been unaware of, overlooked, or ignored—nobody will ever really know which—the effect such a change of course would have on the fire.

The *Morro Castle* traveled 3.1 miles head on into the storm at a speed of 18.8 knots for over ten minutes. In that time, the wind, gusting at over 20 knots, had acted as a giant bellows, fanning and speeding the flames the length of the ship.

Far below the bridge, on E deck, chief stewardess Lena Schwarz finally identified the strange sound she had been hearing: the *Morro Castle* was moaning. The noise of the fire seemed to her like a whimpering child.

Since the alarm had been sounded, Mrs. Schwarz and the other stewardesses had run from stateroom to stateroom, awakening passengers. Mrs. Schwarz's calm did much to reassure them as she offered a hand with life vests, guided people to the quickest route topside, repeating over and over, "there's probably nothing to worry about."

But the deep, sorrowful whine, coming from nowhere, yet everywhere, sent a sudden chill through her.

"Help me!"

The voice came from an outer cabin near the stern.

"Help! Please help me!"

It quelled Lena Schwarz's own panic. She ran toward the voice, plunging from one empty cabin to another. The cry was clearer, but as it came closer, it seemed to come from outside the hull.

The stewardess rushed to a porthole, opened it, and peered ouside. A few feet away, a woman was sitting on the rim of her cabin porthole, feet dangling over the sea, the wind tearing at her nightdress.

She turned and looked at Mrs. Schwarz, abject terror on her face.

"Don't move!" the stewardess shouted. "Just stay there and I'll come and get you."

At that moment the ship lurched, catapulting the woman into the sea.

Mrs. Schwarz caught a brief glimpse of the body bobbing in the ship's wake. Then it was gone. She turned, tears of fear and anguish streaming down her face.


The ship's lurch had been deliberate, the result of another command Warms gave to the helmsman.

"Left wheel!"

The *Morro Castle* rose and fell on the waves as she turned in toward the New Jersey coast.

Warms hoped the maneuver would help contain the main fire in the area of the writing room, where he thought it was still localized. Although the lights were flashing on the fire-detecting system board, indicating intense heat as far down as C deck, he did not believe the situation was critical. He believed the lights only gave *warning* of impending danger; that he still had time to contain the fire; that the heat as far down as C deck was not necessarily a prelude to flames reaching the area.

It was the second, and more tragic, miscalculation the acting captain had made since the crisis began.

"Hard to port!"

The ship tossed and heaved around toward the distant coast. Spray blew across the forecastle. For a moment the liner wallowed, broadside to, and then came onto its new course.

Suddenly a muffled explosion rocked the bridge. Warms rushed to a portside window. A flash burst across the promenade deck near the writing room.

The powder keg for the Lyle gun, hidden in the false ceiling, had exploded.

Yards away from the explosion seaman John Gross heard another seaman screaming: "She's done! We can't do anything to save her now! Oh God, we'll be burned alive! We'll all be burned."

The explosion opened the door to full-scale panic. Passengers stumbled blindly, or walked around in circles, spellbound by terror. Women screamed and men swore like maniacs.

The ship was ablaze all across midships. For a moment her whistle cried. It was the most helpless and despairing sound seaman Gross had ever heard. Then it stopped.

The flames roared on hungrily. The scene was a nightmare. Gross could hear voices crying out in fear, sobbing in dismay, chanting prayers.

The seaman joined a group of other crewmen with axes who were chopping apart deck chairs and tables and stacking them near the rails, where they could later be thrown overboard as floats. The men worked haphazardly with no officer present to direct them.

Dr. Joe Bregstein and his son reached the promenade deck moments after the explosion.

All around the dentist saw general chaos. The crew, panicking, pushed passengers aside—men, women, and children. Bregstein's eyes smarted from the smoke.

The ship was tossing about like a cork.

Shocking red flames seemed to come from every direction, blazing into the sky. The heat on the deck was searing. The dentist could smell the wood burning. Safety glass in the deck doors was melting; metal door frames began to buckle.

The wind appeared to be rising. Large, rolling waves, like hills, lifted the *Morro Castle* up, held it trembling for a moment or two, and then plunged it down again.

Joe Bregstein, young Mervyn clinging tightly to him, felt as if he were in a world of madness. Everything around him assumed strange shapes by the light of the flames.

Some people were making an obvious effort to hold on to their sanity. Bregstein tried to do the same.

As father and son huddled near the open rail of the promenade deck, a gang of sailors appeared carrying ropes. They fastened them to the rail, then uncoiled them over the sides. The ends of the ropes trailed in the water.

A seaman shouted that when rescue came, passengers could scramble down the ropes to safety.

Joe Bregstein looked down at the water. It suddenly seemed much farther away than it had been a few minutes before. He turned, looking aft, his apprehension growing.

Down the deck another father and son had also been watching the sailors snake the ropes over the side.

Then the man lifted his child on to his back, throwing one leg, and then the other, over the railing. For a moment he sat there, holding on with his hands, peering down at the sea. Then he let go of the rail.

Bregstein watched them hit the water. The sea closed over their heads. They seemed to go under forever. Then they shot to the surface. Somehow, the boy still clung around his father's neck. The man snatched at a rope and held on to it, screaming, "Help, help, help us." Passengers who had seen them jump were also shouting for somebody to help the two. But there was nothing anybody could do.

In the glare of the flames Bregstein could see the sea was crashing the pair against the side of the ship. Then a wave swept completely over them and they were gone. The rope hung slack.

Sickened, and now not a little terrified, Joe Brestein clutched his own son close to him and wondered how long it would be before rescue ships arrived.

He automatically assumed that the moment the fire had been discovered, an SOS had been sent.


For twelve minutes George White Rogers sat calmly by the main transmitter, waiting for an official order to summon outside help.

Rogers had been sound asleep in his bunk when the fire alarm sounded. George Alagna had had to shake him quite hard to wake him.

The two men dressed quickly and joined Maki in the radio room.

Rogers tuned to the main six-hundred-meter distress frequency, and threw the switch into a position which would ensure that the transmitter would produce a very broad interfering path.

Evidence of fire was quite apparent from the radio

shack. As far as the radio operators could tell, it seemed to be just below and forward on the port side, by the writing room. The radio room was filling with smoke. When Rogers went to the door he could see the reflection of the flames and hear shouting and confused commands.

But, it seemed to Rogers, the wind carried the commotion, and even the danger, out to sea. The scene gave him a strange sense of detachment, as if he were straddling two ships in a dream—as if he were two different people.

When Rogers noticed that the emergency light was out, he instructed Alagna to unscrew the bulb and test it in a socket where another bulb was burning; there the bulk worked perfectly.

The chief radio officer then signed the radio-room log, saying that he was summoned to duty to take over what was apparently a distress watch.

Turning to Alagna, he said, "Go up to the bridge and see what orders the mate has to give you."

It was just after 3 A.M.

Moments later, Alagna returned, ashen-faced, shaken by what he had seen. "The flames are taller than the radio room," he told Rogers.

"Everything is chaos out there. I heard someone say the pressure is getting low. I tried to get to the bridge, but I couldn't make it."

Rogers took the news calmly. He tried to call the bridge by telephone—without success. Apparently the electrical circuit had broken down. Picking up the speaking tube, he tried to call the bridge again. All he could hear was a loud roaring noise.

Once more Alagna was ordered to go to the bridge and "obtain whatever orders it was possible to obtain."

This time the smoke cleared momentarily, allowing Alagna to reach the bridge. He arrived just in time to hear Warms give the course change for the New Jersey shore, and to see the helmsman frantically spin the wheel.

He yelled to Warms that he had been sent up to the bridge by Rogers.

Warms paid little attention to what Alagna was saying; the radioman had to follow him around the wheelhouse.

When Alagna repeated what he had said, Warms finally answered "All right." He appeared to be saying something else, but Alagna could not hear him in the confusion.

The radio operator suspected that Warms didn't even recognize him. Warms seemed upset, even obsessed, by something of great importance. Alagna assumed it was the fire.

Alagna was wrong. Warms had recognized him, and the sight of the radio assistant had brought to mind all the suspicions he had nursed on the voyage—suspicions that Alagna was a "radical," capable of any act, possibly even arson.

Alagna returned to the radio room and reported what had happened. Already he believed the situation was out of control.

Rogers shook his head.

"Go back to the bridge and ask again for orders when we are to send an SOS," he said.

Alagna made a third journey to the bridge.

In the radio room the smoke was thickening. Maki shifted uneasily.

"Shouldn't we do something?" he asked.

"We wait for orders. That's what the regulations say —and that's what we'll do." Rogers settled back.

Several minutes later he looked at his watch. Alagna had been gone for three minutes. He turned to Maki: "Go soak a towel in the washbasin so that I can breathe through it. Then go to the bridge and find Alagna."

Maki did as he was told, and then left. He would never return to the radio room. For a while he would wander aimlessly around the deck; finally he would jump from the ship.

Alone, Rogers went to the doorway to look at the fire. It was spreading. Black smoke was everywhere.

When he resumed his position in front of the transmitter, he noted the time: 3:13 A.M.

Thirteen minutes had elapsed since the general alarm had been given, and still no order to transmit an SOS had come from the bridge.

Alagna reappeared, trying to maintain his control. "The whole place is on fire," he shouted. "We're going to get caught like rats in a trap in this place . . ."

"What about the distress message? Are we to send it?"

"I dunno. They're a bunch of madmen up there, just running around . . ."

"Go back and ask the mate again," ordred Rogers.

Alagna began a fourth trip to the bridge.

As he left the door, the transmitter crackled to life. Somebody else was using the six-hundred-meter emergency frequency.

It was the radio operator aboard the freighter *Andrea S. Luckenbach,* steaming a parallel course ten miles seaward of the *Morro Castle.*

At 3:14 A.M. her radioman contacted the U.S. Coast Guard station at Tuckerton, New Jersey.

"Do you have any news of a ship burning off Sea Girt?" asked the operator.

"Haven't heard of any," came the reply.

The operator took the reply to the bridge. There he found the *Luckenbach*'s captain and first officer peering west through binoculars.

"There's a glow over there," said the first officer.

The operator reported his conversation with Tuckerton Station.

Both officers lowered their glasses, believing they had made a mistake.

Rogers sat, transfixed by the brief exchange between the cargo ship and the Coast Guard station.

The fire aboard was now visible ten miles away; the situation was critical enough for even the seriously disturbed mind of the chief radio officer to see there was the possibility of becoming a hero.

Regulations governing the sending of distress signals at sea are strict: no SOS can be sent without the express order of the captain. But the rules also allow an operator some leeway. It would have been proper for Rogers to have sent a message such as "Fire on *Morro Castle* off New Jersey. Awaiting orders from bridge."

Such a message would have alerted the outside world. No one could later have criticized such a course of action, confirming the *Luckenbach*'s sighting a serious fire through ten miles of rain. While it was not a formal SOS, it would nevertheless have been a standby call for help. And the time to send it was now.

At 3:15 A.M. the mandatory "listening-out" period for all radio operators at sea began. Instead of a distress signal, Rogers sent:

"Standby. DE KGOV."

KGOV was the call sign of the *Morro Castle*.

"KGOV wait three minutes," ordered Tuckerton radio station.

Rogers immediately stopped sending.

On the bridge, Alagna stood, almost mesmerized by the extraordinary scene before him.

Warms had just discovered Eban Abbott lurking in a dark corner of the bridge.

The acting captain dragged the chief engineer into the center of the area. In his dress uniform, Abbott looked as if he were going to the captain's ball.

Abbott began to shriek, "What will we do? What will we do?"

"What are *you* doing *here?*" Warms screamed. "Why aren't you below to see to it that my engine orders are obeyed and fast—"

"It's too late—"

"God damn it, get below! What about the water pressure?"

"A hundred hoses wouldn't make any difference now—"

"Get below! And stay there until I tell you to come up! We need water! Get the hell down there and organize things!"

"Captain, the water pressure's gone!" Second Officer Clarence Hackney brought the news to the bridge. "It's hopeless down there in places!"

The lack of fire drills had produced its deadly effect. Seamen who abandoned their hoses in the face of the spreading flames had also failed to turn off the hydrants supplying the water. The engine room's capacity to provide something like a thousand gallons a minute of water under pressure was quickly dwindling. In twenty minutes the pressure had been halved, then cut to a third. Now it was only a trickle.

Warms turned to his chief engineer. "What's happened to that pressure?" he screamed. "*Answer* me! D'you hear, *answer* me!"

Horrified, Alagna watched as Eban Abbott paced back and forth, wringing his hands, saying over and over in a shrill voice. "What will we do?"

Warms continued to hound him, shouting, "Answer me! Answer me!"

"Captain! Captain, sir!" yelled the helmsman. "She isn't holding!"

The words stopped Warms in midstride.

"Hard left!" he roared. "Bring it round hard left!"

"Hard to port, sir . . . sir, the wheel isn't responding . . . maybe the line's gone!"

Alagna felt a sense of doom; he could almost smell the fear around him.

"Try the magnetic! The wheel lines are okay!" yelled Warms.

Moments later the helmsman reported that the wheel was again responding.

Alagna glanced around him. Eban Abbott had retreated again into a far corner of the bridge, still wringing his hands.

The radioman stepped toward Warms.

"Mr. Warms. Do you have any orders for the radio room?"

"Orders?"

Alagna nodded.

"Can you send an SOS?"

"Certainly! That's what I've been coming here for—"

Warms turned his back on Alagna, preoccupied.

Desperately, the radioman turned to Clarence Hackney: "What's our position?"

"Sea Girt. And get it off fast," ordered Hackney.

George Alagna left the bridge, convinced it was being run by lunatics.

Father Raymond Egan estimated the crowd of passengers huddled aft on C deck numbered nearly one hundred. Indifferent to the driving rain, their eyes were drawn to the fire raging a few hundred feet away.

The priest moved among them, trying to calm them, urging those who wanted to pray to do so.

"Father." A woman in the crowd touched his sleeve. "My husband. He's still down there."

"Where?"

"D deck. He went back to get a topcoat for me—"

"Stay here. I'll go and look for him."

"I'll come with you, Father." The familiar voice belonged to steward Sydney Ryan.

The two men entered the ship. Ahead the fire crackle from port to starboard.

Near the barber shop a couple of stewards were kneeling beside a badly burned child; the waiters had pulled the boy clear of a burning cabin on A deck. In places the child's flesh had peeled back to the bone. He kept on repeating, *Mi madre! Mi madre!"* As Father Egan knelt to administer last rites, the child died.

The priest rose and said calmly, "Come on. Let's find that husband."

# 12.
## OUT OF CONTROL

Even in his undershirt and shorts headwaiter Carl Wright still retained much of the dignity of his office. He had organized a party of waiters on C deck into an effective search and rescue team. In twenty minutes they evacuated a dozen passengers to safety.

Wright and his men had a problem convincing some of the passengers of the danger. Some were openly resentful at being awakened. One man threatened to report to the line the steward who awakened him.

Some of the passengers were drunk. A young Cuban woman who had been having an affair with one of the men on board was drunk, and quite put out at being taken from her boy friend's bed. Many passengers refused to take the situation seriously.

But by 3:20 A.M., with the arrival of the flames, the mood on C deck changed.

They flashed suddenly through cabin door 226, situated directly below the writing room on B deck.

Wright saw a mushroom of flame and the passengers started to scream. At that moment the lights failed. This time Father Egan was not there to stem the tumult.

Wright anticipated the panic a split second before it came. He had enough time to flatten himself in a cabin doorway.

A tangle of bodies hurtled past him. The loss of elec-

tric light and the awful glare of the flames had robbed
people of the last of their self-control. They clawed
and hit each other, pushing and shoving like animals.
Men hit women, women clawed back.

Forcing his way through the mass to bodies, deflecting them with the handle of his ax, storekeeper William
O'Sullivan and a handful of sailors carried extinguishers
toward cabin 226. They reached it just as its ceiling collapsed.

The firefighters poured their extinguishers into the
flames. Then they, too, turned and ran as the fire leaped
after them.

Headwaiter Wright watched the flames coming down
the corridor, licking first at the ceiling and then shooting down the walls to envelop everything in a roaring
red glow.

Then Wright heard the piercing cry of a child.
He did not hesitate. Bent double, he ran down the corridor. In cabin 234 he found a young girl cowering in a
corner, too frightened to move. Somehow she had been
overlooked in the general panic. Wright picked her up
and ran as the flames came roaring through the walls.

Chief Stewardess Lena Schwarz and stewardess
Ragne Zabola climbed up to D deck.

The older woman was calm, turning to smile encouragement to her friend.

"I wonder where Sydney is?" Miss Zabola asked
more than once. "I hope he's all right."

She and deck steward Sydney Ryan had been good
friends since joining the ship.

"He's fine," said Mrs. Schwarz. "Probably up on
deck waiting for you. When we get there it'll probably
be not half as bad as we think."

But when they reached D deck, her confidence began to evaporate. They found themselves in a corridor ankle-deep in water being washed to and fro with the ship's roll. The spill was gushing from a couple of fire hydrants.

All over the ship hydrants had been uncapped and then, when the flames approached, crew members had abandoned their places at the hoses. Fire had eaten through some of the hoses—and left the hydrants uselessly pouring out water, reducing the water pressure still further. It was all a grim by-product of lax discipline and poor leadership.

Both women noticed the smoke rolling down on them. They squinted their eyes against it without effect.

The smarting pungency came from a combination of layers of heavy paint used in the public rooms, laminated paneling in staterooms, and highly inflammable stain and varnish that had made the *Morro Castle* a thing of beauty, and now helped turn it into a floating charnel house.

The women could hear the fire crackling overhead, interspersed with distant shouts. Lena Schwarz forced a smile. "Sounds like all the action is up top. Let's go and see!"

They were about to continue their climb when the chief stewardess stopped. "What about Mrs. Brown in 507? She can't walk very well."

Mrs. Schwarz turned and began to slosh down the corridor, dimly aware of the wind howling in through a number of broken portholes—ready-made flues allowing oxygen to feed the spreading inferno.

"Lena! The smoke's coming out of the elevator!" shouted Ragne Zabola.

Far above, on B deck, the windows of the ship's lobbies, located fore and aft, had been blown out by the heat. Gales of wind had rushed into the elevator shafts in each lobby, fanning the flames, carrying them downward. No matter how the *Morro Castle* turned and twisted, there was no way of avoiding the wind coming in from port or starboard.

Mrs. Schwarz turned and glanced briefly toward the elevator door, then ran on, finally reaching stateroom 507.

"Oh, Mrs. Schwarz, how good of you to come." Mrs. Brown might have been welcoming a late guest for afternoon tea. "I've been trying to get on my life jacket."

The stewardess fastened the straps, then led Mrs. Brown carefully back down the corridor.

Behind them they heard a sudden dull roar. The fire had reached D deck.

"Which way to lifeboat number ten?" Up on B deck, Dr. Emilio Giro asked the question with polite diffidence.

A sailor shouted over his shoulder, "Forget the lifeboats! Jump!"—then vanished into the smoke.

The doctor turned to his brother-in-law Rafael Mestre. "Jump? But I can't swim."

"It's the only chance," Mestre answered.

Dr. Giro considered the words carefully, as he might consider the second opinion of a trusted medical colleague.

"Very well. I will jump," he said gravely.

The decision made, he took off his jacket, folded it carefully, and placed it on the deck. Next he took off his shoes and placed them beside his coat. He wondered whether he should also remove his shirt and trousers; he would find it easier to swim without them, but there was also the matter of the cold—and the matter of propriety. A few feet away a group of men and women knelt in prayer.

". . . but deliver us from evil, for thine is the kingdom and the power and the glory, for ever and ever, amen."

Turning his back on them, Dr. Giro walked across to the rail. The ship appeared to him to be slowing down, wallowing in the water. The sea was covered with pieces of debris and bodies.

Dr. Giro started to weigh all the factors, applying a sort of scientific discipline to the situation. He knew that his life vest alone would probably not support him in a storm like the one raging around the ship.

A piece of wood, he thought, could become waterlogged. Then it occurred to him—a body. He needed a body to hang onto.

He stared again down into the sea. Then he carefully checked the contents of his wallet: a letter of credit to the Bank of New York for two thousand dollars and snapshots of his wife and baby daughter. He put them back in his pocket. Then he turned to his brother-in-law.

"Take care of Sylvia and the baby for me . . ."

"You'll make it," said Mestre, embracing the doctor.

The two men stepped apart. Giro noticed that Mestre wasn't wearing a life jacket.

"It's okay, it's okay," said Mestre. "I'll jump from lower down. It's okay."

He turned and ran down the deck into the smoke. It was useless to go after him.

Dr. Giro turned, walked to the rail, and sat on it

He swallowed deeply, closed his eyes, and jumped.

The coldness of the water was followed by another sensation—the pounding of air against his ears, the feeling that his stomach was being forced up and up into his chest and then his throat—a terrible choking feeling, as if he were being strangled. Curiously, he had expected this. Something told him that, medically speaking, he was experiencing no unusual symptoms. As long as he didn't open his mouth he was still safe.

He shot to the surface, coughing and spitting, emerging very close to the ship. The black hull rose up like the side of a cliff. Coming down the cliff was the fire, spreading as it came down, showering the water with sparks.

On the decks Giro could see people. From the water they seemed to be dancing, little figures jumping up and down, waving their hands, like puppets in a carnival sideshow. They made no noise, just waved their hands, moving up and down the rail.

But the fire drowned even the noise of the waves, the rain, the wind—everything.

As the waves tossed him around, Dr. Giro felt as if he were going down, being pulled down by the water. He began to swallow sea water, then spat it out and closed his mouth. He kicked and flailed, repeating to himself, "You can't drown. There's Sylvia and baby Sylvia." Then he saw a corpse floating a few feet away, face down in the water.

He reached out and got his arms around its neck. As the body turned over, Dr. Giro could see it was a man, about fifty, dressed in pajamas. His face had been terribly burned.

The doctor knew he couldn't hold on to the body's neck for long; it would sink. Holding on to the neck with one hand, he grabbed the pajama trousers cord with the other. Then he placed both arms around the body's waist and started to kick out with his feet. He kicked slowly and steadily. There was a long way to go to the shore.

Father Raymond Egan and Sydney Ryan emerged from the furnace heat of C deck, unsuccessful in their search for the missing husband. Their eyes streamed from smoke.

The man's wife rushed toward them. She seemed on the verge of saying something when, with a scream of pain, she twisted forward. A great splinter of glass, shaped like a jagged triangle, had pierced her back. She was dead before the priest could move to assist her.

Horror-stricken, seaman John Gross ran forward to catch the woman as she fell. His hands were slippery with blood.

The heavy plate-glass windows of the ballroom had shattered in the heart. Showers of smoke-blackened glass, heavy glass, flew through the air. Any one of the fragments was capable of killing.

"Duck under the thwarts! Duck under them," Gross shouted.

His warning was too late for some: a man and two women were sliced down where they stood.

Amidships on the port side, deckhand Joseph Spilgins, charged with the responsibility of the six port lifeboats, wondered where the officers were, where the lifeboat crews had gone, where the passengers had disappeared.

For twenty minutes, with the flames scorching the

air, he waited to launch the first lifeboat.

Then through the smoke straggled a small group of people: three young women passengers, a few stewards, and a sailor. Spilgins helped the women into the boats. The others scrambled in after them.

Spilgins released the brake and dropped the lifeboat over the side into the sea. The ship was still under way, and he knew that lifeboats are not lowered from a ship under way. But under the circumstances, it seemed essential to use any means of escape at hand.

The wire falls whined in the sheaves as the boat shot down to the sea. The flames roared behind Spilgins. He looked down. Something had gone wrong in the lifeboat. It had not dropped astern as it should have. It was being towed alongside the ship by one of the falls.

Horrified, Spilgins saw that only one fall had been released. The lifeboat was a thing possessed. Its hysterical occupants clung like leeches to a plunging, terrified animal. A man fell over the side and was hauled back on board by the sailor in the lifeboat as it scraped against the *Morro Castle*.

The sailor grabbed a hatchet stowed in the stern and slashed at the wire cable holding the lifeboat fast to the liner. The hatchet struck sparks from the taut wire. Those in the boat were being thrown about like toys. The girls clung silently to the thwarts.

Another lifeboat, red-hot and flaming, came loose from its fastenings and pitched out over the ship's side. Then suddenly the hatchet cut the wire.

They were free.

As they drifted clear of the liner, the burning lifeboat crashed into the sea a few yards away.

Acting Captain Warms was still unaware that at least

one lifeboat had been launched without his authority and that passengers were jumping into the sea.

The calmness which a few hours before had impressed the purser and First Officer Freeman was gone.

It was understandable: Warms had never imagined he would assume command again under such circumstances; nor could he expect his chief engineer to fail him at a crucial moment.

The helmsman spun the magnetic compass wheel to bring the ship onto a new course.

"No response, sir!"

"Now Goddammit, you said that before! *Get* her around!"

"Sir—"

"Get her *around!*"

But the wheel spun slackly. The *Morro Castle's* helmsman had lost control over her rudder.

There was one last option open to Warms: manipulating the engines. Going ahead on one and astern on the other could provide some control.

When Warms ran out to the wing of the bridge to check how fast the stern was swinging, the full enormity of the catastrophe struck him for the first time. A blast of heat scorched his face, singeing his eyebrows and hair. Tall columns of flame leaped as high as the mast amidships and roared forward toward the bridge. Clouds of smoke boiled from the flames and rolled over the ship's side.

Against this background Warms saw blackened figures run and plunge over the side.

That scene was enough to shake the most iron resolve. It numbed Warms. For moments he peered aft, unable and unwilling to believe his own eyes.

"Captain. Fire's totally out of control."

Warms turned at Ivan Freeman's words.

"Ivan. They're jumping back there." Warms shook his head in wonderment. "Get forward and prepare to let go the anchor."

The two men ran back into the bridge, ignoring the chief engineer, still crouched in a corner.

Eban Abbott was muttering, "It's too late. Too late. A hundred hoses wouldn't help . . ."

# 13.
# NIGHTMARE

At exactly 3:25 A.M. Alagna returned to the radio room shouting, "Okay, send it."

George Rogers began to transmit the SOS. *"Morro Castle.* Twenty miles south of Scotland Lightship. Ship afire. Need immediate assistance."

Alagna's and Rogers' versions of events that followed are identical in detail, but Rogers' testimony is more melodramatic and, of course, puts him in a more heroic light.

Heroic he was, even though the motives for his actions may be questioned.

After dealing with a blaze in the radio room, Rogers suddenly became conscious that his feet were so hot he couldn't stand it. He felt the floor with his hand. He withdrew it quickly. And now the bulkhead in the room was beginning to show heat discoloration.

"I had a white towel over my face. I could hardly breathe any longer.

"I had gotten about halfway through the distress message when the corner of the radio-room table that housed the receiver batteries exploded.

"There was a loud puff in the corner and the room became filled with some sort of sulphuric gas from the batteries. Probably the hot deck was boiling the acid as it poured out of them.

"The receiver was completely out of commission. But I continued to send the SOS, realizing that the transmitter was still functioning.

"After sending the SOS, the small auxiliary generator on the table in the radio room suddenly stopped. The connections between that generator and the batteries that ran it had broken.

"I got up from the table and staggered over to the wall. I could hardly breathe, and I hung on to the wall for several seconds. Then I fixed up the connections and I heard the generator start again. Then I lost my way in the radio room.

"I was in a sort of coma. I was just staggering around. The time I don't know. I remember sitting down in the chair and my feet were burning bad. I pulled them back on the chair rungs, and I remember falling onto the towel and feeling the wet towel on my face.

"I was trying to breathe, but the towel was already practically permeated with smoke. I could not hold out much longer.

"Then I heard an explosion in the auxiliary room and the radio generator stopped completely. The apparatus had probably all been blown to pieces.

"I thought to myself, if I am supposed to be dying now, it does not appear to hurt very much! I was just beginning to feel sleepy.

"All of a sudden I felt Alagna shaking me and he was saying, 'Come on, Chief, get out of here. The whole damned place is on fire,' and I remember pushing him away with my arm and saying, 'Go back to the bridge and see if there is anything else! ...'"

Alagna returned to the bridge. There Acting Captain

Warms ordered the radio room evacuated; the ship was being abandoned.

Then Alagna made a highly unusual request: "Captain, what about Wilmott's body? Can I put it in one of the boats?"

Warms was startled.

Why should the man most likely to be suspected of murder want to preserve the evidence? Did he know he was suspected of sabotage and could already foresee arrest? If so, he must have realized what an important part an autopsy of Wilmott's body would play in the proceedings.

Warms got control of himself. "The living are more important than the dead," he said.

Alagna then stumbled back to the radio room. When he arrived, he found Rogers barely conscious. "I remember getting up and Alagna pulled me toward the door. I fell over the door coaming and skinned my leg. I remember lying out on deck for a second. I got up and got hold of the starboard bridge deck rail and pulled myself forward. I looked aft and there was nothing but a sea of fire as far as you could see.

"We managed to get onto the bridge, and I wondered if there was anybody in the pilot house. The air directly on the bridge was very hot, although it was apparently fresher because the ship at that time appeared to be anchored.

"She was covered by the smoke and flames aft. The pilot house was completely afire."

Rogers and Alagna paused, wondering which way to turn next.

On the port side of the bridge, Warms struggled with a passenger. The man had lunged through the smoke, screaming: "Save my girl friend! She's trapped in a cabin."

Warms was the first person he met on the bridge; swiftly other members of the crew disentangled the hysterical passenger.

"Put him in a boat," Warms gasped. "Take him down and put him in a boat."

A few feet from the bridge, a lifeboat had been prepared for lowering. The sailors bundled the man toward it.

Behind them came Chief Engineer Eban Abbott, mumbling, "So we're going to shut off everything. There's nothing more we can do in the engine room without choking to death . . ."

As the sailors dumped the passenger into the lifeboat, Eban Abbott stepped into its stern.

"Lower away," he ordered.

The kindest interpretation of Abbott's action is that he was still deeply shocked. But the fact remains that this lifeboat, with a capacity of seventy, held only eight people when Abbott climbed aboard, six of whom were members of the crew.

The chief engineer was not the only member of the crew who disregarded the safety of the passengers. Of the first eighty people lowered away in lifeboats, seventy-three were crew members.

It was one thing for a poorly paid steward or deckhand with no loyalty to the ship or the Ward Line, and with no sense of seamanship, to adopt such an attitude. It was quite another when the second ranking officer on the ship joined the scramble over the side.

Acting Captain Warms shouted from the bridge, "Don't lower the boat! Keep it at the rail for passengers."

Eban Abbott continued to order the boat to be lowered.

As it slid down its davits, the chief engineer tore off the bars and gold braid from his uniform.

Warms watched the lifeboat hit the water and drift into the night.

"It was a moment of shame for all who believe in the tradition of the sea," Warms said, recalling his fury at the time.

Yet Warms himself was not without fault in at least one critical area of judgment. The nearly thirty minutes he let pass between the discovery of the fire and the sending of an SOS has never been explained adequately.

"The longest thirty minutes in my life," Warms called them. He was never asked fully to account for the gap. His brief public explanation—that he didn't want to alarm the passengers by triggering off an immediate full-scale rescue operation—was accepted.

Some knowledgeable seamen have said that sending an SOS was the last thing a captain would do in those days. He tried to contain an emergency on the ship. He tried not to alarm anybody, and the last thing he did was to send word to his superiors.

Then there was the possibility of a profit motive. An SOS not strictly necessary could be an expensive item and attract undesirable publicity for the line.

A needless rescue operation would undoubtedly also dim the promotion prospects of Acting Captain Warms; the stockholders and directors of the Ward Line were unlikely to look with favor on a request for continued command from a man prone to impulsive behavior.

Whatever the reasons, Captain Warms ignored repeated visits to the bridge by radioman Alagna to get permission to send out an SOS. If it had been somebody other than George Alagna, Warms might have paid more attention to sending an SOS.

The fire spread much faster than Warms—already coping with quite severe weather—had allowed for. Had he suspected the fire had been started intentionally, he might also have acted differently.

There is one inexcapable fact: by the time the SOS *was* sent, the *Morro Castle* was beyond help.

Rogers and Alagna picked their way forward of the bridge. The chief radio operator recalled later that once again as he looked aft, "all you could see was one tremendous sheet of fire. You could hear the big portholes cracking there from the heat inside."

They scrambled to the forepeak, joining a small group of people around Warms, who had a flashlight in his hand.

"Hackney," said Warms, "there is a ship off out there. See if you can raise her."

Hackney started to wink out the call sign of the *Morro Castle* to the steaming *Andrea S. Luckenbach.*

The freighter's blinker system cut in: "Do you need assistance?"

Hackney flashed out: "Immediately. Five forty passengers."

"We will send a boat," came the reply from the freighter's bridge. It seemed an inadequate response, but the *Luckenbach* carried only two.

Warms turned and looked at the superstructure, flaming aft from the bridge, virtually dividing the ship in two. In the forepeak were the other officers remaining on board, Ivan Freeman and Clarence Hackney, as well as Rogers and Alagna, watchman Arthur Pender, storekeeper William O'Sullivan, a handful of seamen, and Dr. and Mrs. Vosseler.

The wind which sent shivers through them also protected them from the blaze roaring through the rest of the ship.

"We'll all be safe soon. I got off the SOS," said Rogers.

C deck, near the stern, was crowded with people. The cruise director was trying to calm them. A priest was praying for them. Somebody had brought a bedspread on deck. The chief stewardess, Mrs. Schwarz, tore it up into little pieces and wet it down so that the people could have a piece to put to their noses to keep the smoke from choking them. Some of the men asked why she didn't jump. "I am *the* stewardess on the ship," Mrs. Schwarz said. "I must stay."

The steward Sydney Ryan and Stewardess Ragne Zabola had been standing, holding hands, by the rail. Mrs. Schwarz turned to give them a strip of cloth, but while she had been tending to others, they had jumped.

Horrified, Mrs. Schwarz rushed to the rail. Far below she watched the couple thrashing desperately to get clear of the water whirling around the stern. Then they were sucked under—as others had been.

"The propellers must have cut them in two," Mrs. Schwarz recalled. "The suction dragged them under. It was horrible, horrible."

Headwaiter Carl Wright sensed that if he didn't jump soon, he and the little girl he still carried would die. But Wright knew the danger of jumping from the stern. He turned and inched his way toward the fire wall, seeking a way toward midships.

It was a nightmare journey. A sailor's hand had been sliced off and he was walking around, appealing for help, trying to use his other hand as a tourniquet. With a scream, the man jumped overboard. A woman passenger lay face down on the deck, either trampled to death or suffocated by smoke. Everywhere there was panic.

Clutching the child tightly to him, the headwaiter jumped into the sea. Swimming steadily, he was carried away from the *Morro Castle*. Around him the sea was filled with corpses and people clinging to debris or swimming. Nearby he could see a lifeboat. He started to swim toward it.

He held the child under his right arm, and when the waves swept over her head, he lifted her and told her to spit out the water. After a while, she moaned and swallowed a great deal of water. Wright listened to her heart but could hear nothing. "I carried the poor little tot on toward the boat because I didn't want to abandon her."

The boat drifted off into the night before he could reach it. Wright clung to the child for two more hours. Other passengers swam up, begging him to release the girl's body and to help the living. "It broke my heart," he said, "when I had to set her body adrift."


Honeymooners Charles and Selma Widder also managed to jump clear of the ship. They landed near Dr. Emilio Giro, who told them to "grab a body" and hold on to it.

They swam for the shore. Soon the couple were tired; the water grew colder. A huge wave swamped them. When it passed, Charles Widder and the corpse he had been clinging to had disappeared.


Patrolman William Price and his wife Mary stood on

C deck. Both agreed the time had come to go over the side.

They had watched others do it—and knew they must do it even though Mary Price was crippled.

It was difficult to get Mrs. Price's limbs over the rail. And there seemed to be no one to help. Finally, with the assistance of a passenger, Patrolman Price got his wife's limbs over the side, tied a life belt around her waist and around a hawser, and lowered her down toward a lifeboat.

The survivors in the lifeboat ignored her. Price kept shouting, "Pick her up! Pick her up!" But instead they shouted for him to jump.

One of the men on deck climbed to the top of the railing as though he was about to jump into one of the lifeboats. Price pulled his gun on him, saying, "If you do you are a dead man." He knew that the man would have gone through the bottom of the lifeboat. The man drew back on deck.

Below, they started to pick up Mrs. Price from the water as William Price slid down a rope. When the policeman got into the boat he found his wife dead.

The other patrolman on board, Charles Menken, had helped his wife jump from C deck, then followed her into the water. He had been stunned by a falling body and nearly drowned.

"When I regained my bearings, my wife wasn't anywhere to be seen. I spent an hour looking for her, swimming from one corpse to another, from one swimmer to another.

"Then I found her, lying on her back, floating like she was in a pool. She just turned her head and looked at me, and said, 'Charley,' and I said 'Annie.'

"Then we just held hands, floating, as the waves kept smashing at us."

"Why don't you take an oar and row, instead of sitting there," a seaman shouted at Chief Engineer Abbott as the lifeboat bobbed helplessly in the sea.

"I can't. I cut my hand."

Eban Abbott held up his left hand to the rest of the boat's passengers. There was no cut. He held up his right hand. Again, there was no mark.

"I can't row. I cut my hand," he repeated. "Nobody can row with a cut hand."

He lapsed into moody silence.

A short distance away, seaman Leroy Kelsey tried to steer his lifeboat toward the shore.

He remembered the darkness and the "sullen waves, white-crested, with breaking foam. They rushed upon us, threatening to capsize us. The girls were sick. One of them had gashed her forehead. The blood matted her hair.

"Then I heard the sound of water slopping under the floor boards. The plug was out—the boat was filling!

"One of the passengers sacrificed his shirt and shivered in the rain. The plug was jammed back in.

"Then, like a monstrous flaming torch, the burning ship, out of control, swung aimlessly around. She bore straight down upon us. She was going to run us down!

"At the last moment she swung away, caught by the sea, a flaming nightmare."

# 14.
# THE RESCUE ARMADA

Cruise director Robert Smith watched as the flames swept through the corridor ahead.

"My friend is still in her cabin," cried the woman passenger beside him. "You must get her out!"

Smith nodded. In the past hour he had answered similar pleas. His heroism had cost him burns on his face, hands, and body.

He edged toward the curtain of flame. "The heat was scorching the inside of my mouth, and I was scared," Smith recalled. Then through the fire he saw it—an isolated moving ball of flame.

"It's my friend!" shrieked the woman behind him.

The fireball staggered down the corridor; the whole body seemed to be aflame.

As the horrified Smith watched, the flames gushed up above the body, and it rolled back along the corridor into the inferno.

Turning, Smith grabbed the woman passenger and ran out to D deck. He scooped the woman into his arms and jumped overboard.

He would support her for hours before both were rescued.

On C deck, a few feet from where Father Raymond Egan knelt, half a dozen passengers were boxed in by fire, trapped in a corridor space of only a few feet. Rescue was impossible; the priest had been called to give final absolution.

Father Egan knelt at the edge of the fire. The heat burned the skin off his knees.

Raising his hand, the priest spoke the words of absolution. Then he rose, clothes smoldering, and ran back onto the deck, tears streaming down his face.

"Father! You've got to jump. Everybody's going!"

The priest nodded to the seaman. It was true: crew and passengers were swarming over the side.

Rafael Mestre had been trying to get himself to jump overboard but his courage failed him. "Then I saw this woman," he recalled. "She was weeping because she had no preserver. I gave her one I found, strapped it on her, cradled her in my arms, and threw her as far out as possible from the side of the ship."

Before he could reconsider, the young Cuban sprang over the side.

He swam steadily for an hour before a rescue boat found him. In it was the body of the woman he had given his life jacket to. She had drowned.

On C deck, Dr. Joe Bregstein still hesitated. The flames were a few feet away. The two girls beside him, Gladys and Ethel Knight of the Concordia Singing Society, seemed to have the confidence he lacked at this moment.

The dentist looked at his son. The child looked solemnly at his father.

"He'll be all right with us," urged Ethel Knight. "We're also good swimmers and we've got our preservers."

"And your little boy's got a life vest," added Gladys

Knight. "Let him come with us. We'll swim with him to the boat."

Joe Bregstein looked at the sisters. He was close to tears.

"I can't swim very well," he began.

"Then all the more reason we should take the boy," said Ethel Knight. "We can make it, sure we can."

From down the deck came a dull roar as part of the superstructure caved in.

"Dr. Bregstein—"

"Okay, young ladies. Take my son. Take good care of my boy."

He bent and kissed Mervyn on the cheek. "You'll be okay, son. They'll get you to the beach."

The child nodded. Supported by the girls, Mervyn Bregstein plunged over the side.

Tears streaming down his face, Joe Bregstein reached a hand out over the rail, the impulse to be with his son overcoming all else. Then he climbed backward over the rail, hanging from deck level over the side.

He felt a sudden, insistent tugging at his ankles. Below, on D deck, a passenger was pulling him down. Bregstein let go. For one awful moment he thought he was falling into a void. Then strong hands grabbed him and swept him in onto D deck.

He rushed to the rail. This time a passenger restrained him. "The rescue boats are coming in. They'll get us off."

Dr. Bregstein looked across the water. Small boats were moving toward the *Morro Castle*.

"They're bound to pick up Mervyn and the girls," he shouted. "They're bound to . . ."

But the rescue flotilla missed the trio drifting toward the shore.

After some hours of swimming, the girls lapsed

into a stupor. They were unaware when the sea snatched Mervyn Bregstein away from them.

His body was never found.

For what seemed hours, Dr. Emilio Giro had been pounded by the sea. He stubbornly clung to the corpse, but he had given up urging other swimmers to seek similar means of support.

Once a lifeboat came close.

"It seemed to be manned by some of the ship's crew. There were people all around in the water, including some children. But the boat didn't stop to pick up anybody, and there seemed to be only a few people in the boat.

"Soon afterward another boat came by. That, too, seemed to be full of seamen and stewards. It was going quite fast toward the beach, and seemed to ignore anybody in the water . . ."

On the forepeak of the liner, Acting Captain Warms muttered: "They needn't have jumped. There's plenty of life gear for everybody . . ."

Theoretically, he was right. There was ample life-saving equipment on board: lifeboats capable of carrying 816 passengers; a dozen balsa-wood floats, able to support 204 people in the water; eighteen lifebuoys.

Panic and inefficiency had rendered much of the gear useless.

"We're getting close to the shore," said Clarence Hackney. "I can smell the land. We'll soon be off."

"I'm not leaving until the line orders me off," said Warms. "That's the rule, and I'm sticking to it."

The others looked at him curiously. Hackney wondered if Warms, in assuming command, had also donned the mantle of the perfect company man.

Seaman Leroy Kelsey peered intently over the prow of the lifeboat. Far ahead a light winked, then was lost, as the lifeboat slid down a trough of water.

"I see it! I see it," he bellowed. "Sea Girt! It's the light at Sea Girt! And look . . . !"

A red star shot up into the sky. Somebody on the shore was firing a rocket to guide them.

Kelsey looked around the boat. Rain was pouring down, and the sea was slopping over the side. He said, "Come on, let's break out the sail, we don't want to be out here forever." They rigged it, and squared away toward the shore. Then Kelsey started to sing.

"Roll, Jordan, roll."

Soon a handful of people picked up his chant:

> "Roll, Jordan, roll,
> I wanna go to heaven,
> When I die, to see ol' Jordan roll."

The night was endless. The *Morro Castle* was a faint glow far on the port side, and the light from Sea Girt blinked more clearly through the murk. Soon they were able to pick out individual lights on the shore.

Then they heard the dull roar of the surf, and there was a new surge. A dark mass of water piled up astern and the boat yawed widely. The sea roared and hissed and the boat pitched skyward and dropped sickeningly in a smother of foam.

"Everybody get ready to jump!" Kelsey ordered.

Into the surf came a man from the shore with a line in his hands. "Jump!" he yelled. "But watch the surf and the undertow."

The men tumbled waist deep into the sea, and then helped the three girl passengers over the side.

The lifeboat survivors were dragged ashore by their rescuers.

. Another man on the shore called out: "Who are you? Where you from?"

Kelsey replied, "Survivors—from hell."


The *Morro Castle*'s SOS came after confused reporting to Coast Guard stations along the New Jersey shore of a "glow in the sky" and "a blaze out there."

Between 3 A.M. and 3:25 A.M., fourteen separate Coast Guard stations received "positive calls" that a large ship was blazing a few miles out to sea. The call included fishermen, a hotel porter, and a group of people playing all-night bridge.

The Coast Guard lookouts scanned seaward. They saw nothing. They decided to wait.

Twenty-five minutes passed before the lookout at Shark River Coast Guard station made a "positive visual sighting of a steamer burning east of here."

Minutes later the radioed distress signal had been picked up by the Navy Radio Direction Finder Station at Manasquan, New Jersey, civilian stations at Rockland, Maine, and Sayville, Long Island, and the Radiomarine Corporation stations at Tuckerton, New Jersey, and in New York Harbor. From these stations a general alert went out along three hundred miles of coast.

By 3:40 A.M. Coast Guard Headquarters in Washington, D.C., was apprised of the disaster. There, the duty officer informed the White House. At 7 A.M., when he awoke, President Roosevelt knew there had been a disaster.

At 3:41 A.M., United Press, Associated Press, Universal Press, City News, the *World-Telegram,* and Fox Movietone News were informed of the SOS by Coast Guard Headquarters in New York—exactly four minutes before the news was relayed to the lookout stations on the New Jersey shore. The media dispatched every available reporter.

At 3:42 A.M., the Coast Guard Radio Station at Rockaway, New York, received a telephone call alerting it. The duty man said there was nothing he could do. Although the station was a vital part of Coast Guard rescue operations, it was being dismantled in preparation for converting it to a U.S. Navy post.

On paper, the Coast Guard commanded a small armada of ships in the disaster area.

Twenty-five miles away from the burning *Morro Castle* cruised the *Cahoone,* a large patrol boat.

The ship had put to sea earlier, short one radioman; the only two operators on board were just out of training school. Their inexperience proved costly. It was 4 A.M. before they picked up the repeated order for the *Cahoone* to speed to the rescue.

At Pier 18, Staten Island, New York Harbor, the cutter *Tampa* was berthed. Her radio team was required, even when in port, to listen out twenty-four hours a day, but the duty operator in the early hours of the morning was a trainee. He completely missed the original order to sail. It was 5:39 A.M. before the *Tampa* finally sailed.

Alongside lay the *Sebago,* her boilers stripped for a routine overhaul, her radio shack deserted. It was 5:22 A.M. before it was manned, and thirteen hours more passed before the *Sebago* sailed.

None of the dozen seventy-five-foot-long patrol boats within the area were equipped with radio to direct them; hours passed before some of them were any use.

Four larger Coast Guard patrol boats, each capable of sixteen and a half knots, had been detached from their regular New Jersey coastal watch to trail a rum smuggler five hundred miles north of New York.

Nobody had anticipated the need to replace them.

The two-thousand-ton cutter *Champlain,* capable of seventeen knots, had been sent off to Greenland to ferry Mrs. Ruth Bryan Owen, American minister to Denmark, back to New York.

The Coast Guard air station at Cape May, eighty-eight miles southwest of the *Morro Castle,* had seven aircraft. One was to be used "only in case of emergency, due to inherent design faults"; another was "in commission, but grounded as unsafe"; two more were out of service. One, the ACRUX twin-engined flying boat, "was the only plane suitable for rescue or observation work off shore." Finally, the station had two pilots. Hours passed before they became airborne.

Commercial ships at sea reacted rather more practically to the crisis when the SOS was picked up.

The freighter *Luckenbach* was the first big ship to the rescue; by 4 A.M. she was picking up survivors.

The liner *Monarch of Bermuda* turned around and raced twenty miles to the *Morro Castle.* The *City of Savannah* also changed course; from the south the *President Cleveland* sped to assist.

In the end, though, it was a Coast Guard boat—a surfboat from Sea Girt—that was first on the scene. Its captain had put to sea simply to investigate "the ball of flame" he had seen. Aboard was a crew of five, including helmsman Warren Moulton.

"We managed to get across the bar and for the next seven or eight miles we had an awful fight until we were

within half a mile of the burning ship," Moulton recalled.

"Then we ran into something I never want to see or
hear again.

"The ocean was fairly lit up by the light of the burning ship, and the water was alive with screaming men
and women.

"We stopped, and it was nearly the end of us and a
great many others, for so many grabbed the boat at
once that we were nearly capsized and sunk.

"I do not know how many times we stopped, but
certainly not more than five, and I heard the skipper
bellowing at me to go ahead on her.

"I got under way, and for the next half mile there
was a fight on that I will never forget.

"Every sea broke over us, washing us from stem to
stern. The crew did all they could to keep others off
and prevent our running over someone in the water.

"The water was so deep that my hands on the gas
throttle were covered. All around—ahead, on each
side, and astern—were men and women, all excited, a
few with their hands stretched out toward us, calling
for help, and we, already overloaded, unable to help at
all.

"As we reached the *Luckenbach* I looked at our cargo for the first time: women back in the stern piled three
deep, men and women over the engine box, cordwood
fashion, all alive. Just how many there were I didn't
know, but we had our hands full to get them aboard the
ship and keep our boat from being smashed alongside."

On the forepeak of the *Morro Castle,* George White

Rogers began flashing out a distress signal on the flashlamp.

Watching him, Clarence Hackney later recalled an expression of "cold amusement" on the chief radio officer's face.

# 15.
# JUMP!

At 4 A.M., radio stations on the east coast interrupted their programs with news of the disaster.

Minutes later, fishermen at Point Pleasant, New Jersey, a landfall about seven miles from where the *Morro Castle* now drifted, heard a local radio station announce that everybody on board had been rescued.

The fishermen decided to wait for daybreak before investigating the fire glowing out at sea.

At a dozen inlets nearby, a similar decision was taken by other fishermen who also heard the radio announcement.

The news flash puzzled James Bogen. At the age of twenty-six he was skipper of the thirty-ton *Paramount,* and one of the youngest sea captains on the coast. He had a reputation for boldness and flair which drew respect from older men.

From the wharf at Manasquan Inlet he watched the fireball on the horizon and wondered how anyone could know for certain that everybody had been rescued. At 4:30 A.M. Bogen telephoned the local Coast Guard station.

"Go on out there as fast as you can," urged the duty officer. Minutes before, the station had received a report of survivors coming toward shore.

Bogen spread the news through the dozen broad

beamed fishing boats moored around the *Paramount*. Swiftly he mustered a crew made up entirely of fishing boat captains. And at 4:40 A.M. the *Paramount* surged out to sea.

From Manasquan Inlet a fisherman alerted other boats. Soon a small armada of smacks, their engines chugging through the swell, followed the *Paramount*.

But the false local radio announcement had cost nearly forty valuable minutes. Time enough for the sea and the *Morro Castle* to claim further victims. Some of the fishermen believed nearly seventy could have been saved if they had put to sea earlier.


Steward Daniel Campbell jumped from B deck and found himself buffeted by flotsam. The water around the liner was strewn with broken chairs and tables; a film of hot ash coated the sea.

Campbell had plunged into a confusion where survival was literally a matter of the fittest. Swimmers clung to anything buoyant. There were sometimes brief and bitter struggles over a piece of wood; several passengers recalled seeing two men struggling for possession of a deck chair. The tussle ended with one of the men kicking himself free and vanishing into the night.

Radio operator Charles Maki was in the water an hour before he reached a lifeboat. The Finn was a powerful swimmer and seemed unaware of anything around him; he concentrated on nothing but reaching that lifeboat.

At its helm was seaman Joe Spilgins. Spilgins had behaved with remarkable coolness during the crisis on board. He marshaled passengers and crew into the boat.

One woman demanded, "Are you an officer, giving us orders like this?"

Spilgins had brushed aside her protest. To everybody he said, "You're under my command."

Spilgins resisted until the last moment demands to lower the boat. Then, with perhaps a dozen half-dressed passengers, helped by a couple of stewards and engine-room assistant Antonio Bujia, he maneuvered the life-boat down to the water level. It was the last lifeboat lowered from the *Morro Castle*.

As it drifted clear of the burning hull, it also attracted the stronger swimmers. In all, another dozen scrambled aboard. Among them were some members of the Con-cordia Singing Society, Rafael Mestre, Charles and Annie Menken, and three corpses, all passengers, hauled over the gunwales by Father Raymond Egan.

The arrival of radioman Maki encouraged those in the wallowing boat. He picked up an oar and urged the other men to do the same. In broken English he told them to help him row toward the shore. Soon the life-boat was slopping with some purpose through the dark-ness.

After a while Father Egan asked those who weren't rowing if they would like to sing to encourage the oars-men. Uneven voices blended into a chorus whose reper-toire ranged from the Episcopalian hymn "Autumn" to "Tea for Two."

They were still singing when the boat beached, hours later.

Dr. Emilio Giro had devised a simple experiment in concentration: estimating the time between swallowing a mouthful of salt water and its affecting his alimentary system. He guessed, after a number of mouthfuls, that only a couple of minutes elapsed between a swallow and the onset of diarrhea.

The doctor managed to keep his wits and stamina, believing it would not be long before rescue came. In the meantime "the issue was clinically simple: could I stay alive until then?"

He knew how easily the icy water broke a man's resistance. He had seen it happen several times in the past few hours.

Alone again on the dark swell, headwaiter Carl Wright experienced a strange tranquillity. The *Morro Castle,* the inferno, the bodies—all were forgotten for the moment. He was still in that state of euphoria when the *Paramount* fished him aboard.

"Long before we reached the *Morro Castle* we were picking up survivors. We didn't bother with the bodies. We only picked up the live ones," said *Paramount* skipper Jimmy Bogen. "They were all over. If they had on life preservers we got them with grappling hooks. Otherwise we had to jockey the boat alongside and grab them."

Nobody really knew what happened to many of the people on the *Morro Castle.* From the water, those still on the ship looked like puppets. The marionettes on the forepeak did not move; those on the stern jerked spasmodically, like figures in some old newsreel.

Even close in, it was impossible to say exactly in many instances what did happen.

Dr. Van Zile, the ship's surgeon, was the subject of a number of different legends concerning his death. All were heroic; none could be verified.

One account placed him in the ship's surgery waiting for casualties that never came. Another had him standing on the bridge, passing around a flask of rum before perishing in the flames. A third version took him over the side of the ship; in the water he took off his life jacket and strapped it on a child—an extraordinary feat of gymnastics even for the fittest man. One passenger said she saw the doctor raise his hand "in brave salute," and then roll over and drown.

Incredible stories were told of others as well.

A bedroom steward was credited in some reports as diving repeatedly from a lifeboat to rescue swimmers; the same man was also reported as being "the last person off the ship's stern."

The ship's manicurist, Ella Jacoby, died, witnesses swore, trying to rescue the liner's parrot in its cage on the verandah cafe; the story went that she freed the bird only to die in the flames herself.

A ship's musician would be immortalized for playing ragtime jazz through the corridor on B deck—long after the area was a solid mass of flame.

A cabin steward, a bellboy, and a deckhand were each separately credited with sacrificing their lives trying in vain to save the Saenz family from Havana. Mrs. Saenz and her three children died in the tragedy—but there is no shred of evidence to show that anybody else gave his life attempting to save them.

During the first streaks of daylight, there was no time for storytelling among the hundreds of people scattered over a couple of square miles of turbulent sea around the *Morro Castle*.

Aboard the Coast Guard surfboat, helmsman Warren Moulton received orders to head for land to refuel. On the way he came across another Coast Guard vessel, stranded in the swell with a broken engine.

"I got aboard her somehow and straightened up to

take a look around. I saw a dead woman lying across the stern, dead, lying on top of the cabin; the port side of the deck and cabin were red, dripping blood. In the after cabin were the most forlorn men and women I have ever seen, and all with hardly a rag on.

"Bilge matter was on the after cabin floor and in the engine room forward, and everywhere one of the worst smells I have ever smelled where they had vomited."

When the engine was fixed, the search and rescue operation continued as both boats made for the shore.

"We could find nothing but dead, with life preservers on. We picked up a few of them, but it was such a job to get them on board, and they would soon be on the beach anyway.

"The fellow in charge thought it best to get those down in the cabin to a doctor, and leave those already dead alone.

"How many we pulled out of the water, I don't know. I kept count up to fifty-six; the skipper said one hundred and sixteen in all."

At daybreak Mrs. Hiram Hulse, wife of the missionary bishop to Cuba, puzzled over a new sound. It was a deep rumbling that seemed to come from beneath the waves.

She struggled feebly in her life jacket. She and her husband had been separated when they jumped from the ship. The impact with the water had knocked Mrs. Hulse unconscious; when she awoke, there was no sign of her husband.

"He's drowned," she repeated. "He's drowned. It's the Lord's way . . ."

Nearby, cruise director Robert Smith, who had spent

several hours keeping a woman passenger afloat, also heard the sound—and identified it as the engines of a large ship. He shouted encouragement to Mrs. Hulse.

She mumbled: "Go away. My husband's dead. It's the Lord's way . . ."

A few hundred yards from her, the Right Reverend Hiram Hulse looked around him. He, too, mumbled a misquotation from the scriptures: "Plucked from the valley of death into the arms of safety."

The seaman looked at the old man kindly. In a broad Cockney accent he asked: "Like a cuppa, sir?"

Hiram Hulse was the first passenger to be picked up by the *Monarch of Bermuda.*

On the bridge, Captain Albert R. Francis gently nudged the Furness Line cruise ship until it was less than two hundred feet from the *Morro Castle.*

In the gray light of dawn the extent of the disaster silenced the passengers and crew lining the rails of the *Monarch of Bermuda.*

"The flames licked up into the sky from the *Morro Castle,*" Captain Francis recalled. "She was anchored, bow into the wind, keeping the flames from the forepeak where a small group of people stood. The rest of the ship was in flames. But you could still hear the screams and cries of the passengers. It was horrible . . ."

The sight also raised in his mind the question of whether even his ship could cope adequately with disaster on such a scale.

When the duty operator had awakened Captain Francis with the CQD message, he had bolted to the bridge in pajamas and dressing gown, ordered the ship around, and then, after issuing the order, worked out the fastest course to the *Morro Castle*.

While he plotted, he fired off a volley of orders: the engine room was to cram on every ounce of steam; the first officer was to prepare lifeboats for lowering.

Other deck officers were given specific tasks: to open all gangway doors; to rig chair slings for the injured, canvas slings for hauling up children, cargo nets for the more agile; to pile blankets up on deck; to fix pilot ladders and side ladders at all gangways; to man forward derricks in case there was time to pick up cargo, mail, and baggage.

The ship's doctor and nurse were ordered to set up a casualty clearing station in the first-class lounge; the purser and his stewards, to man all gangways and channel survivors to the lounge for medical checks; other stewards, to help the galleys prepare urns of coffee, tea, and soup; the chief steward, to break out the liquor store and have brandy and whiskey ready; all passengers, to provide spare clothes for the victims.

Captain Francis told the radio room to supply him with fullest details of other rescue ships in the area. When the *Monarch of Bermuda* was still some ten miles from the scene, the *Andrea S. Luckenbach* had arrived; still steaming northward was the *President Cleveland*.

The *Monarch of Bermuda*'s crew responded swiftly to their captain's instructions. The engine-room watch crammed on enough speed to send the liner slicing through the water at twenty knots.

Up on the bridge Captain Francis, now fully dressed, waited. "That was the hardest part," he remembered. "We all just stared and strained ahead for the first sight of the ship."

At 7 A.M. they saw the glow. Twenty minutes later

the Right Reverend Hiram Hulse was hauled aboard, wrapped in a blanket, and taken to the first-class lounge. There he received a medical check, was put to bed, and was given coffee laced with rum.

On the *Morro Castle,* Acting Captain Warms and the others grouped around him watched the five lifeboats bobbing toward them from the *Monarch of Bermuda,* just two hundred feet away.

Clarence Hackney and George Alagna both recalled the excellent seamanship of the lifeboat crews. "The seamen had a calmness and control you only get in a good British ship."

Warms looked at Dr. and Mrs. Vosseler, the only passengers to have reached the forepeak.

"Time for you to go," he said.

The couple nodded and shook the hands of those remaining on board. Then they made the difficult descent down a Jacob's ladder to a lifeboat.

"Anybody else?" called a voice from below.

"No. We are staying," said Warms steadily.

"We are all staying," echoed George White Rogers.

In the time the chief radio operator had been on the forepeak, he laid the foundation of a legend that would survive his lifetime.

A number of gestures established it. There had been two theatrical, and abortive, attempts to find a way through the wall of flame stretching back from the bridge to the stern. The heat had beaten Rogers back.

Next had come an attempt to rescue a woman passenger trapped in a porthole just forward of the bridge. This, too, he used to full dramatic effect. First he swung himself out over the side, supported by a couple of seamen; for a while he dangled there like a monstrous jellyfish. Then he was hauled back aboard.

Next he took off his shoes and prepared to swing on a rope, Tarzan fashion, down the side of the ship, to rescue the woman. When it came to the final leap, Rogers decided the rope was not strong enough to support his bulk.

While he thought out a new way to reach the screaming woman, she freed herself, fell into the sea, and drowned.

Unabashed, Rogers busied himself with the signal lamp.

"He was so cool," First Officer Ivan Freeman remembered. "He had a limitless supply of advice," Hackney recalled.

It seemed to night watchman Arthur Pender and storekeeper William O'Sullivan that the chief radio officer was "working at top speed and keeping up our spirits."

George Alagna watched Rogers with growing unease. He wondered why the chief radio officer seemed to be positively enjoying the tragedy all around him.


The lifeboats from the *Monarch of Bermuda* fanned out in a circle around the stern of the *Morro Castle*.

Through a megaphone an officer urged those remaining on board to jump. He added, "We'll get to you. Have no fear."

Dentist Joe Bregstein, standing on D deck, felt a "sudden reassurance" at the sound of that voice. "It was so English, so calm, so authoritative."

He didn't hesitate. Dropping over the side, he floundered in the water for moments until strong hands pulled him into a lifeboat.

Stewardess Lena Schwarz leaped over the side and

surfaced beside another lifeboat.

As soon as she was aboard, she began to concern herself with the rescued passengers. When the officer in charge gently suggested she should rest, Mrs. Schwarz replied, almost fiercely, "I still have a job to do."

# 16.
# SHE'S WORTH A FORTUNE
# TO THE TOWN

Chief Engineer Eban Abbott sat stiffly in the lifeboat which carried him to within sight of the shore.

He spoke to no one: he seemed oblivious to the cold, the rain, and the pounding of the seas.

Around him the other occupants of the lifeboat shivered and shook. There were now twenty-nine people in the lifeboat. Only three of them were passengers.

The crew, mostly stewards and seamen, found the lifeboat difficult to handle, and in the hours it took to approach shore, a considerable amount of water had been shipped.

Waiter Milton Stevenson recalled: "Some of us were pretty yellow around the gills. The nervous strain and excitement had gotten to us all."

Stevenson, like the others, eyed the chief engineer curiously. Abbott's only response was to look away.

Then suddenly the sound of the surf breaking a few hundred feet away awoke new fears in him. "Row away from here!" he cried. "It's too dark to go ashore! The shore's too rocky! Row away!"

Dr. Charles Cochrane, one of the three passengers in the lifeboat, himself deeply shocked at the loss of his invalid sister, felt sorry for the ship's officer. "In the darkness I had heard him mutter that he would be jailed for his behavior, and that if he came ashore with so few passengers he would be arrested."

Abbott was still urging the oarsmen to put out to sea when the lifeboat was caught by the crest of a wave and sent scooting onto the beach.

Waiting there was a group of fishermen, who pulled it farther up on the sand.

Eban Abbott, in full dress uniform, was the first man ashore. He ignored the fishermen. Turning to the lifeboat's complement he said, "Remember. None of you should talk to newspapermen. They would never understand."

Then he turned and walked up the beach, tears streaming down his face.

On the sundeck of the *Monarch of Bermuda* others wept that morning for different reasons. By 8 A.M., the liner's lifeboats had picked up over fifty passengers—the final count was seventy-one rescued by the *Monarch*.

As boatload after boatload came alongside, the survivors already on board peered down, seeking familiar faces. For some the agonizing wait was mercifully brief, the reunions little short of miraculous.

Mrs. Hiram Hulse was spotted by stewardess Lena Schwarz: "The old woman was on the point of death when they got her on board," said Mrs. Schwarz.

Mrs. Hulse recovered remarkably quickly when she found her husband; she and the reverend wept openly.

Cruise director Robert Smith and the woman passenger he had supported for hours in the water were picked up. They also burst into tears when they stepped on to the *Monarch of Bermuda*.

Otherwise there was virtual silence on board the rescue ship.

"The rescue operation performed by the Furness Line ship and its crew," a later commendation stated, "was in the highest traditions of the sea."

So, too, was the work of the crews of the *Andrea S. Luckenbach,* which had twenty-six survivors aboard, and the liner *City of Savannah,* whose lifeboats rescued sixty-five people from the water.

The same could not be said for the Dollar Line of San Francisco's *President Cleveland.*

The ship's captain, Robert F. Carey, had been on the bridge when the SOS came. An hour later, the ship was abeam of the *Morro Castle.* Forty more minutes passed before she lowered two lifeboats. Both made a brief circuit of the *Morro Castle;* the officers in charge concluded there was nobody on board, and they returned without a single survivor—or corpse.

Later, the ship's four senior officers announced they would refuse to sail with Captain Carey again.

By breakfast time part of the New Jersey shore took on a strange aspect as thousands of people moved along it, keeping pace with the pall of smoke. It was all that could be seen of the *Morro Castle,* drifting about five miles off the beach.

The throng moved up through Brielle, Manasquan, and Sea Girt, growing all the time. There was an almost carnival atmosphere among the onlookers. Vendors of hot dogs, soft drinks, and coffee did brisk business. Restaurants, cafes, and coffee shops had an end-of-season boom. Few of the watchers actually saw a survivor, or a victim. If they did, it was only a brief glimpse.

After a slow start, the land-controlled rescue operation had become a massive and coordinated effort between Coast Guard, civilian and military spotter planes, police, fishermen, National Guard, local hospitals, and mortuaries.

The Saturday editions of the newspapers were already printed when news of the disaster broke: radio had a clear lead—and was quick to seize it.

All three networks had mobile units in the area, broadcasting on-the-scene accounts across America. Edited versions were later beamed around the world.

It was the first major sea disaster the media had covered. It did so brilliantly.

An NBC reporter told his listeners:

A little shack on the New Jersey shore has been transformed in minutes into the humming headquarters of a great rescue station. At the post of command is a man who until now was an obscure Coast Guard officer. He is Commander S. S. Yeandle. Called from his bed early today, he went into action at once. Driving down the coast from his home near Sandy Hook, he stopped to organize rescue forces whenever boats and seamen were on hand.

Fishing boats, pleasure craft—anything that can be used to save the lives of those out there has been commandeered.

From his shack Yeandle has sent out orders by radio and telephone. But the one that is most often repeated is the call for manpower.

At Sea Girt, A CBS reporter described the scene:

Since daybreak, Coast Guard boats have pitched and tossed through the whitecaps, making tortuous progress toward that dreadful pall on the horizon.

Sometimes you can see the flames, but generally they are shut out altogether by the squalls of rain that must be making it hell for everybody out there.

The rescue fleet has come from such famous vacation spots as Shark River, Beach Haven, from Barnegat and Sandy Hook, from Monmouth Beach and Spring Lake and Deal and Long Branch.

We don't know how many boats have gone out. But one fact has just been confirmed by the Coast Guard: Their pullboats, dories manned by four oarsmen, are having trouble getting through the surf.

But the bigger boats are getting through those staggering walls of dirty green water.

WCAP, a local station at Asbury Park, told its listeners:

A call has gone out for all Coast Guard men to be rushed to the area by automobile and truck to man fishing and pleasure craft.

First reports are coming in of survivors coming ashore at various points—and we hope soon to bring you the first eyewitness accounts as to what happened.

While radio relayed a constant stream of instant information, scores of newspaper reporters were also piecing together a first impression of the calamity.

There were dozens of angles to follow up. A team from the *New York Times* began the job of assembling information that enabled the newspaper later to print:

At least five married couples, and probably more, jumped hand in hand from the decks of the burning *Morro Castle* and started to swim for shore.

Two couples, both young, were successful and reached the Jersey coast in safety. In another case both husband and wife were picked up by rescue craft, though for several hours each thought the other dead.

In the case of the other two couples, both middle-aged and both from Philadelphia, the wife was saved from seeing her husband drown.

The *New York Herald Tribune* reporter had driven straight to Spring Lake, New Jersey, and found an immediate angle:

Soon after dawn this morning the first boatloads of survivors from the flaming *Morro Castle* drew up on the sandy beach in front of the southern bathing pavilion of this seaside resort, and in that instant the village, usually deserted this late in the season, began to assume the aspect of a beleaguered community.

The gray breakers lashed the shore, driven by north-east winds. Through the surf, from time to time emerged exhausted swimmers, singly, in pairs and in groups, clinging to logs, rafts and life preservers.

Private homes all along the shore took in the sea-battered survivors, put them to bed, and furnished warming drinks until medical aid could arrive.

But it was radio's day. The airwaves were filled with reports:

CBS:

As the day wears on and the storm increases, the crowds grow thicker as families and friends of those on board come down from New York seeking news.

So dense has the crush become along the shore that the local American Legion has been called out to help police with traffic control.

New Jersey state troopers are also here escorting doctors and nurses and the injured.

Nobody knows yet how many have lived—and how many have died. It will be some hours, perhaps even days, before the final toll becomes known. Survivors and bodies are coming ashore along a wide stretch of coastline. . . .

NBC:

At nine o'clock this morning it was announced that a morgue will be established at Camp Moore, the New Jersey National Guard training quarters. Already the first bodies are being taken there. . . .

WEAF-NY:

The New York Chapter of the Red Cross has mobilized its Disaster Relief Service to care for survivors. . . .

CBS:

. . . a mongrel puppy, mascot of the crew, jumped to the beach as one of the first lifeboats made the sand today. . . .

NBC:

. . . the first bodies are arriving at the morgue in Camp Moore. Eighty cots have been set up in the building, and in adjoining buildings others have been prepared. Ambulances and undertakers' cars began to arrive soon after the preparation of the cots. . . .

WCAP, Asbury Park:

We have just heard that the National Guard have three planes over the sea spotting for survivors. In one of them is Governor Harry Moore. . . .

The open-cockpit military two-seater banked and skimmed over the sea. Bracing himself, the fifty-five-year-old governor of New Jersey stood up in the rear seat and waved a red flag to guide the scores of rescue ships toward people in the water.

It was a flight that Moore would never forget. "The waves were extremely high and the boats had difficulty in sighting those in the water. I could see many of them had life belts improperly adjusted. When I spotted a swimmer, the pilot would drop a smoke bomb nearby.

"I shall always recall one man. He was struggling feebly, partly submerged, when he heard our plane and looked up. I waved to him."

Dr. Emilio Giro did not return the wave. He knew he could not afford even such a simple gesture. His strength was going. He had spent many hours in the water, clinging to a corpse. But the will to stay alive had been steadily drained by the cold, the salt water, and his constant seasickness and vomiting.

227

He sensed rather than heard the aircraft; moments later a smoke bomb plopped into the sea.

Captain James Bogen of the *Paramount* had spent an hour chasing from one bomb burst to another; frequently the result was a corpse to be hooked and dragged aboard.

This time he was luckier. Dr. Giro was alive, though barely, when Bogen pulled him out of the water.

Ashore, the survivors found themselves surrounded by reporters eager to create heroes.

Seaman Leroy Kelsey thrilled the readers of the *New York Times* with his graphic portrait of "the crew and everyone else doing all they could to save the passengers."

Only later, at the official investigation, away from the guidance of the press, did Kelsey admit that his lifeboat contained only three passengers.

Another seaman, Joseph O'Connor, told a reporter: "I was the one who discovered the fire and turned in the alarm. I then joined the ship's fire brigade, and when all hope of putting out the fire was abandoned, I took a lifeboat.

"There is a heavy loss of life among passengers because at least a third of them had been seasick, and the fire spread quickly through the corridors cutting off escape from the cabins."

Steward Joseph Markov told of fighting the fire until he was "forced to take to the lifeboats."

"Showered with hot broken glass from the upper decks, we drifted in the surf. We saw nothing in the water but the red glare of the flames. The smoke was streaming from the port side of the boat.

"As we managed to row the lifeboat around the ship we could see that the decks were filled with passengers, screaming, crying and waving frantically. We rowed for an hour with what few oars were available. We had lost some overboard while we were trying to lower the lifeboat.

"We thought the *Morro Castle* would blow up any minute. It was a terrible sight and it was a terrible night. We did not see any other ship and we didn't know what had happened to those on board. I lost everything I had except a belt and that isn't mine."

The boat he was in brought two passengers—and eighteen members of the crew—ashore.

The *New York Herald Tribune* news team reported that "One member of the crew declared that for some peculiar reason a draft encircled the *Morro Castle,* driving outward in all directions—stopping lifeboats going back to rescue those passengers on board."

It made a good headline, in any case.

On the promenade at Asbury Park a handful of the resort's officials peered out to sea. Far down the coast the pall of smoke was slowly moving closer; keeping pace with it on the shore were an estimated fifty thousand people.

"Just supposing," one of the officials said, "they beached her here. She's worth a fortune to the town."

# 17.
# ABANDON SHIP

The *Morro Castle* drifted northward, dragging her anchor. With the rudder inoperative, the ship was at the whim of wind and waves. From time to time the sea canted the hulk to port or starboard with sickening force.

The men on the forepeak had divided into two groups. Acting Captain Warms and the deck officers drew to one side; the crew were gathered around storekeeper O'Sullivan. Between the groups stood George White Rogers and George Alagna.

With one exception they were silent, even morose, as the enormity of the catastrophe became clear.

The chief radio officer continued to act with some degree of forcefulness; later, some of those around him wondered at the pointlessness of much that he did.

At one point Rogers attempted to find a way down into the hull through the forward cargo hold; he told Warms that "maybe he could find a way to lead us all to safety." Because of the heat emanating from the bridge, it was clearly impossible for anyone to remain in the vicinity of the hold long enough to remove its cover. Even if the cover had been removed, nothing would have been gained, because the hold was filled with cargo that needed power winches to haul it clear. Only when it was removed could Rogers have possibly opened a bulkhead door at the foot of the hold and worked his way into the hull.

When O'Sullivan and night watchman Arthur Pender both pointed out the futility of his plan, Rogers ignored them and continued to make attempts to remove the hold cover.

In the end, complaining that the heat was almost choking him, he gave up and began flashing a series of SOS signals. Warms put a stop to that activity, pointing out that the area was filled with rescue craft, that undoubtedly more were on the way, and as the group on the forepeak intended to stay there, the signals would cause confusion.

Receiving the order to stop signaling, Rogers assumed another role—cheerleader. The rain, the cold, the wind, the threat from the fire raging just over a hundred feet away—all these things, he declared, were small discomforts. God had singled them out. They were "being tested"—they must not fail.

It was the first time George Alagna had heard the chief radio operator express his religious convictions; Alagna found the fervor and righteousness with which he did so disturbing.

Others would also remember Rogers' manner and speech. He displayed the domineering aggressiveness and inconsistency which make the maniac at best socially exhausting, and at worst—as in the case of Rogers—frightening. A number of the seamen muttered uneasily when he invoked God. Warms detected their fear and told Rogers to "take it easy." Whereupon the radio chief promptly found a new game: looking for survivors.

Clarence Hackney remembered that Rogers "just yammered on, beginning and not finishing an idea and getting edgy with any suggestion that didn't match him. I just thought he was trying to cover up his own fears."

It was Rogers who noticed the anchor dragging. The consternation over that had hardly abated when the chief radio operator asked aloud what a number of others were thinking at that moment.

Staring intently at the pall of smoke, Rogers asked: "How come it got a hold so quick?"

"It was set!"

Hackney's accusation got a chorus of agreement.

"I'm positive it was set! It spread too fast," repeated Hackney.

Arthur Pender thought it looked like a chemical fire. "The flames in the writing room were blue-white, just like you get with chemicals."

Rogers listened carefully to the conversation. When he was asked his opinion, he shrugged apologetically. "Guess I was too busy getting out the SOS to notice the color of the flames."

Acting Captain Warms killed further speculation: "If it was set, I guess I know why." He glanced at Alagna. Baffled and still unaware of Warms' suspicions about him, the junior operator looked uneasy.

Rogers interrupted the tension momentarily by asking Warms if there was any message to be sent to any of the rescue ships nearby.

Warms peered out across the port side. The *City of Savannah* was a few cable lengths away.

"Rogers," said the acting captain, "use your lamp to ask her to contact the line as to what I should do."

Rogers blinked out the message.

It was a strange request for Warms to have made.

The command he longed for—master of a luxury cruise ship—had been the shortest in maritime history. Barely seven hours elapsed between the death of Captain Wilmott and Warms' having to evacuate the bridge.

Any orders he could give now were virtually meaningless: the *Morro Castle* answered only to the elements.

Warms became increasingly morose. In his mind he reviewed every order, every course change, every step he had taken, "and I knew I had done everything correctly."

Probably he had. If anything, he had gone too much by the book. His seamanship had been technically excellent. His failure had been in not anticipating that the fire could spread so quickly. Such anticipation would have produced orders to close all the fire doors on board; if nothing else the flames would have been delayed. Anticipation would have meant asking for outside help sooner.

Exhausted and acutely depressed, Warms turned to the Ward Line for his next orders.

They never came. The officers and crew on the *City of Savannah* were far too busy settling survivors to pay attention to the flashlamp blinking from the forepeak of the *Morro Castle*.

Aboard a *City of Savannah* lifeboat, Thomas S. Torresson, Jr., third assistant purser on the *Morro Castle*, tried to organize his jumbled thoughts.

Torresson's father, the marine superintendent of the Ward Line, would be facing a major crisis ashore, trying to explain how the disaster could have happened to "the safest ship afloat."

The Torresson family history was closely associated with that of the Ward Line. Young Torresson's grandfather had been a line captain; two uncles served as chief engineers, and another as a master. The line was "a way of life," Torresson recalled. "To serve in it was almost a family tradition."

233

The disaster destroyed eighteen-year-old Thomas's image of the line "with the greatest record for safety in the business."

He recalled his own attempt to save the life of a young passenger. "I jumped from C deck, taking a young boy with me. He died in the water, after many hours, from shock, exposure, and the pain of the burns. When the lifeboat picked me up, they wouldn't take the boy's body; there was scarcely room for the living."

The media embraced the young hero eagerly.

Others, Torresson recalled, found themselves written up in newspapers not unduly concerned with accurate reporting. When the *City of Savannah* docked, two women were photographed with two children they were said to have "rescued from the fire." The children had never been on the *Morro Castle*.

By midmorning, September 8, further legends had obscured the picture even more.

From Havana, the Associated Press reported that Captain Oscar Hernandez, the Port of Havana chief of police, had "positive information" that the fire was the result of a Communist plot. The captain's allegation and his "revelation" that other American ships were scheduled for similar destruction caused weeks of panic along the east coast.

From Sea Girt a reporter from another wire service filed a story of a body washed ashore with a bullet hole in its forehead. There is no official record of that body, but even today the story persists that a sailor was shot on board for looting when the fire broke out.

No detail was too small to be reported or embellished. The order of the day was heroism: four survivors were credited with swimming ashore, running temperatures of

104°; a Cuban mess-boy was hailed for a nine-mile swim without a lifebelt.

Captain James Bogen of the *Paramount* was heading for the ship when the Coast Guard ship *Cahoone* raced past on his starboard side. Some of the fishing boat crew felt the *Cahoone*'s speed was dangerous under the circumstances. There were still people in the water; the patrol boat's wash could have swamped them.

The *Cahoone* disappeared into the mist and the *Paramount* resumed fishing for bodies and, occasionally, a living person.

When it came to collecting these survivors, Captain Bogen's foresight in picking the most experienced crew available paid off: "It was a ticklish business running the boat close enough to a man or a woman, or a group of three or four, in that rough water, without bumping one of them, and yet getting close enough for a crewman to throw a line with certainty, or even—in the case of the weaker swimmers—to reach out and seize them.

"We were so busy with the rescue work and managing the boat that we had little time to devote to those we hauled on board. Those who had the strength we directed below. The others, the exhausted, the unconscious, the dead, we laid out on deck."

With fifty-five on board, Captain Bogen gave the order to head for the beach.

A mile astern, the *Cahoone*—which had taken four and a half hours to reach the scene—reduced speed.

The Coast Guard patrol boat watched the *City of Savannah* steaming off toward New York. The *Cahoone*'s captain believed this, coupled with the general view of the situation, conveyed the impression that all passengers had been rescued.

It was an unhappy mistake. Another followed. The

*Cahoone* called up the *Monarch of Bermuda*. The *Cahoone*'s log recorded: "*Monarch of Bermuda* so busy handling press radio traffic that we cannot break in with a call." The *Monarch of Bermuda* later denied the charge; its radio operators insisted they were only transmitting names of survivors and dead.

Next the *Cahoone* approached the Morro Castle. The patrol boat's log documents another curious incident: "Held verbal conversation with the crew of the *Morro Castle*, grouped on forecastle deck. When asked if they wanted to be taken off, some member of the crew, apparently an officer, replied they were going to stand by for a tow to port."

The Official Coast Guard report on the *Cahoone*'s role makes equally strange reading: "Had the *Morro Castle* or the *Monarch of Bermuda* given the *Cahoone* any information that lifeboats had gone ashore or that passengers had jumped over the side, the *Cahoone* could have gone inshore to search, and *possibly some lives might have been saved by that vessel*." (Author's italics)

In all, the *Cahoone* spent ninety minutes floundering around the *Morro Castle* before going off to search for swimmers. In the end it recovered two bodies.

On the forepeak, the group watched yet another boat approach the *Morro Castle*. It was a New York Harbor tug that had buffeted down the New Jersey coast. It jockeyed alongside the hulk's bow, and a man leaned out of the pilothouse with a megaphone.

"My name's Swenson," he called up to the forepeak. "You wanna be taken off?"

"No!" Warms shouted down.

"Okay. You wanna tow?"

"A tow?"

"Sure. We'll tow you and it won't cost you a thing."

"Can *you* tow *us?*"

"Sure."

"What kind of line you got?"

"Eight-inch," said Swenson.

Warms looked around him. Hackney and Freeman shook their heads in disbelief. The idea that the tiny tug could tow the twelve-thousand-ton stricken liner into New York Harbor was sheer nonsense.

But the exhausted acting captain said: "You heard that, fellows. He said it won't cost us anything for a tow. You know, after they land us in harbor these fellows forget things like that."

Nobody answered him.

Before Warms could accept the tugboat captain's offer, the Coast Guard cutter *Tampa* swept past. The 1800-ton boat, with a crew of one hundred under the command of Lieutenant Commander Earl G. Rose, rounded in the wind and came up on the *Morro Castle's* port side.

"Do you want a tow?" The magnified voice boomed out from the *Tampa*.

"Yes," bellowed Warms.

"All right," replied the mechanical voice. "We will put a twelve-inch hawser on board you and tow you to New York. Understand?"

"Yes."

From somewhere behind the bridge came a crashing rattle of metal, and a huge tongue of flame forked up through the smoke.

Warms paid no attention to it.

The arrival of the *Tampa* galvanized George White Rogers. As he watched the *Tampa* lower a surfboat to bring the tow hawser over to the *Morro Castle,* he kept up an elated chant: "They're coming, they're coming, they're coming . . ."

The surfboat, crewed by eight Coast Guardsmen, was rowed across to the *Morro Castle*'s bow. A heaving line was thrown down to haul up the hawser. Then the handful of men on the forepeak began doing a job usually performed by powerful winches.

They went at it like a tug-of-war team, with Rogers as the anchor man. Warms urged the men to pull. Inch by inch, foot by foot, yard by yard, almost fifty fathoms of hawser was pulled up and made fast first around the bitts, and then the mast.

It took two hours.

By then the weather had worsened. The rescue flotilla withdrew toward the shore. Only the *Tampa* and the New York Harbor tug remained alongside the *Morro Castle.*

"Now slip the anchor chain." The metallic voice from the *Tampa* brought the men on the forepeak staggering to their feet.

The order was unintentionally ironic. The anchor was dragging along the sea bed, but the forepeak crew had no mechanical power either to raise it or to "slip" it into the sea. The only way was to cut it.

The *Tampa* was equipped with the latest steel-cutting equipment. In spite of the running sea, it would have been possible for the cutter to have sent over a team to do the job on the *Morro Castle.* Even if they could not have climbed up the numerous ropes dangling from the forepeak, the cutting gear could have been hauled up.

Commander Rose later maintained that since he received no request from the *Morro Castle* for such help, he did not think it was his place to volunteer it. In any case he had his hands full just keeping the *Tampa* alongside the hulk. The gale had freshened considerably during the morning, and forty-mile-an-hour winds drove squalls of rain at both ships.

Acting Captain Warms' reasons for not requesting help from the cutter are equally unsatisfactory. He had not anticipated that the *Tampa* would carry such gear. Even so, he declared later, it would not have been feasible to ferry it across in such weather.

It was Rogers who hurried to the carpenter shop beneath the forecastle and reappeared triumphantly, holding a hacksaw.

He insisted on taking the first turn at cutting through the forged steel link. Soon, he tired of the task and handed the saw to a seaman.

Then he wandered off, whistling to himself.

Psychiatrists who later examined Rogers or studied his own account of these events have been struck by the marked disturbance of his thinking. A disturbed or psychotic personality suffering from this "thought disorder" has tremendous difficulty separating the relevant from the irrelevant, recalls and remembers everything, describes events in almost incredible detail.

Rogers' description of what happened to him when he left the bridge clearly displays this condition: "There had been a canary down in the hold of the ship. It belonged to the boatswain. I had seen the canary there. I was looking for a pair of shoes. I had lost mine overboard.

"I got the canary and put a towel around the bird and came up. He was the only living thing down there. I got halfway up and the heat was terrific. I went all the way with the flashlight and I noticed there was a space of about four feet on the bulkhead that was beginning to glow, turning red."

Clutching the canary, he shuffled back to the deck

and delivered the "news that the place was glowing hot down there and it's a shame to use a five-and-ten-cent method to saw through the chain." Suddenly the steel link snapped. In all, five hours had passed since the *Tampa* first offered help.

"Everybody be ready to leave," came the magnified order from the *Tampa*'s loudspeaker.

Taking the strain on the hawser, the cutter moved ahead of the hulk; astern, the tugboat, hooked onto one of the ropes trailing over the side, acted as a jury rudder—keeping the rope taut and so providing some steerage.

Immediately alongside the bow of the *Morro Castle*, one of the *Tampa*'s lifeboats waited to lift off the last of the liner's crew.

One after the other, the seamen scrambled over the side.

Then it was Rogers' turn. 'The sea was quite choppy because the ladder was actually hanging over the forward overhang of the boat and was swaying back and forth. One minute the boat was down in a trough and then on the crest of a wave. It looked like she was bouncing up and down at least twelve or fifteen feet."

Suddenly he saw something that terrified him. On the trip across from the *Tampa,* the lifeboat had picked up three bodies. They lay, bloodied from being smashed against the side of the *Morro Castle,* in the bottom of the lifeboat.

"Jump! Goddamn you! Jump!" The command from the lifeboat's officer broke Rogers' hold on the Jacob's ladder.

He fell into the boat, sprawling across the bodies. He shrieked and fainted.

Warms was the last man into the lifeboat.

# 18.
# BEACHED

At 11:55 A.M., Commander Rose of the *Tampa* was satisfied. The *Morro Castle*'s captain and crew were safely below, wrapped in blankets, sipping coffee. The ship's pharamacist, who examined Rogers, discovered that he was suffering from acute nervous exhaustion and over-inhalation of smoke, and had the chief radio officer put to bed.

Commander Rose ordered "full speed" and the Coast Guard cutter headed for New York.

In Manhattan, thousands of people had already lined the waterfront, looking expectantly to the mouth of the harbor.

Ward Line offices on Wall Street were besieged by newsmen, relatives, and friends.

At midday came the first public confirmation that the tragedy was vast. The first list of known dead was posted by the line—eight men and five women. The body count came from the *Monarch of Bermuda*. Thirty minutes later the number of dead rose to forty as reports came in from the New Jersey shore. By nightfall, the list would grow to one hundred—thirty-four short of the final toll. In proportion to their numbers, twice as many passengers as crew died.

Reporters badgered Ward Line officials for some reaction to the disaster. Reports about the timing of the SOS, the officials conceded, were "confusing"; the death of Captain Wilmott was "baffling"; the news from Cuba of possible Communist sabotage was "disturbing."

The New York press used the words to full effect.

At 3 P.M., the *City of Savannah* steamed past Staten Island and a huge mass of watchers on the Battery.

As she edged toward Pier 46, at West Tenth Street, a crowd of several thousand jammed the area for blocks back from the waterfront.

A reporter from the *Herald Tribune* stood in the crowd in the pouring rain as the gangplank was raised and Customs men and doctors began to swarm around. He described the scene:

> Several of the *Morro Castle* survivors were standing in the shelter of an overhanging deck—girls with water-soaked hair straggling over sweaters and sweat shirts loaned them by members of the crew, their numb-looking bare feet protruding from beneath rolled-up khaki pants or borrowed dungarees.
>
> The press and impetus of the boarding party was so great that it pushed the forlorn line of survivors —eager to get ashore at the earliest opportunity to reassure relatives who were trying frantically to learn whether they were alive or dead—out into a torrent of water descending from the deck above.
>
> Yet so abject was their state from shock and fatigue that they seemed scarcely to notice the added hardship unintentionally forced on them.

Passenger Nathan Feinberg stormed that "a majority of passengers felt that the crew had been negligent in not giving the alarm." It was a cry other passengers took up.

First-class passenger John Kempf, a New York fireman for fourteen years, told reporters that the crew "didn't understand the first and simplest principles of fighting a fire."

Late-afternoon headlines passed on to the public the accusations against crew members:

FIRE ÁLARM LATE SURVIVOR ASSERTS
FIREMAN HOLDS CREW IGNORANT OF FIREFIGHTING

GIRL DECLARES OFFICER FIGHTING FLAMES
ASKED HER NOT TO AROUSE PASSENGERS

There was no limit to speculation.
The *Herald Tribune* wrote:

> Captain John Diehl of the *City of Savannah,* asked if there had been any electrical display in the storm during which the *Morro Castle* was overtaken by disaster, replied "plenty" with an intonation and emphasis that spoke volumes.

The *Morro Castle* had clearly not been struck by lightning. But it was a novel twist. Within hours it was republished in a dozen capitals around the world.

Late in the afternoon there was another development to report.

NBC broke the story in an early-evening radio news bulletin:

> Martin Conboy, United States Attorney for the District of New York, has announced that he is to be-

gin urgent investigations to discover, and we quote, whether there is any criminal angle in the disaster, unquote. Already several members of the *Morro Castle* crew are being questioned.

The investigation followed reports from Havana early that afternoon that Captain Oscar Hernandez and his agents were about to unmask the Communist plotters who had not only sabotaged the *Morro Castle,* but were about to strike against Pan American Airways services from Cuba to the United States.

Captain Hernandez was quoted as saying that the FBI was sending agents from Washington to the island —a move the FBI swiftly denied.

Captain Hernandez never caught his plotters. After a week of headlines around the world he faded back into obscurity.

But by then the damage was done. The investigators in New York were convinced that all they had to do was prove a member of the crew was a Communist and the case would be solved.

The *Monarch of Bermuda* docked at West Fifty-fifth Street in Manhattan.

Dentist Joe Bregstein, dodging newsmen, was met by his fiancée Muriel Rubine with the news that there was no word of young Mervyn.

Cruise director Robert Smith and stewardess Lena Schwarz managed to slip ashore before newsmen caught them. While others sought out reporters, Smith and Mrs. Schwarz maintained a dignified silence.

With the news columns filled, the feature writers took over. The time had come to begin apportioning blame for the calamity.

At Point Pleasant, on the New Jersey shore, Lionel Hauser of the *New York World-Telegram* wrote a story beginning:

> Where the tall wild rice and green rushes feather the mirrors of the marshes, forty fishermen dried their heavy nets and spoke with angry head shakes of the failure of the United States Coast Guard. . . .

In New York, a *Sun* writer expressed widely held sentiments:

> The policy of governmental economy has struck the Coast Guard a hard blow. The slash in wages paid men leaves little inducement to enlist in a service steeped in traditions of bravery. Traditions are all very well, but without the hope of earning sufficient money to marry and lead the life of an average, normal male, it is small wonder that the grumblers are calling the Coast Guard "school boys."

The Associated Press reported a "mounting storm" over the delay in getting Coast Guard spotter planes into the air to aid the disaster-stricken ship.

It was also the time for official pronouncements.

In Washington, the Secretary of Commerce drafted a statement saying he believed that in the future it should be mandatory for all large liners to carry experienced firefighters to train and direct the crew in emergencies.

From his summer home at Hyde Park, New York, President Roosevelt announced he advocated the construction of foolproof passenger vessels which would make impossible a repetition of the *Morro Castle* disaster.

During the afternoon William Warms, dressed in borrowed oilskins, spent most of the time alone at the *Tampa*'s stern, watching the burning *Morro Castle* being towed a few cable lengths behind.

George White Rogers slept the whole afternoon. The other survivors sat silently, shrugging off questions from the curious Coast Guard men.

At 6 P.M., the *Tampa* towed the *Morro Castle* abeam of Asbury Park. A few hundred yards away on the port side lay the resort's brightly lit Convention Hall and the group of hotels clustered around it. Car lights winked along Sunset Avenue.

At that moment the tugboat's hold on the liner's stern was severed suddenly, leaving the *Morro Castle* without a jury rudder. The hulk dragged around to come broadside to the gale, increasing the tension on the towing rope.

At 6:01 Commander Rose radioed Coast Guard Headquarters in New York: "Derelict unmanageable in increasing gale."

The barometer had dropped to 29.85 and was still falling rapidly.

At 6:02 P.M. the *Tampa*'s helmsman reported that the *Morro Castle* was holding the wind increasingly on her starboard side.

At 6:03 Rose ordered an increase of the *Tampa*'s engine speed at 100 rpm.

A minute later soundings showed the depth of water under the *Tampa* had decreased to ten fathoms.

At 6:05 Commander Rose radioed Coast Guard Headquarters: *"Morro Castle* in danger of grounding." At the same time he ordered an increase of engine speed to 110 rpm, sending a shudder through the length of the cutter.

For seven minutes the *Tampa* struggled to turn the *Morro Castle* seaward. Suddenly there was a loud crack —and the *Tampa's* engines died.

The hawser had snapped and coiled around the cutter's propeller shaft. Commander Rose ordered anchor to be dropped and summoned urgent tow by radio.

In the cutter's stern, Acting Captain Warms watched the *Morro Castle* shudder at its new-found freedom. Then, trailing smoke and flame, it seemed to gather speed and head directly for the Convention Hall at Asbury Park.

It was 6:23 P.M.

Radio Station WCAP, the voice of Asbury Park, broadcast from the Convention Hall. Station staff had an excellent view of the sea.

At 7:30 P.M. duty announcer Tom Burley was about to give a station identification when he glanced out into the night.

"She's here!" he shouted. "The *Morro Castle's* coming right toward the studio!"

When the survivors aboard the *Tampa* finally reached New York, they were met by a battery of reporters and photographers.

Warms refused to talk to them. The others gave only perfunctory answers.

George White Rogers, the last to leave, was carried off the cutter on a stretcher to a waiting ambulance.

Newsmen demanded of Hackney: "Who's he?"

"That's the hero of the day," replied Hackney.

In a convoy of cars the reporters chased after the ambulance. At the Marine Hospital they were temporarily held at bay. Rogers was installed in a private room. Then, with a nurse at his side, he posed in bed for photographers, and made a brief statement that he only "did what anyone else would have done."

George Alagna refused to accompany other survivors to the meeting with Ward Line lawyers.

Instead he went in a car with journalist Damon Runyon. Later Runyon startled readers of the New York *American* with his exclusive story: Alagna believed "there might have been a chronic pyromaniac on the ship."

Alagna's statement required the most urgent investigation. District Attorney Martin Conboy and his aides chose to ignore it. They were preoccupied with hunting Communists.

The *Morro Castle* ran aground less than three hundred feet from where radio announcer Tom Burley sat.

By then he had recovered enough to give listeners a graphic description of the burning ship and the throng watching it on the seafront at Asbury Park.

Mayor Carl Bischoff and the resort's civic leaders, like everyone else, stared in amazement.

"Carl," someone said to the mayor, "she's in our front yard. This is the biggest thing's ever happened to us. They're going to come from all over to see it. Raise a city flag on her to stake our claim!"

# On the Beach

# 19.
# INDICTMENTS

By midday, Sunday, September 9, 1934, Asbury Park was experiencing an unprecedented boom. The weather —it was a mild, sunny day—helped to draw an estimated twenty-five thousand people to the resort.

The main attraction was the *Morro Castle*.

Roads leading into the town were posted with signs reading "Two Miles to the *Morro Castle* Wreck," "Come and See the *Morro Castle,*" and "Asbury Park —the Home of the *Morro Castle.*"

Concessionaires lined all approaches to Convention Hall with frozen-custard and hot-dog stands, bingo stalls soft-drink booths, children's rides, and shooting galleries.

The town's restaurants and cafes opened early, as did cocktail lounges in the Berkeley-Carteret, Monterey, and other hotels.

Inside Convention Hall, boxer Primo Carnera, training for a tour of South America, put on extra sparring sessions. "Everybody's getting in the act—why not us?" his manager explained.

Over Convention Hall a hurriedly painted banner flapped in the breeze:

22 CENTS TO SEE THE S.S. MORRO CASTLE
BENEFIT OF THE FAMILIES OF THE DEAD

The signwriter's English may have been faulty, but his business acumen was sound. By lunchtime, ten thousand people had paid for a closer view of the liner.

There was little to see besides the blackened hull and the burned-out superstructure. The fire was out.

Reporter David Garmey, one of over a hundred newsmen waiting to go on board, described the hulk as "a huge mass of twisted steel, a useless reminder of the dreadful disaster. There were buckled steel plates, gaunt black funnels, and a maze of charred, rusted framework."

Each newsman paid five dollars to use the breeches buoy rigged between the ship's stern and the ground floor of Convention Hall. A gas mask cost another five dollars; a flashlight, one dollar. The money went into a fund to buy liquor for the firemen on duty.

Garmey found no firemen when he went aboard. Although newsmen were supposed to remain in the stern area of B deck, Garmey and a few others were able to slip past the Ward Line officials and local policemen to go below.

We found ourselves in a long dark passageway, clogged with ashes, broken bits of steel, the walls bent and the floor, ripples of warped steel.

Thousands of rivets protruded from the distorted decks, forced out by the incomprehensible heat which waved the metal like sheets of paper. Girders supporting the superstructure and the floor below sagged terribly.

He descended a metal stairway—"all of the wooden ones have disappeared completely"—and arrived on C deck. "Once there were staterooms here. Piles of black ashes are all there is left; even the iron walls have melted."

Finally, he reached the boat deck.

Five lifeboats still hang from their davits, un-used, unwanted now. One of them hangs from one of its supports. Evidently someone tried vainly to lower it. Another is doubled into a V, prob-ably from the intense heat of the fire. Still another is lying on its side.

Sickened, the reporter left the ship.

Forward, a handful of men continued their search for the body of Robert Wilmott. Two days passed before a handful of bones were sifted from the ashes and de-clared to be those of the dead captain.

Ashore, the ghoulish exploitation continued. House-holders rented their rooms, their lawns, their garages. When Asbury Park's mayor was pressured to do what he could to ensure that the hulk would become a perma-nent exhibit, he rejected the scheme as macabre.

William Warms and the other officers of the *Morro Castle* spent Sunday closeted with lawyers of the Ward Line.

Company attorneys also visited Rogers in the hospital and called on Chief Engineer Eban Abbott at his home.

What happened at those meetings is not known. Ab-bott's widow, Ada, reported that the company's lawyer ordered her husband to "button up"; similar instruc-tions were given to William Warms and the other deck officers.

By early Sunday afternoon, the lawyers had put to-gether a series of statements to show that the fire had not been caused by any inefficiency on the part of the line or the crew, and that once the fire had been discovered, every officer and crew member behaved in an exemplary manner.

Warms' statement contained the remarkable information that he "ordered" his chief engineer into a lifeboat when Abbott "collapsed from the effects of the smoke." There was no mention of their feuding.

In the affidavits, Rogers emerged as the hero, lauded by his colleagues as a perfect example of how the liner's officers and crew behaved.

Ward Line officials visited the Seamen's Institute in downtown New York, where most of the crew was recuperating. There they offered free clothing and money to all crew members who signed statements confirming their good impression of the officers.

The one flaw was George Alagna's interview in the *American*.

SHIP'S CHIEFS IRRESOLUTE, CREW IDLE, AIDE CHARGES
Wireless Operator Declares Captain Failed to Command
While Panic Ruled Liner
Hints Firebug on Vessel

The story under the headlines ran counter to almost everything in the sworn affidavits.

Understandably, the story produced consternation.

It began in the offices of Burlingham, Veeder, Clark & Hupper, attorneys for the Ward Line. The lawyers saw that, at the very least, Alagna's allegations were a serious nuisance. Apart from the damage they could do to the Ward Line's image, the accusations would be seized upon by attorneys representing claimants; they could invite countless suits for punitive damages.

Burlingham and partners asked for an urgent meeting with their client. Chauncey Clark was chosen to explain to the line the financially crippling situation it might face. Clark, an experienced trial lawyer, was a man with a deserved reputation for no nonsense.

In midafternoon on Sunday, Clark arrived at the line's office on Wall Street. He detailed the serious situation to vice-president H. E. Cabaud. Cabaud contacted Franklin D. Mooney, president of AGWI, the line's parent company.

One course of action emerged clearly from the flurry of discussion and argument that followed: the line would maintain that Alagna's allegations were totally untrue and they would be contested at any hearing.

Given this tack, it was necessary to answer another question: Why had he made them?

Clark discounted financial gain. His inquiries showed the *American* made only a token payment for the interview.

Somebody mentioned the reports of a Communist plot. Mooney and Cabaud seized upon the idea of a plot, especially a Communist one. If the fire had been set, as Alagna hinted, then it was a Communist, or a sympathizer, who had set it, the men decided.

That afternoon the Ward Line lawyers interviewed Warms, Rogers, and Hackney again. By early evening Chauncey Clark had a new—and more complete—picture of Alagna's behavior since he had joined the *Morro Castle.*

Rogers filled in the finer details: "Ever since he tried to call that strike, Alagna was looked upon as an agitator and a vengeful person." The words "radical," "troublemaker," and "difficult" appeared repeatedly in the chief radio officer's statement.

Clark advised Rogers that it was his duty to repeat the allegations to District Attorney Martin Conboy. It was a shrewd move. Conboy had rumbled all day that the Ward Line attorneys were keeping material witnesses away from the official investigators.

On Sunday evening, Rogers made a statement to the district attorney. So did Warms.

The move to discredit George Alagna had begun.

In Washington, the Secretary of Commerce announced that an official investigation into the disaster would open in New York. Dickerson N. Hoover, assistant director of the Bureau of Navigation and Steamship Inspection, headed a board that promised "a thorough and full inquiry."

The hearings began in room 135-B in the Customs House, New York, on Monday, September 10, 1934.

Acting Captain William Warms was the first witness. He told the board he believed "some unidentified person willfully started the fire that destroyed the ship and cost so many lives."

Supporting evidence for the theory was provided by Clarence Hackney and Ivan Freeman.

Then George White Rogers took the stand. His testimony presented a picture of George Alagna as a dangerous agitator.

Alagna was arrested next day as a material witness and lodged in the House of Detention in New York. His bail was fixed at three thousand dollars.

The hearings dragged on for weeks. Warms and Abbott, barred from going to sea until the investigations were concluded, received full salary from the Ward Line. The other deck officers received half salaries. Some members of the crew whose testimony the Ward Line regarded as crucial also received payments.

By the end of September, the *New York Herald Tribune* told its readers:

"A clearer picture of what happened aboard the *Morro Castle* is beginning to emerge. Officers of the Ward Line felt for the first time the sting of official criticism and were subjected to a biting cross-examination."

The questioning was uneven. Several times the board of inquiry pressed for answers and then suddenly switched its tack—particularly on the question of whether the fire was set. Early on, the board seemed to discount the possibility. Dickerson Hoover made the curious statement that "we, of this organization, are more interested in the failure of matters pertaining to our responsibilities. Especially is this so in connection with the prevention, detection, and extinction of the fires."

Apparently, arson did not fall within any of those categories.

But a great deal did come to light: the cargoes of arms; the lack of boat and fire drills; Warms' previous suspension; Abbott's removing his insignia.

In one session sensational evidence was given that inflammable polish was unlawfully carried on the ship by stewards. They found it easier for cleaning brass and woodwork. The stewards' department was then subjected to rigorous questioning about how a ship should be kept clean. The board strained to show that the polish had caused the fire—a conclusion that would have neatly tied up loose ends. But the theory could not be substantiated.

Other avenues were explored. Passengers were suspected of starting the fire. There was talk of "wild parties" and "sex orgies." Titillating though it was, it was soon clear that passengers had not started the fire, either.

Balked there, the board turned to another possible

explanation—that the fire was accidental, caused by electrical short-circuiting. Volumes of evidence were presented outlining the nature of the ship's wiring. Then abruptly—within one session—the board switched tack yet again.

This time it was to pursue the matter of an "explosion in the engine room." Seaman Charles Angelo mentioned it as a casual afterthought near the end of his examination. The board snapped it up, and for hours Angelo was grilled. He failed to come up with anything new to support the story. Others were called; only after several days of ponderous questioning was the "explosion" forgotten.

When Joseph Spilgins mentioned the unseaworthiness of the lifeboats, he was subjected to a barrage of technical questions. Doggedly, Spilgins stuck to his story that the lifeboat tanks—designed to keep the boats upright and afloat when loaded—were almost rusted through, and there would have been holes in them if the rust had been scraped off before a coat of paint was applied.

Again, the board did not pursue this to its logical conclusion: detailed questioning of Acting Captain Warms and his fellow deck officers. By the time they gave evidence, Spilgins' testimony seemed to have been forgotten.

Not a day passed without a passenger attacking the crew for panicking or a seaman counterattacking that passengers had often been too drunk to comprehend orders.

George White Rogers caused a sensation when he was reexamined and testified that the SOS "should have been ordered forty-five minutes earlier than it was."

What prompted Rogers to make this statement is not

clear. There are two possibilities. First, the Ward Line refused to treat him the way he felt a public hero should be treated (the line had refused his request for a new wardrobe of clothes and a bonus for his heroism). Second, and more likely, his statement about the SOS was a perfect opportunity to attack Warms who, Rogers believed, had been part of the "plot" to remove him from the ship.

Rogers' testimony had one good effect: the release of George Alagna from custody. The chief radio officer now testified that his assistant had repeatedly gone to the bridge.

Calmly Rogers told the hearing: "I want it to be known that the earlier testimony at this hearing was given with great reluctance on my part and had no bearing whatsoever upon George Alagna's conduct or his responsibility to me who was his direct superior on board. I can remember no instance where he was ever insubordinate. He was a man I was proud to have as my first assistant. I realized that [my earlier] testimony would be misconstrued, which in every newspaper report I read has apparently happened. At times Mr. Alagna may not have been tactful in dealing with members and officers of the ship's crew. But I would say from my association with him that he was a perfect gentleman, and his character, to my knowledge, was irreproachable."

A reporter wrote: "It is good to know that America can still produce heroes like George White Rogers."

A whole new life had opened up for the chief radio officer during the month following the disaster. The Radiomarine Corporation of America withdrew his dismissal notice, and a dozen shipping lines let it be known that Rogers was welcome to sail with them. He politely declined the offers. He told the Veteran Wireless Operators Association, which gave him a medal for heroism, that his wife preferred to have him at home.

Yet he spent little time in September with her in Bayonne, New Jersey. Most of his time was occupied with making public appearances. At a lavish official reception given by the mayor of Bayonne, Rogers found himself surrounded by dignitaries from all walks of life.

Among them was Bayonne Police Officer Vincent Doyle. Doyle, usually modest and soft-spoken, had a reputation for blunt speaking when aroused. He had been invited because he was a former ship's operator. On land, Doyle established something of an international reputation among policemen by designing and installing the first two-way radio system in the world in the Bayonne Police Department.

Instinctively, he felt suspicious of Rogers—and he made it known.

Doyle recalled, "I turned to face Rogers. 'Rogers,' I said, 'you were quoted in the newspapers as saying that you were dragged out of the radio room aboard the *Morro Castle* when it was so hot in there that the solder melted out of the terminals of the panel of your transmitter. Was that statement of yours true?'

"He did not answer me, but just glared at me. I waited for an answer about fifteen seconds. The answer did not come.

" 'Since you have not answered my question,' I went on, 'and since I have never seen or heard of a demand by you that the statement be retracted, I must assume that your answer should be that it was a true statement. I am sure that, in your position as a radio operator, you have used a soldering iron many times. I am also sure that you had to wait many times for your iron to get hot enough to melt the solder that was to do the job. Do you know or have you any idea how hot your iron must be before solder will be melted by heat? Have you ever tried to hold an iron that hot in your bare hand?'

"Still no answer.

" 'I was invited here tonight to meet you and to welcome you home as the hero of the *Morro Castle*. I met you and I welcome you home. You have had a trying experience. My conscience, however, will not allow me to call you a hero. A hero, in my humble opinion, should be modest and truthful. You are neither and I feel sorry for you. Good night.'

"I apologized if I had made any of the guests uneasy and left."

The next day, Rogers left Bayonne for New York to meet a theatrical agent. A few days later, wearing a spanking-new white officer's uniform, Rogers made his stage debut at the Radio Theatre. He split his thousand-dollar-a-week salary with the agent.

Outside the Rialto, posters announced:

IN PERSON!
RADIO HERO ROGERS
TELLS INSIDE STORY
OF MORRO CASTLE
DISASTER

Standing in the footlights, Rogers told his audiences: "You people have made a hero of me . . ."

After a week, interest waned. Plans for Rogers to tour America were abandoned.

By October 1934, an estimated one hundred thousand people had paid to view the *Morro Castle* from the vantage point at Convention Hall.

The Women's Club of Asbury Park issued a statement that the display was outrageous: "This thing is too much of a tragedy to think of making an entertainment of it."

Two young men were arrested aboard the hulk and charged with looting the abandoned staterooms. They pleaded that they had gone on board as a "dare." As they appeared to have stolen nothing they were released with a reprimand.

In New York, the federal grand jury investigating the tragedy spent months listening to testimony similar to that given before the Dickerson Hoover panel.

On December 3, 1934, the grand jury handed out indictments. Accused of willful negligence were Acting Captain William Warms, Chief Engineer Eban Abbott, and Ward Line vice-president Henry E. Cabaud.

In the preamble to the charges against Warms, the indictment declared: "Members of the crew were without discipline and did not know what to do, and the passengers were left to help themselves; the passengers in large numbers were pushed into the water or jumped in the water or perished in the fire."

Warms was accused specifically of failing to observe the law in ten matters:

1. To divide the sailors in equal watches.
2. To keep himself advised of the extent of the fire.
3. To maneuver, slow down, or stop the vessel.
4. To have the passengers aroused.
5. To provide the passengers with life preservers.
6. To take steps for the protection of lives.

7. To organize the crew to fight the fire properly.
8. To send distress signals promptly.
9. To see that the passengers were put in lifeboats and that the lifeboats were lowered.
10. To control and direct the crew in the lifeboats after the lifeboats had been lowered.

Chief Engineer Abbott was accused of:

1. Failure to assign members of his department to proper posts during the fire.
2. Failure to report to his own station in the engine room and consequently giving no instructions to his men.
3. Failure to hold proper fire drills.

"Abbott had charge of the water pressure, and knew it to be inadequate," the indictment asserted, "but did nothing to increase it. He also was responsible for the ship's lighting and generators, and did nothing when they failed."

The chief engineer's decision to abandon ship was also attacked: "He did not report at his lifeboat station; he failed to direct passengers to the boats; as a matter of fact he left the vessel in lifeboat one, and when he got in the lifeboat made no effort to rescue anyone else."

Cabaud was charged with "willfully and knowingly causing and allowing the violations of the law" that Warms and Abbott were charged with.

In New York, at 4:30 in the afternoon of December 4, 1934, Warms and Abbott were arrested by a deputy United States marshal at a prearranged meeting. Abbott said nothing. Warms repeatedly asked the marshal: "What's it all about?"

After being fingerprinted, the two men were arraigned before Commissioner Garret Cotter. By then both had learned they could face prison sentences of up to ten years and fines totaling ten thousand dollars.

Prosecuting Attorney Francis W. H. Adams told the court that both men "are accused of a crime of the most serious nature—conduct which caused the loss of life of upward of fifty persons."

It was a curious figure to have arrived at in view of the final death toll of 134 persons.

Adams then asked Warms: "You were captain of the *Morro Castle,* weren't you?"

"No," mumbled Warms. "I wouldn't say that."

Abbott was not questioned. Ward Line lawyers posted bail bonds of $2500 for each man.

Onlookers might have wondered at the coldness between the two men—or the way the line's lawyers were always on hand to keep a distance between them.

The rift between Warms and Abbott had grown to active hatred. All that bound them was the continued pressure from the Ward Line to maintain a united front and the knowledge that any division would be exploited by the prosecution.

In Washington, the Hoover Board of Inquiry found that negligence on the part of the two officers had caused the ship's destruction.

In its summary, the board dismissed the possibility of arson: "Considerable testimony to the effect that explosions disconnected gas lines, infers this to be the cause. But in running down possibilities of malicious acts, nothing definite was revealed."

At their home in New Rochelle, New York, Mrs. Ada Abbott tried to brace her husband for the future.

"It was a cruel thing they did to him," she recalled. "He wasn't the sort of man who deserved it. Christmas was coming, and we took our small boy to see Santa Claus, and my husband said to the boy, 'Don't tell him your name, son.' You see, Eban had named the boy after him—and my husband had become ashamed of his own name."

# 20.
# THE VERDICT

By Christmas 1934, over three hundred claims totaling $1,250,000 had been filed against the Ward Line by survivors and relatives of the dead.

The Ward Line asked the federal court to limit the total of any single claim to $20,000 and offered $250,000 as a full and final settlement. Lawyers for the line based their case on the "limited liability" law that had been on the statute books since 1851. The 1851 law was clear that in the event of disaster, "only by proving the owners to have possessed knowledge of the unseaworthiness of the vessel or the inadequacy of the crew before sailing," could passengers collect.

A game of legal bluff began. Lawyers for the survivors created—by judicious hints, feints, and countermoves—the impression that they could positively prove unseaworthiness and inadequacy. The Ward Line flinched at the prospect of another public hearing—one that promised to reveal still more unfortunate aspects of the company's methods. It made an offer of $500,000.

The survivors' lawyers rejected the offer.

From London came another, more subtle, pressure. Lloyd's of London, the principal underwriters of the *Morro Castle,* raised their eyebrows at reports reaching them of the Ward Line's attitude.

Seventy-one insurance companies, a third of them

British, carried insurance on the ship. As the word spread that the Ward Line was in a protracted battle with lawyers for the survivors and relatives of the dead, more than one underwriter wondered why—was there something shady about the whole episode?

Word reached the Ward Line that it could be assailed soon from all sides and that it might be years before the line could collect the $4,200,000 insurance on the *Morro Castle*.

It suddenly increased its offer to the claimants to $890,000. This was accepted.

In London, Lloyd's underwriters settled $2,500,000 in insurance liability. In the end the Ward Line collected $4,188,999 in insurance.

The line sold the *Morro Castle* to Union Shipbuilding of Baltimore for $33,605 as scrap iron.

On the day the hulk was towed away from Asbury Park, George White Rogers opened a radio-repair shop in Bayonne, New Jersey.

It was the first time he had worked in some months. Customers found Rogers a bombastic shopkeeper, fond of telling them how lucky they were to have their radio sets mended by him. His business dropped off.

One day in February 1935, Rogers left the shop "to get a breath of air."

Shortly afterward it caught fire.

Bayonne police files reveal: "An inventory made by Rogers disclosed equipment had suffered damage to the extent of $1200. Arson was suspected. But no proof existed to warrant an arrest. He collected from the insurance company."

The police inquiries had been perfunctory; even the slightest serious probing into Rogers' background would have uncovered his previous attempts at arson. Just why the Bayonne Police Department failed to make those inquiries is a matter of supposition.

Increasingly, George White Rogers seemed to live in a world of his own; for him, the laws of cause and effect might never have existed. A strange thread of irresponsibility ran through all his behavior.

Dominated by his impulses, and with such a deficiency in his sense of reality, Rogers continued to be capable of the most bizarre or dangerous acts, apparently without realizing their incongruity.

After his return to Bayonne, he showed no signs of wanting either the company or the friendship of even those few who offered it.

The destruction of the *Morro Castle* and the ensuing worldwide headlines had made Rogers feel that he counted—that he was tough, important. The notoriety had been only a palliative. When the headlines faded, Rogers' feeling of inferiority remained as strong as before.

After the Bayonne police completed their inquiries into the fire at his repair shop, Rogers dropped out of public sight. Exactly what the state of his mind was during the next year is difficult to say. His continued preoccupation with the Leopold-Loeb case might have been some indication. The defendants in that case were two young men from highly respected families who had shocked America in 1924 by their murder of a young boy. After killing him, they assaulted him and then skinned the corpse with acid. Rogers carefully collated the story.

Early in 1936, he reappeared in the headlines when he gave evidence at the trial of William Warms, Eban Abbott, and Henry Cabaud, which had been delayed until then by a series of legal moves and countermoves.

At the trial, reporters noted Rogers had aged considerably; he was fatter, his hair thinner, his dress shabbier. Only his voice remained the same—oddly feminine and gentle. He told the now familiar story of the delay in sending out the SOS and how he stayed at his post.

After completing his evidence Rogers brushed aside questions about what he was doing with his life—and disappeared again.

Some little time later Rogers had a chance encounter with a Bayonne businessman who was present at the reception at which Police Officer Vincent Doyle had publicly called Rogers a liar. The man told Rogers he thought Doyle's behavior had been uncalled for.

Afterward, he had offered Rogers friendship, unaware of the insulation Rogers had long ago built into his personality. Now, the businessman tried again to befriend Rogers.

Rogers accepted an invitation to dinner. It must have been a painful experience for Rogers to maintain the semblance of human contact which he had excluded for so long from his pattern of life. But by the end of the evening Rogers had become excited by an extraordinary turn of events. The businessman suggested he should help him get a new start in life—as a patrolman with the Bayonne Police Department.

The verdicts in the criminal trial arising out of the *Morro Castle* disaster caused a new sensation. William Warms was sentenced to two years imprisonment; Eban Abbott received four years; Ward Line vice-president Henry E. Cabaud was fined five thousand dollars and given one year's suspended sentence.

The Ward Line filed an immediate appeal on behalf of Warms and Abbott. The acting captain told newsmen: "It's hard for a jury to understand the conditions which confronted me. Having no knowledge or experience of the way of the sea, the jury probably didn't comprehend what it means to suddenly battle against a raging sea, the worst storm for years along the Atlantic Coast, and a fire which was sweeping the vessel.

"Then again, only in this country are such cases tried by laymen juries. In England and other foreign countries they are heard and tried before admiralty courts."

Chief Engineer Abbott declined to make any statement.

In June 1936, George White Rogers joined the Bayonne police force. He was assigned as assistant to Vincent Doyle in the radio department.

How he came to be taken on is now impossible to ascertain. Present-day police officers have told us that the likeliest explanation is that Rogers' businessman friend had sufficient influence to "bulldoze his man" onto the force.

In the job he was assigned to, Rogers' physical condition was no barrier; he was not subjected to any physical examination before being accepted, though nobody can now say positively why. Nor—and this is more incredible—was any account taken of his known past. On more than one occasion he had come under grave suspicion as an arsonist. But all this seemed to have been forgotten on the morning George White Rogers reported for duty.

If Doyle was amazed to see Rogers, he hid it well. His clash with Rogers at the civic reception almost two years before might never have happened; the suspected arson was forgotten.

The relationship between the two men was slow in

forming. Doyle was a warm, outgoing man; Rogers was an affectionless character, unable to form relationships with anybody.

Gradually, though, Doyle managed to establish contact with his assistant; they found common ground in their seagoing experiences and an interest in things electrical. As the barriers came down, Doyle became aware of Rogers' arrogance.

"He just couldn't stop telling me how clever he was, how he just knew he was right about almost everything."

After some months, Doyle detected a recurring theme in most of Rogers' talk: a preoccupation with exploding devices. Doyle was both fascinated and worried as Rogers explained the theory of timing devices and how explosions could be triggered to go off at an exact moment.

"George, is that how it was on the *Morro Castle?*" Doyle asked at the end of one lengthy explanation.

Rogers looked at Doyle and smiled.

In April 1937, the United States Circuit Court of Appeals, in a unanimous decision, set aside the conviction of Warms and Abbott.

"Warms," said the Appeals Court, "maintained the best tradition of the sea by remaining on his vessel until the bridge burned under him and all others had left."

The court held that Abbott's behavior in leaving the ship was "caused by suffering from smoke, and therefore he was not responsible."

Following the decision, Warms told reporters in an uncustomary burst of eloquence, "It was the judgment of God. I was innocent and God knew it. While patience is bitter, it bears sweet fruit, as the Orientals say, and I have been patient for two years and seven months awaiting the decision."

News of the verdicts brought a marked change in Rogers. He became almost obsessive in his desire to discuss the fire on the *Morro Castle*. Increasingly, he dwelt on how the blaze had been set.

Doyle began to keep a record of his assistant's statements. Finally, he noted: "George knows that I know he set fire to the *Morro Castle*."

Doyle decided to wait. He knew that what Rogers had told him was not strong enough to obtain a conviction. If questioned, Rogers could always escape by pleading idle boasting, something his police colleagues knew he was capable of.

Vincent Doyle told no one of his suspicions. But he continued to question Rogers on every aspect of the *Morro Castle* disaster, and began to form a picture of Rogers which was remarkably in tune with later psychiatric reports.

The strange cat-and-mouse questioning went on until early March 1938. Then, on March 3, a quiet Thursday afternoon, Doyle and Rogers sat down for yet another discussion on the peculiar fate of the *Morro Castle*.

At the end of it Doyle knew "exactly how Rogers set the fire. He told me how to construct an incendiary fountain pen; how it had been placed in the writing-room locker. . . ."

Doyle wondered how best to present his sensational evidence to his superiors. He was still worrying over it next afternoon when he met Rogers outside the police radio department. Rogers seemed pensive and withdrawn.

"There's a package for you," said Rogers.

Doyle nodded and went into the department. Rogers remained just outside the doorway.

On the workbench was a package. Doyle unwrapped it and found a heater for a fish tank. There was nothing unusual in that; from time to time Doyle used the department's facilities to repair electrical equipment for his colleagues.

Attached to the fish tank was a typed label:

> This is a fish-tank heater. Please install the switch in the line cord and see if the unit will work. It should get slightly warm.

Doyle was puzzled by the instructions and by the fact that they carried no signature. He looked again at the label. It had been typed on the standard office machine of the radio department. This also puzzled him.

He turned toward the door, intending to ask Rogers for a comment. Rogers had disappeared. Doyle shrugged and turned back to the heater.

For a moment he toyed with the heater, then plugged it into the workbench's double-outlet plug. He flicked the switch on the outlet plug.

The resulting explosion broke windows in the workshop, and shook the main police headquarters building over two hundred feet away.

It was a miracle that Doyle escaped death. His left hand, left leg, and right foot were smashed. His left eardrum was fractured. He was rushed to Bayonne Hospital, where he underwent an emergency operation.

The next day Rogers visited Vincent Doyle in the hospital, and asked through his tears: "How can I get the guy who did this to you?"

Two weeks later Rogers was charged with the at-

273

tempted murder of Vincent Doyle.

After eighteen weeks in the hospital, Vincent Doyle began to assemble a formidable dossier on Rogers' background. It brought to light a great deal of his criminal record. The prosecution decided to exclude it, and concentrate solely on the attempt on Doyle's life.

It was a curious decision, one that caused considerable bitterness among Doyle and his colleagues. Equally unusual was the agreement between the prosecution and defense that the report of the psychiatrist appointed to examine Rogers should remain largely confidential.

Neither decision can be explained with absolute certainty. A study of the pre-trial prosecution case indicates that the district attorney regarded it as "an open and shut case." To introduce Rogers' background would "unnecessarily complicate the neat and clear line of attack." The attitude toward the medical evidence is best summed up by a note attached to the bulky police files on the case: "Don't need a fancy doctor's report to tell us that R. is a nut." The note was unsigned. Since the defense was not entering a plea of insanity, it would not wish to complicate its case, either, by introducing as evidence the psychiatrist's report.

That document indicated that to some extent Rogers' repressed sexual wishes probably caused his criminal behavior. There was a suggestion that he might have given vent to his repression in a symptomatic form; just as a man who is otherwise impotent can achieve an orgasm by violence, so Rogers had found relief in sending the fish-tank exploding device.

How much notice the judge took of this medical opinion is not known. By any accounts he was an unusual judge. At the end of the trial, he summoned Doyle to his chambers. "As the victim of the crime, he asked my opinion on a just punishment for Rogers," Doyle recalled. "I did not hesitate to suggest that he be given the maximum sentence allowed by law."

On December 15, 1938, the judge passed sentence:

"Your crime is one of the most diabolical nature and it fell short of murder only by the intervention of Divine Providence. It is the type of crime executed only by the mind of a fiend.

"I hereby sentence you to serve from twelve to twenty years in the State's Prison at Trenton."

On May 15, 1939, Rogers lost an appeal before the New Jersey State Supreme Court. Again, before the Court of Errors and Appeals, in February 1941, his conviction was upheld.

On September 3, 1942, the New Jersey State Court of Pardons granted Rogers parole to "join the armed services." The announcement caused a storm of protest. The protest was ignored. On November 24, 1942, Rogers was released from Trenton State Prison after serving less than four years.

The American Navy refused to accept him. But once again his business friend, the man who had helped get him onto the Bayonne police force, came to his aid. "He still believed in Rogers," Vincent Doyle stated. "Why I don't know—nor will anybody else. But the day Rogers was released, this man took him to New York."

Next day the Federal Communications Commission gave him a ninety-day permit to operate as a radio officer at sea. The Radiomarine Corporation of America assigned him to a ship sailing from San Francisco to Australia.

The voyage ended with Rogers' arrest in Darwin, Australia. His exact crime was not made clear. There is a veiled reference to "enemy alien activity" in the files of Vincent Doyle. But the FBI, which would undoubtedly have been involved at some level in such a charge, emphatically denied any involvement.

Afterward Rogers went to work in a war plant in Jersey City. He was dismissed from there on suspicion of stealing. He went to work in another war plant in Brooklyn.

Soon afterward a number of employees showed signs of poisoning after drinking from a water cooler near where Rogers worked.

Again, there was no positive proof, but once more Rogers found himself out of work.

With the last of his capital, Rogers again opened up a radio-repair shop in Bayonne. By 1945, he managed, against all expectations, to develop it into a thriving small business.

In May 1952, he was finally discharged from parole. By then his business was in financial difficulties.

Soon afterward he formed a relationship with an elderly couple living a few doors away. They were William Hummel, an eighty-three-year-old retired printer, and his unmarried daughter, Edith.

Rogers had sold them a second-hand television set, and discovered that Hummel and he shared a common interest in electrical gadgets.

Over the months Rogers became a regular caller at the Hummels'. On his own admission, he found William Hummel sympathetic to a new preoccupation Rogers had developed—that he had been framed by the Bayonne Police Department all those years before because they were jealous of having a genuine hero among them.

It was an extraordinary piece of convoluted thinking, but Hummel seemed to accept it. As time passed, Rogers dwelt increasingly on this delusion, embellishing it as fancy took him.

In all probability the Hummels unwittingly encouraged Rogers in this fantasy; certainly they spent many hours together going through the Bible looking for "proof" (as Rogers later put it) that the change in his life situation could be traced back to the police.

The delusions became more grandiose as well as paranoid; the police were hostile and vile, and the world at large full of dangerous pitfalls.

Rogers received not only emotional, but also financial, support from the Hummels. When he told them the police were "keeping customers away from the shop," William Hummel offered to subsidize the loss. By June 1953, Hummel had loaned Rogers $7500.

Then the relationship between the two men underwent a change. In his diary Hummel wrote: "It has been unwise on my part to continually advance Rogers money. He is very temperamental, and I am in constant fear he might renege, and I would lose everything."

In June 1953, William Hummel put his home up for sale. He planned to move with his daughter to Florida. In his diary he wrote: "Must collect loan from G."

On July 1, 1953, acting on a tipoff, the police broke into Hummel's home. They found father and daughter savagely bludgeoned to death.

Suspicion quickly fell on Rogers. After painstaking police investigation, Rogers was arrested.

Postponement followed postponement as the defense lawyers pleaded for time to prepare their case. The trial finally began on September 13, 1954.

Days later the jury found Rogers guilty of murder in the first degree and recommended life imprisonment.

Police Captain Vincent Doyle, still bearing the marks

of Rogers' murder attempt, was in court to hear sentence passed.

On March 4, 1955—seventeen years to the day since he tried to murder Vincent Doyle—Rogers appealed the sentence of life imprisonment. The appeal was swiftly denied, and Rogers withdrew even further, avoiding contact with anyone.

At 6 A.M. on January 10, 1958, George White Rogers died in prison of a brain hemorrhage.

# Appendixes

# ACKNOWLEDGMENTS

This book is the result of almost three years' work.

Research fell naturally into two main stages. The first was collating all the published material available on the subject. By the end of that phase, we had assembled some 2.8 million words of newspaper stories, magazine articles, technical journals, official reports, and books. The second part involved the task of locating the American, British, European, and Cuban participants in the drama of the *Morro Castle*.

It involved some one hundred thousand miles of travel across America and in Western Europe.

From the outset the most difficult task was to establish the truth. It became clear that the official records did not tell the whole truth—nor did some of the people who testified at the public hearings. There were three major inquiries into the peculiar fate of the *Morro Castle*, as well as numerous investigations by newspapers and interested parties. Those who conducted them paid little or no attention to the mass of circumstantial evidence indicating arson. One inquiry took as its subject the possibility that Communist plotters were behind the fire, but the case was not proven.

Yet we believe that had the allegations of arson been seriously followed up by competent police officers and had those suspected been brought to trial before a court of law, there would have been little doubt that the strange story of George White Rogers would have taken a different course. There is ample evidence that the burning of the *Morro Castle* was his moment of supreme madness—perhaps, too, his moment of truth.

Because Rogers was never tried, we were not able to state the "truth" about what he did in a legal sense; it is a broad axiom of the practice of criminal law that "truth" is what remains beyond a reasonable doubt after the case has been presented.

Nevertheless, we could see that, at the very least, there was a strong implication of guilt, although Rogers had never been tried and convicted. Lawyers we have consulted believe that some of the testimony against Rogers, properly presented by the prosecution, would have been unassailable.

Alas, it was never tested; in that respect, justice was not done to Rogers. If he had been tried and found guilty, we believe there is a real possibility that he would have been sent to an asylum for the criminally insane.

At the outset, we realized that Rogers was probably mad; expert medical witnesses amply confirmed our suspicion by the end of the research period. Yet it also became clear that this book would not be a case study in insanity. There was a history of tragic errors and, in the case of George Alagna, injustice.

But above all we discovered a story of ordinary people caught up in an extraordinary situation.

Far from setting out to produce a judicial assessment, we hoped those people would be helped a little to a better understanding of the hurt that such a tragedy caused —and still causes.

In the end literally hundreds gave us assistance—for the most part gladly.

Many had been on the *Morro Castle*. Others had helped with the rescue work. Still more had worked behind the scenes. A few—like Mrs. Ada Abbott and the family of Acting Captain William Warms—had lived a large part of their lives with the recollection of what the disaster did to their loved ones.

Some of the Cuban passengers were reluctant to talk because they feared it might somehow compromise relatives they had left behind in a Cuba long dominated by Fidel Castro. One Cuban woman believed we were from the Central Intelligence Agency; another had difficulty in believing that we were not Communist agents. Both were people of average intelligence who had allowed their experiences aboard the *Morro Castle* to color, probably forever, their view of events. Both believed there was political agitation behind the fire.

But for the majority of interviews, we were well received by men and women who seemed to have only one interest—that at last the full story of a great sea disaster should be told. They went to extraordinary trouble to contribute far more than we could ever hope to use. To have included every reminiscence was impossible.

A very special debt must be acknowledged to the family of the late Captain Vincent Doyle. His widow made available to us all her husband's files on George White Rogers; his daughter Jane and his son-in-law Jack patiently helped to fill in a number of small, but important, details.

Edward S. Adamski, deputy chief of police of the Bayonne Police Department, proved especially helpful by making available hitherto unpublished material on Rogers. Mr. Adamski, together with Captain of Detectives Thomas Lavin, submitted uncomplainingly to our questions as we searched to comprehend the strange behavior of the man.

Mr. John A. Reynolds, director of individual treatment at the State Prison, Trenton, New Jersey, gave us a morning during his busy schedule to fill in further gaps in the life of Rogers.

A particular debt is owed to the many doctors who helped us to understand Rogers and his severe illness. Some of them had treated him as a patient while he had been in prison. To them we give special thanks for their professional guidance. Because of medical etiquette they have to remain anonymous.

Psychiatrists, like Dr. James Pearce and Dr. Andrew McFie, were invaluable guides to understanding a psychotic mind such as Rogers'. Acknowledgement must also be made to the published work of Dr. Andrew Crowcroft and Dr. Howard Jones, who describe so well a criminal like Rogers and his disturbed thinking.

Professor Francis Camps, consulting pathologist and a world authority on forensic medicine, offered valuable guidance in dealing with the death of Captain Robert Wilmott.

In Dublin, the National Library provided some fascinating material on arson that completed our portrait of Rogers.

In New York, the distinguished lawyer Mr. William Standard made available to us all his private files on the *Morro Castle* disaster. Mr. Standard served as a member of the *Morro Castle* Proctors' Committee. This committee defeated attempts by the owners to limit their liability to twenty thousand dollars. They were ultimately forced to pay the victims and their survivors more than eight hundred thousand dollars. Mr. Standard has been general counsel to the National Maritime Union of America, CIO, since its organization in 1937, and was chairman of the Admiralty Law Committee of the National Lawyers Guild. He went to great pains to give us the *feeling* of what it was like for the average seaman sailing in the days of the Depression.

Douglas Whiddon of the Seamen's Institute, New York, and Donald King at the National Archives in Washington provided a score of useful avenues to explore.

The Federal Bureau of Investigation was helpful because of its repeated denial of any involvement; its attitude encouraged us to press our inquiries elsewhere. We did not have such luck with the U.S. Secret Service. Though they are listed in the New York telephone directory, a call only produced a vague promise of "we'll call you back if we can help." They never did call back.

The United States Coast Guard proved friendlier and more helpful. In Washington, Captain John S. Lipuseck and Lieutenant Michael Robinson made available their precious and only copy of the Dickerson Hoover report.

But in the end it was the people who had been directly involved who made this book possible.

Dr. Joe Bregstein sat with us in his spacious home in Miami, Florida, and re-created the painful days he spent on the *Morro Castle*.

There is a similarly haunting echo of the past in the recollections of Dr. Emilio Giro. We found him in Apple Creek, Ohio, a kind, gentle man, still having difficulty with the English language. With the help of his daughter, Sylvia—who had just been born when Dr. Giro booked passage on the *Morro Castle*—we were able to have a rare glimpse of life on the liner.

A chance call to the Chancery Office of St. Patrick's Rectory in New York led us to the story of Father Raymond Egan, a brave man and priest.

The New Jersey coast between Atlantic City and Asbury Park became familiar ground; we got to know it in relative comfort thanks to Ed and Dolores Corcoran, who seemed to know every shortcut.

Our research took us to unexpected places: in an apartment at the foot of Fifth Avenue we came across Captain George Seeth; a journey to Neptune, New Jersey, added a new dimension to the story of William Warms. His son, Donald, with unfailing kindness, brought his father to life in a way that hundreds of thousands of previously published words had failed to do. In New Rochelle, New York, we sat with Mrs. Ada Abbott, a gracious lady, who, while recognizing her husband's human weaknesses, rationalized them. At the end of our long interview, she gave us a photograph of Eban Abbott—"so you can see what a fine man he was."

We made contact with Cuba; of that we can say no

more except that in the end it helped us to weigh what we had heard more carefully.

From it all we have tried to present an accurate and honest picture of what really did happen on the *Morro Castle*.

If we have succeeded in nothing else but that, then we will have achieved what we set out to do.

# SPECIAL THANKS

*Individuals:*

Mrs. Ada Abbott
Matthew Ackle
Andrew Adams
Elsie Adams
James Adams
Edward S. Adamski
Felicity Alagna
Arthur Beadle
Ralph Bennett
Robert Beresford
Alexander Bogen
James Bogen
Richard Bosenheim
Frank Braynard
Dr. Joe Bregstein
Mrs. Muriel Bregstein
Rosemary Broward
George H. Brown
Richard Buck
George Bullard
E. A. W. Bullock
Francis Camps
John M. Cannon
Kevin Canter
John Clark
Maurice Cohen

Richard Collin
Dorothy Connor
Edward Cook
Gavin Cooke
Standard Copley
Dolores Corcoran
Edward Corcoran
Herbert Cox
James T. Cox, Jr.
Ramon Cunnella
John Dowling
Mrs. Vincent Doyle
Reverend Vincent J. Doyle
Ethel Driscoll
Michael Drysdale
Peter Durso
Oliver Duval
Charles Eames
Charles Elliot
Ernest Engelder
Patrick Evans
Barry Factor
Oliver Fergusen
Angel Fernandez
Edward Fitzgerald
Guillermo Galanea
Fred Gerkyn
Dr. Emilio Giro

| | |
|---|---|
| Mrs. Sylvia Giro | Michael Mitchell |
| Miss Sylvia Giro | Frank Mountier |
| Joseph P. Glynn | Michael O'Driscoll |
| Joseph Hardy | Shirley O'Neil |
| Oliver Harman | Patricia A. Pauly |
| William Hernandez | James Pearce |
| Nelly M. Houston | Gilbert Perrine |
| Ian Hudson | Gouverneur M. Phelps, Jr. |
| Terence Hughes | David Phillips |
| Aubrey Hunt | William Post |
| Loretta Husman | Herbert Pringle |
| Albert Hutchins | Arnold Puzzoza |
| Stanley Jackson | Steven Race |
| Jack Jacob | Norman Raithel |
| Peter Johnson | J. A. Reynolds |
| Idris Jones | Michael Robinson |
| John Kalso | Captain William Ross |
| William M. Keegan | Jack Schabile |
| John Kent | Jane Schabile |
| Shirley Kent | Barbara Seanes |
| George Kentera | Captain George Seeth |
| Captain Robert Kessel | Pat Shapiro |
| Arthur King | Francis Sheridan |
| Donald King | Charles Snow |
| Peter Kooner | Estes Sofroniou |
| Thomas Lavin | Adele Springer |
| Lawrence F. Ledebur | William Standard |
| William E. Lind | Mrs. Daymar Stickle |
| John S. Lipuseck | Harvey Stricartz |
| Eugene L. Lora | William Sutphin |
| Michael T. Mahon | Curt Templer |
| Arthur Mainbrace | Thomas S. Torresson, Jr. |
| Elliot Martin | Patrick Unger |
| Roger H. McDonough | Robert Unwin |
| Carl McDowell | Richard Usk |
| Andrew McFie | Charles A. Van Hagen, Jr. |
| P. J. McGee | James Venebles |
| Richard Medale | Jerry Walker |

Donald E. Warms
Pauline Warms
Morris Weisberger
Douglas Whiddon
Robert Whitmore
Doris Wilde
Murray Wilkes
George Witterschein
Peter Woods
H. Yeager
Stanley Young
Peter Yuffey

*Organizations, Societies, and Institutions:*

American Bureau of Shipping
American Choral Foundation
American Hull Insurance Syndicate
American Marine Insurance Syndicate
American Maritime Association
American Radio Association
Bayonne Police Department
*Bayonne Times*
Bigham, Englar, Jones & Houston, New York
British Broadcasting Corporation
British Museum, London
*Brooklyn Spectator*
Catholic Central Library, London

City of New York Fire Department
City of New York Police Department
Cunard Lines
Department of Commerce, Washington
Department of Institutions and Agencies, State of New York
Fireman's Fund American Insurance Co.
Furness Withy & Co. Ltd.
General Accident, Fire and Life Assurance Corp. Ltd.
Harvard University
Honourable Society of the Middle Temple, Law Library, London
Industrial Union of Marine and Ship Building Workers of America
Jersey City Police Department
Joseph Conrad Library
Library of Congress, Washington
Library, United States Information Service, London
Library, University of Maryland
Lloyd's of London
Lloyd's Register of Shipping
London *Times*
Marine Division, Radio Corporation of America

Marine Insurance
  Association of America
Maritime Law Association
Maritime Museum, Mystic,
  Connecticut
Massachusetts Institute of
  Technology
National Archives,
  Washington
*Newark Daily Ledger*
*Newark Evening News*
New Jersey State Prison,
  Trenton
Newport News Shipbuilding
  and Dry Dock Co.
New York Public Library
*New York Times*
Penn Central Transportation
  Co.
*Philadelphia Enquirer*
Public Library, Washington
Radio Officers' Union
Republican Party National

Committee
Research Library of the
  Performing Arts
Sailors Snug Harbor, Staten
  Island, New York
Sailors' Union of the Pacific
Seamen's Church Institute
  of New York
State of New Jersey Library
United States Bureau of
  Prisons, Washington
United States Coast Guard
United States Department
  of Justice
United States Embassy,
  London
United States Information
  Service, London
United States Salvage
  Association, Inc.
United Telegraph Workers
Wireless Telegraph Section,
  Post Office, London

# BIBLIOGRAPHY

## Newspapers and Magazines

Only the sinking of the *Titanic* came near to matching the intense press interest that surrounded the *Morro Castle* disaster. Like the sinking of the White Star liner, the disaster involving the flagship of the Ward Line led to a great deal of sensational and inaccurate reporting.

The *New York Times* did a solid, workmanlike job, but other metropolitan newspapers were guilty of headline chasing.

Better coverage came from out-of-town newspapers. In Philadelphia, the *Enquirer* did a sound job of reporting; in San Francisco, the *Chronicle* also produced reliable reports; abroad, the London *Times* led the field in its thorough coverage.

At the other end of the scale, the Cuban press produced the wildest and wooliest crop of stories; many of them are recounted to this day. A careful check through a good newspaper library shows how the bogey of a Communist plot against the *Morro Castle* continues to attract journalists.

Contemporary magazines did rather better; good examples of pictorial journalism can be found in the pages of the *Illustrated London News* and *Harper's Weekly*.

We have listed here only some of the prime sources we consulted; credit must also be given to the many individual reporters who, in one way or another, reported the running story.

*New York Times,* "Program of Red 'International,' " July 1928.

*New York Times,* "Communists and Criminals," January 1930.

*New York Times,* "Red 'Internationals,' " March 1930.

*New York Times,* "Red 'International' Shifts World-Wide Aims," May 1930.

*New York Times,* "Red Data Called Gold Brick," May 1930.

*New York Times,* "Cuban Labor Got Moscow Funds," June 1930.

*New York Times,* "Communist Group Cheers Cuban Reds," June 1930.

*New York Times,* "Moscow Still Firm for World Revolt," July 1930.

*New York Herald Tribune,* "The Ward Line's New Ship," August 1930.

*New York Herald Tribune,* "New Liner Shows Speed," August 1930.

*New York Times,* "World Negro Rising Said to Be Soviet Aim," August 1930.

*Marine Engineering,* "The Turbo Electric Morro Castle," September 1930.

*New York Times,* "The Red Plotters," November 1930.

*New York Times,* "Red Plots to Bomb Shipping in Harbor," November 1930.

*New York Times,* "Communists in South America Have Far-Flung Organization," April 1932.

*New York Times,* "Soviet and the U.S.A.," July 1932.

*New York Times,* "The Moscow Whip," October 1932.

*New York Times Magazine,* "Four World Ideas Vie for Domination," June 1934.

*Illustrated London News,* "The Burning of the Morro Castle," September 1934.

*Literary Digest,* "Morro Castle Disaster Challenges Investigation," September 1934.

*New Republic,* "The Morro Castle Disaster," September 1934.

*Newsweek*, "Disaster," September 1934.

*New York American*, "Morro Castle Officers," September 1934.

*New York American*, "Lifeboats Unseaworthy," September 1934.

*New York American*, "Last Log of the Morro Castle," September 1934.

*New York Herald Tribune*, "The Woman Who Swam Four Miles," September 1934.

*New York Sun*, "Coast Guard Criticized by Fishermen," September 1934.

*New York Times*, "Fireproof Ships," September 1934.

*New York Times*, "Fishermen Get Heroes' Praise," September 1934.

*New York Times*, "Cuba Seizes Six in Morro Castle Tragedy," September 1934.

*New York Times*, "Moore's Flight," September 1934.

*New York Times*, "Blaze Laid to Reds by Cuban Official," September 1934.

*New York Times*, "Cubans Push Ship Inquiry," September 1934.

*San Antonio Sunday Light*, "New Sea Salvage Law Demanded," September 1934.

*San Francisco Chronicle*, "Off on a Junket," September 1934.

*New York Sun*, "The Morro Castle and the Ferry," September 1934.

*Sunday Graphic*, "The Morro Castle Was Burnt by the Fire Bugs of Havana," September 1934.

*London Times*, "Fire Disaster at Sea," September 1934.

*New York World Telegraph*, "Rogers . . . Vaudeville Turn," September 1934.

*New York Evening Post*, "The Morro Castle: a Whitewash Job on the Ward Line," October 1934.

*Lookout*, "Stories of the Morro Castle," October 1934.

*New Republic*, "Rescue at Sea," October 1934.

*New York American*, "New Morro Castle Risk," November 1934.

*New York Herald Tribune,* "Six Days at Sea," November 1934.

*New York Herald Tribune,* "New Shipowner Rules," January 1935.

*Scientific American,* "Fire at Sea," February 1935.

*New York Sunday News,* "Ward Line Disaster Spurs New Sea Laws," February 1935.

*Fortune,* "Havana Cruise," March 1935.

*Scribner's Magazine,* "Fire on the Bridge," March 1935.

*New York Daily News,* "Sea Survivors Urge Ship Liability Boost," April 1935.

*American Magazine,* "Lifesaver," May 1935.

*New York American,* "The Dead Are Remembered," September 1935.

*New York World Telegram,* "Congress and Sea Tragedy," October 1935.

*New York Times,* "The Morro Castle Loss," January 1936.

*New York World Telegram,* "Morro Castle in Drydock Only Once in 174 Trips," January 1936.

*New York Herald Tribune,* "Better Times Seen for Shipyards," April 1936.

*New York Times,* "The Morro Castle Appeal," April 1936.

*Los Angeles Times,* "Morro Disaster Made Ships Safer," May 1936.

*Newark News,* "Morro Castle Hero Joins Police," June 1936.

*Mid-week Pictorial,* "Two Years After the Morro Castle," September 1936.

*New York Herald Tribune,* "A Monument to the Morro Castle," April 1937.

*London Times,* "The Morro Castle Case," April 1937.

*Bayonne Times,* "A New Face in the Rogues Gallery," March 1938.

*Time,* "Heroes," March 1938.

*Nautical Gazette,* "Distribution of Settlement Fund," February 1939.

*New York American,* "Morro Castle Settlement," April 1939.

*New York Times,* "Clarence Hackney of Morro Castle,"
April 1939.

*New York Times Magazine,* "Thirty Years Ago—a Ship
Named the Morro Castle," September 1964.


*Periodicals, Pamphlets, Reports, Etc.*


We were privileged to be allowed access to much official
documentation that has never been published before; this
material provided some of our most valuable written evidence.


Blueprints, Ward Line, 1930.

Reports, American Bureau of Shipping, 1930.

Handbook, Wireless Telegraph Operators RG 67, London,
1932.

Dispatches, Commander U.S. Coast Guard, New York
Division, 1934.

Documents, Registrar General of Shipping & Seamen, Car-
diff, 1934.

Documents, Casualty Section, Board of Trade, London,
1934.

Documents, Federal Maritime Commission, 1934.

Log, U.S. Coast Guard patrol boat *Cahoone,* 1934.

Log, U.S. Coast Guard cutter *Tampa,* 1934.

Log, U.S. Coast Guard cutter *Sebago,* 1934.

Log, Cape May Air Station, 1934.

Log, Press-Radio Bureau, New York, 1934.

Log, U.S. Coast Guard Rockaway Radio Station, 1934.

Logs, U.S. Coast Guard life-saving stations at Shark River, Manasquan Beach, Long Branch, Sandy Hook, Deal,
Monmouth Beach, Bayhead, Spermaceti Cove, 1934.

Log, S.S. *President Cleveland,* 1934.

Report, S.S. *Andrea F. Luckenbach,* 1934.

Report, S.S. *City of Savannah,* 1934.

Report, S.S. *President Cleveland,* 1934.

Report, S.S. *Monarch of Bermuda,* 1934.

Paper, Morro Castle Safety at Sea Association, 1934.

Report, The Maritime Association of the Port of New York, 1934.

Report, U.S. Coast Guard Board of Investigation, 1934.

Report, U.S. Coast Guard cutter *Champlain*, 1934.

Report, Commander, U.S. Coast Guard, Eastern Section, 1934.

Report, American Red Cross, 1934, 1935.

Reports, Lloyd's Weekly Casualty, July-December 1934.

Reports, Radiomarine Corporation of America, 1934.

Report, Salvage Association, 1934.

Reports, Governor of New Jersey (Harry A. Moore), 1934.

Reports, Morro Castle Survivors Association, 1934.

Reports, New York Fire Department, 1934.

Report, Dickerson N. Hoover Board of Inquiry, 1934.

Reports, American Maritime Association, 1934/35.

Reports, U.S. Maritime Law Association, 1934.

Reports, U.S. Bureau of Shipping, various.

Report, London Salvage Association, 1934.

Report, U.S. Shipping Board, 1934.

Transcript, Lena Schwarz, 1934.

Transcript, William Francis Price, 1934.

Transcript, William O'Sullivan, 1934.

Transcript, Dr. Joseph Bregstein, 1934, 1971.

Transcript, Charles S. Cochrane, 1934.

Transcript, William Warms, 1934.

Transcript, Charles Menken, 1934.

Transcript, Dr. G. M. Phelps, 1934.

Transcript, G. Morris Phelps, Jr., 1934.

Transcript, Paul Arneth, 1934.

Transcript, Sol Livingston, 1934.

Transcript, Katherine Liebler, 1934.

Transcript, George Alagna, 1934.

Transcript, Antonio Bujia, 1934.

Transcripts, George White Rogers, 1934, 1938, 1954.

Transcript, Manuel Garcia, 1934.

Transcript, Antonio Georgio, 1934.

Transcript, John Gross, 1934.

Transcript, Aubrey Hunt Russel, 1934.

Transcript, Thomas Charles, 1934.

Transcript, Leroy Kelsey, 1934.

Transcript, Joseph O'Connor, 1934.

Transcript, Robert Beresford, 1934.

Transcript, Arthur Stamper, 1934.

Transcript, Robert J. Smith, 1934.

Transcript, William W. Tripp, 1934.

Transcript, Charles A. Maki, 1934.

Transcript, Ivan Freeman, 1934.

Transcript, Clarence Hackney, 1934.

Report, U.S. Salvage Association, Inc., 1935.

Report, U.S. Senate, 74th Congress, First Session, Report No. 776, 1935.

Report, Committee on Merchant Marine and Fisheries, House of Representatives, 74th Congress, First Session, 1935.

Hearing, No. H.R. 4550, 74th Congress, House of Representatives, 1935.

Memorandum, U.S. District Court, 1936.

Report, U.S. Department of Commerce advisory conference on the making of passenger vessels more safe from destruction by fire, 1936.

Transcript, Eban Abbott, 1934, 1935.

Aides-mémoire, William Warms, 1930-1940.

Aides-mémoire, Dr. Joseph Bregstein, 1934, 1938.

Collection, Captain Vincent Doyle, 1938-68.

Transcript, Edward S. Adamski, 1971.

Transcript, George Seeth, 1971.

Transcript, John Reynolds, 1971.

Transcript, Dr. Emilio Giro, 1971.

Transcript, William Standard, 1971.

Transcript, Donald Warms, 1971.

Transcript, Mrs. Ada Abbott, 1971.

Recording, Robert Beresford, 1971.

*Books*

Allen, Clifford, *Sexual Perversions and Abnormalities,* Oxford University Press, New York, 1949.

Allen, Kenneth S., *The World's Greatest Sea Disasters,* Odhams Books, London.

Armstrong, Warren, *Last Voyage,* Frederick Muller, London, 1956.

Bard, Philip, *Medical Physiology,* C. V. Mosby Co., New York, 1956.

Barnaby, K. C., *Some Ship Disasters and Their Causes,* Hutchinson, London, 1968.

Best, Charles H., *The Physiological Basis of Medical Practice,* Williams & Wilkins Co., Baltimore.

Brown, Riley, *Men, Wind and Sea,* Carlyle, Garden City, New York, 1939.

Cameron, Norman, *The Psychology of Behavior Disorders,* Houghton, Mifflin and Co., Boston, 1947.

Campbell, Meredith, *Urology,* W. B. Saunders Co., Philadelphia, 1954.

Crowcroft, Andrew, *The Psychotic,* Pelican Books, London, 1967.

Edmunds, C. W., and Gunn, J. A., *Pharmacology and Therapeutics,* J. & A. Churchill Ltd., London, 1936.

Foster, William Z., *History of the Internationals,* International Publishers, New York, 1955.

Gallagher, Thomas, *Fire at Sea,* Frederick Muller, London, 1969.

Glaister, John, and Rentoul, S., *Medical Jurisprudence and Toxicology,* E. & S. Livingstone Ltd., Edinburgh, 1966.

Gonzales, Thomas A., *Legal Medicine: Pathology and Toxicology,* Appleton-Century, New York, 1954.

Jones, Howard, *Crime in a Changing Society,* Pelican Books, London, 1965.

Leighton, Isobel (ed.), *The Aspirin Age,* Bodley Head Press, London, 1950.

Manrara, Luis, *Communist Methodology of Conquest,*

N.C.C.C. Publishers, New York, 1966.

McFee, William, *The Law of the Sea*, Faber and Faber, London, 1951.

Rushbrook, Frank, *Fire Aboard*, Technical Press, London, 1961.

Smith, Sydney A., *Forensic Medicine*, J. & A. Churchill Ltd., London, 1938.

————*Mostly Murder*, George Harrup & Co. Ltd., London, 1960.

————, and Glaister, John, *Recent Advances in Forensic Medicine*, J. & A. Churchill Ltd., London, 1938.

Snow, Edward Rowe, *Great Gales and Dire Disasters*, Dodd, Mead & Co., New York, 1952.

Standard, William, *Merchant Seamen*, International Publishers, New York, 1947.

Williamson, John, *Dangerous Scot*, International Publishers, New York, 1969.

Wilson, R. M., *The Big Ships*, Cassell & Co. Ltd., London, 1956.

Wolf, William, *Endocrinology in Modern Practice*, W. B. Saunders Co., Philadelphia and London, 1940.

Wolfe, Stewart George, and Wolff, Harold George, *Human Gastric Function*, Oxford University Press, New York, 1960.

Wright, Samson, *Applied Physiology*, Oxford University Press, New York.

# DELIVERANCE

## by James Dickey

This novel, by one of America's finest poets, is a tale of violent adventure and inner discovery. Four men embark on a canoe trip down a wild section of a river in the heartland of today's South. When two of the group are attacked viciously and perversely by mountaineers, a mildly adventurous canoe trip explodes into a gruesome nightmare of horror and murder.

"The limit of dramatic tension . . . a novel that will curl your toes!" *The New York Times*

*Now a major motion picture from Warner Brothers starring Burt Reynolds and Jon Voight*

A DELL BOOK   $1.25

If you cannot obtain copies of this title from your local bookseller, just send the price (plus 15c per copy for handling and postage) to Dell Books, Post Office Box 1000, Pinebrook, N. J. 07058.

If you enjoyed *The Anderson Tapes*
this is your kind of book!

# 11 HARROWHOUSE

by GERALD A. BROWNE

Here is a novel in the Hitchcock tradition of
high adventure, romance, and suspense, a story
combining an ingenious *Rififi*-like theft with an
ensuing chase that moves across many of the
exotic faces of Europe. The place is 11 Harrowhouse, a dignified structure in London's posh
Mayfair district. The target is deep within its
subterranean vault—some thirteen billion dollars' worth of diamonds. J. Clyde Massey, a man
whose personal wealth runs into billions, com-
missions the heist not for love of money but
for the pleasure of revenge. For his operatives
he selects a most unlikely crew: Chesser, a diamond merchant, and his sensuously beautiful
mistress, Maren.

A DELL BOOK $1.50

If you cannot obtain copies of this title at your local bookseller, just send
the price (plus 15c per copy for handling and postage) to Dell Books, Post
Office Box 1000, Pinebrook, N. J. 07058.

**The big bestseller about cops—by a cop!**

## a novel by Joseph Wambaugh

THE NEW CENTURIONS is the work of a new and powerful American writer, a ten-year veteran of the Los Angeles Police Force. Joseph Wambaugh neither exaggerates nor whitewashes a cop's life. It is fiction, but everything in it is real.

It is the story of three men: Serge Duran, the tough, competent ex-Marine who learned everything fast—except how to escape his Chicano identity; Gus Plebesly, the baby-faced youth who was tops at entrapping prostitutes, and painfully unsure of his own manhood; Roy Fehler, who liked to think of himself as a liberal, until he came face to face with his own true feelings about blacks. . . .

They were men with money troubles, women troubles, all kinds of troubles. They were also cops, part of the new breed who had to deal with the unrest and violence of a society coming apart all around them.

32 weeks on *The New York Times* Bestseller list!

*Now a major motion picture*
*starring George C. Scott.*

### A Dell Book   $1.50

If you cannot obtain copies of this title from your local bookseller, just send the price (plus 15c per copy for handling and postage) to Dell Books, Post Office Box 1000, Pinebrook, N. J. 07058.

# HOW MANY OF THESE DELL BESTSELLERS HAVE YOU READ?

1. **THE MAN WHO LOVED CAT DANCING**
   by Marilyn Durham $1.75
2. **THE BRAND-NAME CARBOHYDRATE GRAM COUNTER** by Corinne T. Netzer $1.50
3. **GEORGE S. KAUFMAN** by Howard Teichmann $1.95
4. **THE TRUTH ABOUT WEIGHT CONTROL**
   by Dr. Neil Solomon $1.50
5. **MEAT ON THE HOOF** by Gary Shaw $1.50
6. **MAFIA, USA** by Nicholas Gage $1.75
7. **THE WATER IS WIDE** by Pat Conroy $1.50
8. **THE OSTERMAN WEEKEND** by Robert Ludlum $1.50
9. **11 HARROWHOUSE** by Gerald A. Browne $1.50
10. **DISRAELI IN LOVE** by Maurice Edelman $1.50
11. **WILL THERE REALLY BE A MORNING?**
    by Frances Farmer $1.50
12. **A PSYCHIATRIST'S HEAD**
    by Martin Shepard, M.D. $1.50
13. **THE SUPERLAWYERS** by Joseph C. Goulden $1.75
14. **EXECUTIVE ACTION** by Donald Freed and
    Mark Lane $1.25
15. **DO YOU REMEMBER ENGLAND?**
    by Derek Marlowe $1.25